WHERE THE JOBS ARE

Other Avon Books by
John W. Wright

The American Almanac of Jobs and Salaries

WHERE THE JOBS ARE

JOHN W. WRIGHT

with
Don Clippinger
Mary Quigley
John Rosenthal

AVON BOOKS ◆ NEW YORK

WHERE THE JOBS ARE is an original publication of Avon Books. This work has never before appeared in book form.

AVON BOOKS
A division of
The Hearst Corporation
1350 Avenue of the Americas
New York, New York 10019

First Avon Books Printing: June 1992

AVON TRADEMARK REG. U.S. PAT. OFF. AND IN OTHER COUNTRIES, MARCA REGISTRADA, HECHO EN U.S.A.

Printed in the U.S.A.

RA   10   9   8   7   6   5   4   3   2   1

For Jeanie and Gerry,
for their love and support

Contributors

This is clearly a book requiring work by many hands. An important part of our strategy was to tap into the first-hand knowledge of people who actually worked in specific fields. It is a pleasure to acknowledge their special contributions: Robert L. Spring (engineering), Jennifer K. Wright (the securities industry, health care), Mary Quigley (newspapers and magazines), Christopher D. Stack (computer industry, management consultants), David Lay (working overseas), Ray Porfilio (architects), Ellen Chodosh (book publishing), Patricia Szczerba (teachers, college and university faculty), and Maureen Chiofalo (librarians).

For state and local area information we also, whenever possible, utilized the services of people who were living in the region. Don Clippinger brought an experienced journalist's ability to "crack the code" of how to research this topic first in Kentucky, Tennessee, and Ohio, but then branching out west and south to wherever he was needed. Pam Hait (in the southwest) and Richard Gilbert (Indiana, Illinois) provided very important contributions here in terms of research methods as well as writing particular state and metro area sections.

The other excellent on-site writers and researchers were: Karen Augé (Pennsylvania, Delaware), Gerard Canavan (San Jose, Sacramento), John Connelly (Connecticut), Matt Forbeck (Michigan), Allan Freedman (Maryland, Virginia),

Elizabeth Fried (Massachusetts, Rhode Island), Glen Gendzel (San Francisco), Ellen Goldlust (Minnesota, Wisconsin), Evie Jones (Maine), John Kretzschmar (Nebraska), Jack Kucera (Georgia), David Lay (Florida), Ken Merritt (the Carolinas), Dunston Prial (Colorado, the Dakotas, Idaho), Christine Schlesser (Oregon), Ruth Bayard Smith (New Jersey), Linda Stutzman (Washington), Sally Webb (Houston).

Senior Editor and Writer: John Rosenthal

Staff Writers and Researchers: Ellen Chodosh, Greg Dimitriadis, Jerold Kappes, Benedict Leerburger, Edward Myers, Mary Quigley.

Acknowledgments

First and foremost we wish to thank Yolanda Strozier and the staff at Arizona State University's Economic Outlook Center for providing us with their excellent monthly surveys, *The Job Growth Outlook*, and *The Western Blue Chip Economic Forecast*, and for granting us permission to quote from them liberally. A special thanks to Ruth McClarnon for her help and cooperation.

At the U.S. Bureau of Labor Statistics we received a great deal of help from Tom Nardone and Neil Baxter, who provided data quickly and answered questions thoughtfully.

We would be terribly remiss if we didn't acknowledge the help and cooperation of all those people who work in state and city government who provided us with mounds of information about their labor markets, always with a courtesy and professionalism that gives the lie to all the bureaucrat bashing one hears. In addition we wish to thank the economists and analysts at various chambers of commerce and occupational associations who submitted to telephone interviews and gave us up-to-the-minute assessments of the local and national job opportunities.

Michael Zapf, Melissa Wright, and Sherry Repp took time out from hectic schedules to help us find information that would have remained uncovered without them.

A special note of thanks (once again) to our friend Dorothy Green for her help in preparing the manuscript under less than ideal conditions. Danielle V. Holloman, Victoria Wright, and Marian Spring helped enormously when it counted most.

Finally, this book would not have existed had it not been for the patience, tenacity, and guidance of Jody Rein, our editor at Avon Books. To her and the entire staff at Avon, we offer our sincerest thanks.

Contents

Where the Jobs Are
by Occupation

Where the Jobs Are in Major Industries

Where the Jobs Are
in the Public Sector

Where the Jobs Are
in Special Areas

Introduction

This book has been written in direct response to today's headlines:

"GM to Cut 71,000 Jobs"

"IBM Will Lose 21,000 Jobs"

"Only Three Major U.S. Airlines Likely to Survive"

"County Payrolls Slashed"

"Employment in Service Industry Falters"

"20,000 Construction Workers March for Jobs"

No wonder all the soothing assurances of President Bush and his advisers that the economy is basically sound have brought only sneers, derision, and plummeting public approval ratings. In the context of a deepening recession, millions of Americans have become economically paralyzed by the fear of not having a job in the near future.

Economists might assert, quite accurately, that unemployment levels remain significantly lower than the last major recession (1981–82) but the hard truths are that blue-collar unemployment has been over 10 percent for a year or more—higher in some areas of the country—and unemployment among blacks has been over 13 percent, more than double the 6.5 percent for whites. White-collar unemployment has also risen significantly (to 4.5 percent for 1991) and the total reshaping of American banking, as well as the restructuring and downsizing of U.S. corporations, have made once-secure mid-level managers far more vulnerable than at any time in the recent past.

Whether one blames all this on the baby boom, the Japanese, the deficit, or Ronald Reagan's "voodoo economics," the net result has been that jobs are simply much harder to find today and chances are that situation won't change for some time, even after recovery takes place. With that in mind, we have set out to provide serious job seekers with the most accurate, up-to-date information about employment opportunities in every state and many of the major metropolitan areas in the United States, as well as detailed descriptions of the current situation for all key white-collar occupations, including the traditional professions and the major jobs in science and technology.

Compiled by researchers in every region of the country, our information has been derived from sources as diverse as the U.S. Bureau of Labor Statistics, the U.S. Commerce Department, state labor and employment development agencies, local chambers of commerce, employment experts (Korn/Ferry, for example), and, of course, the major associations representing the nation's key industries and occupations.

How to Use This Book

To get the most out of this book, you should see it as a snapshot—a Polaroid if you wish—of the U.S. job market taken during the first two months of 1992. The subject of the photograph has been arranged according to the two most important factors related to your finding a job: what you do and where you are.

The two are always related, of course, but as a glance at the accompanying tables will show, location is much less crucial if you have been highly educated in computer science, engineering, or mathematics, or highly trained in medicine, the law, or accounting. These jobs have unemployment rates of less than 2.5 percent and opportunities are available in almost every part of the country.

Moreover, tens of thousands of jobs exist for people who are qualified to work in these fields at the support level. In the law, for example, there is an exceptionally strong demand for legal assistants (usually called ''paralegals'') as well as for legal secretaries. In medicine, registered nurses, physical therapists, and medical technicians are needed everywhere. In fact, almost every occupation in the health services sector of the economy is growing, most especially in the relatively new field of home health services. Fourteen of the 30 fastest-growing occupations in the U.S. are in health care services.

A full description of the opportunities in health care can be found in the section called ''Where the Jobs Are By Industry.'' So too can other fast-growing occupations listed in the tables, most of which are in retail sales, including eating and drinking establishments. While these are usually low-paying jobs they give millions of people access to work in every part of the country. But a wide range of industries is included in this section, the purpose of which is twofold: to show the immediate prospects for jobs that are industry-specific, in other words, jobs that exist only in this particular field (flight attendants and pilots obviously only work for the airlines, etc.), and to give a sense of the current state of the industry for people in accounting, human resources, etc., who are looking for jobs now. It should also be of some help in long-range career planning. Both the banking and computer industries, for example, will be going through years of turmoil that will include the loss of many jobs, especially at the support level. This includes clerical staff, marketing and sales people, even accountants and other key white-collar professionals.

Job opportunities for these occupations as well as for many others can be found in a separate section, ''Where the Jobs Are By Occupation.'' Although it includes both blue-collar and white-collar jobs, the main emphasis is on career opportunities for people with education levels beyond high school. The reason for this is simply that, for the most part, jobs are immediately available for most of these occupations, especially in the professions, sciences, and in the human resources departments of most large corporations. Clerical workers and most office staff personnel are almost always in demand but even in good economic times the need can fluctuate dramatically from region to region. The same is true for all blue-collar workers but most especially those in construction and manufacturing.

In a country as vast and economically diverse as the United States, regional employment levels can be as different as winters in Maine and Arizona, and as volatile as the price of a barrel of oil. In 1991, for example, the unemployment rates in many parts of New England topped 10 percent while the rates in almost all of the western states and many upper midwestern states were below 6 percent. By the early months of 1992, however, Nevada's economy had slowed down considerably and Southern California's was sinking faster than Darryl Strawberry's batting average. In fact, by February California's unemployment rate was higher than that of Massachusetts.

These shifting currents and local variations are all addressed in the book's largest section, "Where the Jobs Are By State and Metro Area." Americans are probably the most mobile people on the planet (over 3 million *households* move from one metropolitan areas to another each year) so this section can help many people pondering a move to make informed decisions about job possibilities throughout the country. For every state, many major metropolitan areas as well as some smaller ones, they will find information about the general health of the local economy, specific job opportunities, major local employers, and relevant facts about the key employment sectors, especially construction, manufacturing, retail sales, finance, insurance, and real estate, and most importantly health care. In every instance the emphasis is on job growth or the potential for job growth in the near future.

Growth is stressed because it means new jobs are being added so opportunity is expanded. In the accompanying map we have identified those states and metropolitan areas we believe have strong potential to add new jobs over the next few years. Some readers will be surprised that Los Angeles, San Diego, and other well-known Sunbelt cities aren't on the list, while small midwestern cities such as Omaha, Indianapolis, and Cincinnati are. But bear in mind that growth is a relative term and the job growth explosion of the 1980s—especially in the Sunbelt states—will not be seen again for the foreseeable future.

During the 1980s the increase in the number of jobs resulted in part from two factors: population growth, much of it in the Sunbelt due to migration, and dramatic increase in defense spending. Since both of these elements have now changed considerably the nation is heading into a period of uncertainty, one where job growth will be much slower than in recent times.

This does not mean, however, that jobs will be extremely scarce even in those large cities like New York, Chicago, and Philadelphia, where times have been tough recently. Because of the size of the labor force in these cities the number of job openings (as opposed to new jobs) is enormous due to retirements, deaths, firings, and other forms of so-called separations. On the national level the Bureau of Labor Statistics estimates that about 2 million jobs a year become vacant just from deaths, retirements, and people leaving the work force.

The changing nature of that work force is the final consideration for job seekers to ponder. It is important for all working people to realize that for the foreseeable future all job growth in the U.S. will be in the services sector of the economy, not the goods-producing sector. In other words, manufacturing will continuously dwindle in importance while legal services, business services (e.g., payroll providers, temporary employment agencies), retail stores, health care facilities, etc., take precedence.

Officially, the U.S. Department of Labor projects an increase of over 24 million jobs over the years 1990 to 2005, virtually all in services; 500,000 jobs in manufacturing are projected to be lost. This continues a trend begun in the early 1970s as the service sector's share of the work force rose from 70.5 percent in 1975 to 77.2 percent in 1990. By 2005 the percentage of all U.S. wage and salary workers will be 81 percent.

Policy makers, politicians, and pundits will debate the wisdom of this carefully planned obliteration of the U.S. manufacturing base for some time to come. But even if the current flood of lost manufacturing jobs can be stopped, the implications of the long-range trends for job seekers—especially younger ones—should be clear. Learning how service organizations are structured, what kinds of jobs are available, and what level of education and training you must pursue are the basic facts they must acquire. Purchasing this book is a great beginning.

Job Decline by State, Jan. 1991 vs. Jan. 1992 (in thousands)

State	Number of Jobs Jan. 1991	Number of Jobs Jan. 1992	Job Decline	Percent Change
New York	7,850.6	7,598.0	−252.6	−3.10%
California	12,771.4	12,620.8	−150.6	−1.18
New Jersey	3,468.8	3,384.4	−84.4	−2.43
Massachusetts	2,811.0	2,740.0	−71.0	−2.53
Ohio	4,747.3	4,680.6	−66.7	−1.41
Pennsylvania	5,027.6	4,965.2	−62.4	−1.24
Florida	5,303.2	5,244.2	−59.0	−1.11
Connecticut	1,561.1	1,508.0	−53.1	−3.40
Maryland	2,071.4	2,021.5	−49.9	−2.41
Michigan	3,826.2	3,788.3	−37.9	−0.99
Illinois	5,151.4	5,114.2	−37.2	−0.12
Virginia	2,803.8	2,780.7	−23.1	−0.82
South Carolina	1,494.5	1,479.2	−15.3	−1.02
Missouri	2,254.0	2,239.6	−14.4	−0.64
Rhode Island	423.4	410.5	−12.9	−3.05
New Hampshire	478.6	469.3	−9.3	−1.94
Maine	506.6	499.3	−7.3	−1.44
Delaware	338.1	334.4	−3.7	−1.09
Vermont	248.1	245.9	−2.2	−0.89

Note: These are nonagricultural jobs.

SOURCE: *Job Growth Update*, a monthly publication of Arizona State University's Economic Outlook Center. Reprinted with permission.

Job Growth by State,
Jan. 1991 vs. Jan. 1992
(in thousands)

State	Number of Jobs Jan. 1991	Number of Jobs Jan. 1992	Job Growth	Percent Change
Texas	7,041.0	7,172.5	131.5	1.87%
Washington	2,103.4	2,150.5	47.1	2.24
Louisiana	1,578.5	1,611.1	32.6	2.07
Kansas	1,063.0	1,094.5	31.5	2.96
Arkansas	905.5	935.3	29.8	3.29
Colorado	1,513.3	1,541.9	28.6	1.89
Wisconsin	2,232.8	2,259.7	26.9	1.20
Kentucky	1,435.3	1,460.9	25.6	1.78
Idaho	379.5	402.8	23.3	6.14
Oregon	1,216.7	1,238.8	22.1	1.82
Oklahoma	1,185.2	1,191.8	6.6	0.56
North Dakota	262.2	268.1	5.9	2.25
Alaska	223.3	228.9	5.6	2.51
Hawaii	536.1	541.4	5.3	0.99
West Virginia	616.0	620.9	4.9	0.80
Nebraska	720.4	724.8	4.4	0.61
New Mexico	570.8	573.6	2.8	0.49
Georgia	2,918.4	2,921.0	2.6	0.09
Wyoming	192.4	194.9	2.5	1.30

Note: These are nonagricultural jobs.

SOURCE: *Job Growth Update*, a monthly publication of Arizona State University's Economic Outlook Center. Reprinted with permission.

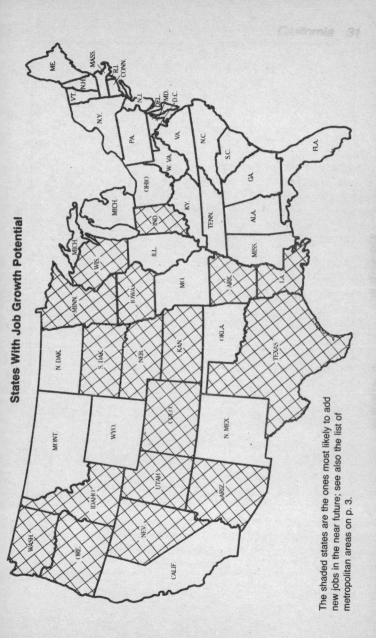

States With Job Growth Potential

The shaded states are the ones most likely to add new jobs in the near future; see also the list of metropolitan areas on p. 3.

WHERE THE JOBS ARE

STATE AND
METRO AREA

The following list represents, in our estimation, areas that have very good potential for job growth in the near future. Not all of them were outstanding in this regard during 1991 but all either weathered the recession fairly well or were not significantly affected. (A fuller description is found in Part I.) We've divided these into larger and smaller areas since fewer jobs are created in areas with smaller populations.

Large Metro Areas
Atlanta, Georgia
Cincinnati, Ohio
Columbus, Ohio
Denver, Colorado
Houston, Texas
Indianapolis, Indiana
Milwaukee, Wisconsin
Minneapolis-St. Paul,
  Minnesota
Orlando, Florida
Phoenix, Arizona
Portland, Oregon
Salt Lake City, Utah
Seattle, Washington

Smaller Metro Areas
Ann Arbor, Michigan
Baton Rouge, Louisiana
Boise City, Idaho
Des Moines, Iowa
Evansville, Indiana
Fort Myers-Cape Coral,
  Florida
Little Rock, Arkansas
Madison, Wisconsin
Nashville, Tennessee
Naples, Florida
Omaha, Nebraska
Provo-Orem, Utah
Sioux Falls, S. Dakota
Terre Haute, Indiana
Tucson, Arizona
Wichita, Kansas

Alabama

Although not seriously affected by the 1991–92 recession, Alabama offers a mixed outlook for the job seeker. Its unemployment rate was 6.2 percent near the end of 1991, but the jobless rate was kept below the national average by a declining work force. From a work force of roughly 1.9 million, Alabama lost 3,300 jobs—3,100 product-producing positions and 200 in the service-producing sector—in the year ended November 1991. Nonetheless, Birmingham and Mobile in particular are expected to have steady business expansion and job growth through the decade.

Over the next several years, the state's employment is projected to grow at a modest 1.55 percent annual rate, with the strongest expansion in its metropolitan areas, which are projected to grow by 1.85 percent annually. For the remainder of the state—in the rural areas outside Birmingham, Mobile, Huntsville, Montgomery, Tuscaloosa, Florence, Anniston, Gadsden, Dothan and Decatur—job growth is projected to be an anemic 0.82 percent annually.

Moreover, changes in American trade laws and reduced federal spending for defense and aerospace cast some doubt over Alabama's job outlook. Changes in trade regulations, particularly relating to imports from Mexico, will reduce employment in the state's textile trade. In all, textiles accounted for 41,000 Alabama jobs in late 1991, down 400 from a year earlier. Wage scales are modest, from $6.43 to $8.32 an hour, but the fear among state employment officials is that inexpensive imports will close down some cut-and-sew operations.

Federal-spending cuts pose a danger to a smaller but better-paid segment of the Alabama economy. The state has several defense installations, and U.S. Defense Department employment totaled 30,600 at the end of 1991. Total federal-government employment was 64,300, making it Alabama's second-largest employer after the state itself. Huntsville, home of the Alabama Space and Rocket Center, would be adversely affected by cuts in NASA funds.

Should the space appropriations continue, Huntsville—in the state's northeast corner and located 90 miles north of Birmingham and 120 miles south of Nashville, Tennessee—would be poised for strong growth in professional employment, particularly for engineers. Total employment was projected to grow by 2.5 percent annually through the decade, one of the highest rates in the state. In addition, the demand for professional and technical workers was projected to advance by 3.2 percent annually, with more than 2,000 job openings a year.

Based on projected job openings, the eight fastest-growing occupations in the Huntsville area are technical or professional, ranging from 265 annual openings for engineering technicians and 245 openings for electrical and electronic engineers to 30 openings a year for computer operators. The projected growth rates, all above 3 percent annually, outpace even retail salespersons, whose job openings are projected to grow by 3.72 percent annually, or 340 positions.

In a state with widely divergent job needs, those technical positions do not register as high-growth jobs in other regions. In the Tuscaloosa region, for instance, mechanical engineers rank 10th among fastest-growing occupations, with only 10 projected openings a year. The top growth category in the west-central portion of the state covers accountants and auditors, with a projected increase exceeding 5 percent and 35 annual openings. With a projected annual job growth of 1.8 percent, Tuscaloosa has strong demand for retail salespersons, low-paying positions with about 200 annual openings; and for registered nurses, with 100 annual openings—half of them new positions.

Montgomery, the state capital, has a 2.1 percent projected annual growth rate, with highest numerical demand for retail salespersons and truck drivers, mirroring the state as a whole. Among technical and professional employees, demand is projected to be good for registered nurses and engineers.

SPOTLIGHT ON BIRMINGHAM

Over the years, Birmingham has had several nicknames. For years, it was the Pittsburgh of the South because its iron, limestone and coal provided all of the raw materials for steel making. A substantial portion of the steel industry is gone now—Birmingham's basic-steel employment plunged from 18,000 workers in 1970 to 5,000 two decades later—although the city now makes more steel than Pittsburgh itself.

Birmingham also has been called the Magic City, and it indeed worked some magic by diversifying away from steel before the domestic industry collapsed in the 1970s and 1980s. While somewhat within the economic sphere of influence radiating out of Atlanta, Birmingham has developed as a center for financial services, medical care, biomedical research, insurance and engineering.

Health care, in particular, has become Birmingham's principal employer, providing jobs for one of every nine persons in a work force approaching a half-million people. The largest employer, with a 13,765-worker payroll, is the University of Alabama at Birmingham, which operates one of the great medical centers of the world, Baptist Medical Centers and three other hospitals—Carraway Methodist Medical Center, St. Vincent's Hospital and AMI Brookwood Medical Center—are all among the region's top 25 employers.

As a result, healthy demand exists for health workers. The region is projected to need 400 new registered nurses each year, with more than half of them filling newly created positions. The area also is projected to need almost 250 nurses aides-orderlies, 235 licensed practical nurses and 180 physicians each year. Jobs for other health-service workers also will grow vigorously. Demand for medical technicians is projected to grow by more than 5 percent a year, and increases for home health aides will approach 4 percent annually.

Among business services, the Birmingham region is projected to have openings for 170 accountants and auditors each year, with 70 of them filling new jobs. Among the area's fastest growing occupations is computer systems analyst, with an annual demand of 60 workers for 50 new posts and 10 vacancies. Of 105 computer-related openings each year, 80 will be newly created jobs. Birmingham also is projected to need 200 engineers annually, with the heaviest demand for electrical engineers.

Although growth has been strongest in service-producing jobs, Birmingham has maintained modest gains in its manufacturing sector. USX, the former U.S. Steel Corp., employs 2,200 in Birmingham at its Fairfield Works, where it has a seamless pipe mill and a new continuous slab caster. The region's companies also produce about 55 percent of the cast-iron pipe made in America each year.

SPOTLIGHT ON
MOBILE

A large Gulf of Mexico port, Mobile is the state's second-largest metropolis with a work force of about 200,000 and a projected annual job growth rate of 1.9 percent. Assisted by a diverse economy and an aggressive development program, Mobile enjoyed some insulation from the 1991–92 recession. Retail sales in the third quarter of 1991 were more than 8 percent above the same 1990 quarter, and the value of building permits issued during 1991 jumped 25 percent over the previous year.

With a 45-foot-deep channel through Mobile Bay to the Gulf, Mobile and its region benefit from the busy port. A major export point for Alabama's forest products, Mobile has operations of Scott Paper and International Paper. The U.S. Coast Guard has three separate operations in Mobile, and the port has been designated as a home port for four Navy vessels. The home port designation, part of the Navy's base-consolidation efforts, is expected to result in 3,000 civilian and military jobs. The city also has several ship-building operations as well as chemicals, textiles, oil and gas production, computer manufacturing and seafood processing.

Mobile also has a growing health-services industry whose largest employer is the 800-bed University of South Alabama Hospitals and Clinics. With other hospitals and clinics, Mobile is a strong market for health professionals. Demand for registered nurses is projected to grow by about 5 percent a year, and 125 of 200 annual openings will be newly created positions. Therapists, nursing aides-orderlies, licensed practical nurses, home health aides and medical technicians will also be in demand.

Alaska

In 1968 oil was discovered on the North Slope near Prudhoe Bay and a decade later the 800-mile trans-Alaska pipeline was completed. Oil has been the centerpiece of Alaska's economy ever since and it has proven to be a mixed blessing. During periods of higher oil prices there are always an expansion in the state's economy and an increase in both the state's population and labor force. Unfortunately, according to John Boucher, a labor economist with the Alaska

Department of Labor, since the end of the Gulf War, oil prices have dropped, and the state's two largest oil producers are reducing operations.

The state's recession surprisingly has not slowed the number of people coming into Alaska from the lower 48 states. Between 1990 and 1991, 20,000 moved to Alaska, making it second only to Nevada in population growth. As a result, many have found it difficult to get jobs, and Alaska's unemployment rate threatened to reach double digits for the first time since May of 1988. More than 25,000 of the state's 255,459 workers were out of a job in 1991.

Yet, despite all the signs of recession, several sectors of Alaska's job market showed growth in 1991. The service-producing industry posted the largest gain, with 6,000 more jobs than in 1990. Of those jobs, 1,100 came in the retail trade area, while 1,800 came from the business services, medical services and engineering and management services industries. Government also posted large employment gains in 1991, rising by 3.27 percent, or 2,500 jobs over the previous year. Many of those jobs, such as temporary workers hired to conduct local elections and part-time and student employees at the University of Alaska, do not, however, reflect long-term job growth. But the influx of new residents brought with it a respective increase in personnel in the state's local government and school districts. In all, Alaska's nonagricultural employment level grew by 2.5 percent, or almost 6,000 jobs in 1991.

More than half of Alaska's work force remains concentrated in Anchorage, the state's largest city, and the neighboring borough of Matsu. An additional 31,000 workers are employed in Fairbanks, Alaska's second-largest city. Agriculture represents 7.2 percent of the work force, down more than a full percentage point from the year before.

Despite Alaska's well-publicized problems, many people seem to be intent on moving here. The careful job seeker would be wise to stay put—unless there is a job waiting for him or her.

Arizona

"Population is the key to understanding the long-term outlook for Arizona," writes Lee R. McPheters, director of Arizona State Economic Outlook Center, in *Arizona Business*, January 1992. "Part of the stimulus for growth comes from migration by those looking for jobs as the local businesses expand and other employers relocate into the state. However, some of the stimulus for growth is not job-related, but is simply embedded in the American culture, which has encouraged Westward migration since the Pilgrims first set foot on Plymouth Rock."

Like its sister frontier states, Arizona has capitalized on the Western mystique. In the last 100 years, the state grew more than any other in percentage of population. In 1991, Arizona's population was 41 times larger than a century ago. During the last 10 years, it increased its population by more than one-third making Arizona the third-fastest growing state in the country.

In 1990, Arizona ranked eighth in the nation in production of new jobs. While population growth is predicted to remain at a slower pace during the 1990s, the state will continue to grow faster than most of the country, assuring that Arizona will continue to be a leader in creating new jobs.

Even in a poor economy, Arizona continues to rank among the top ten states in rate of growth of trade and service sector jobs. The "Arizona Blue Chip Economic Forecast (December 1991)" notes that of the 22,000 total jobs added in the state between September, 1990 and September, 1991, three-quarters were in service.

As for 1992, this forecast sees a gain of 3.2 percent in employment, a rosier labor market outlook than any time during the past four years.

Growth, however, has always been a two-edged sword for Arizonans. The state delivers the promised climate, lifestyle and opportunities, but it hasn't fared as well providing good wages and high income for its residents. Both wage and per capita income fall below the national average. More significantly, both lost ground during the 1980s. The average wage of Arizona employees in 1990 was 8 percent below the national average.

Several factors contribute to this reality. Probably most important, Arizona continues to be a right-to-work state with relatively few strong unions. Because people move to this state by choice and often for perceived quality of life advantages, residents are often willing to accept lower wages in order to continue to live here. Finally, the state's industrial mix is tilted more toward low-wage industries than is true of most of other states, which skews the earnings picture even more.

Arthur L. Silvers, Ph.D., of the College of Business and Public Administration of the University of Arizona, points out in his report, "On the Edge of the 21st Century," that for the last 50 years, Arizona's industrial makeup has differed significantly from that of the rest of the nation. Arizona has a much higher share of jobs in service-producing industries and a much smaller percentage of jobs in manufacturing. In 1969, manufacturing made up 18 percent of all jobs. Today, that number is 12 percent. And experts predict manufacturing will continue to take up an even smaller proportional piece of the Arizona pie. The Arizona Occupational Profile of Manufacturing (1991) notes that today, manufacturing ranks behind services, trade, and government in terms of numbers of employees.

Still, electronic manufacturing is big business in Arizona. More than half of those employed in manufacturing help produce electronic computing equipment. Electronic machinery will continue to be the greatest area of new manufacturing job growth in the state through 1994. In addition to semiconductors and related products, Arizona manufacturers produce machinery, defense and aerospace equipment, and in the next few years, experts predict strong growth in firms manufacturing chemicals and allied products (pharmaceuticals, etc.).

Printing and publishing is another strong area of consistent growth. In 1991, printing and publishing employed some 17,000 Arizonans, up a whopping 54 percent over the 1980 figures.

All predictions indicate that the hot future spot will be F.I.R.E. (finance, insurance, real estate and services). By the year 2000, this category will be responsible for one out of every two new jobs.

Government, a major statewide employer which traditionally reflects population growth, is expected to diminish in percentage share by the turn of the century. In 1990 government accounted for 17.3 percent of all new jobs. By 2000, this number will drop to 12.7 percent of non-farm payroll jobs.

Health and related services is also expected to boom. More than 8 percent of all new jobs created between 1989 and 1994 are predicted to be in Arizona's health care delivery system. While part of this may be attributed to growth (Arizona's population is expected to increase by 29 percent by 2000), some of this increase will reflect the needs of an aging population. In terms of the average age of its residents, Arizona is a young state today. By the turn of the century, however, the population of Arizonans 75 years or older will .grow by 46 percent.

Not surprisingly, the Arizona Occupational Profile 1991 for Hospitals expects hospital employment in Arizona to increase 3.4 percent *annually*. Areas seeing special growth include acute, geriatric and long-term care. What does this mean for specific career opportunities? R.N.s should be able to write their own tickets. More than 7,310 jobs for R.N.s are expected to open up in Arizona between 1989 and 1994. Nursing aides, orderlies, clerks and practical nurses will also be in demand.

In the final analysis, Arizona's future growth is predicated upon a healthy national economy. While historically this state has led the nation—both experiencing and recovering from downturns before the rest of the country—the rules have changed recently. During the boom and bust days of the 1960s, 1970s and 1980s, construction—both residential and commercial—always propelled Arizona out of its economic doldrums. No longer. As economist Lee McPheters of ASU notes, "This time Arizona must ride the wave of the national economy. Until there is a national momentum, there will be no strong Arizona rebound."

Still, until sunsets, sage and *saguaros* go out of style, Arizona will retain its allure, making it a favorite of new employers for locations and new employees seeking work.

SPOTLIGHT ON PHOENIX

Economists report that the Valley of the Sun is still out-performing most other large metropolitan areas of the nation.

Why? When the question is jobs, the answer is Maricopa County, the county which encompasses all of metro Phoenix. Three out of every four new jobs created in Arizona open up in Maricopa County. In 1992, Maricopa County will add 33,000 new jobs to the state's economy.

For a region accustomed to booming population and a blooming economy, the immediate outlook for this sun-drenched Valley appears less than golden. Tied to the national economy, some economists see 1992 and 1993 as transition years. While each year will be better economically than 1991, 1994 is generally viewed as the first year when the economy will swing back into its "normal" fast pace.

What may help kick the economy into high gear is the work of a two-year, statewide planning effort, ASPED (Arizona Strategic Planning & Economic Development). Driven by citizens who met all over the state, ASPED is recommending legislation in several areas. The committee is also identifying specific actions that must be taken by the public and private sectors to create healthy "clusters" (economic sectors) and "foundations" (infrastructure plus a host of other considerations including telecommunications, education and training, etc.) for Arizona. With this comprehensive study moving into the implementation phase, ASPED is expected to make a difference in the state's economy.

Although this group focused on economic clusters such as tourism, health, transportation and industry, at present government remains the biggest business of Greater Phoenix. The City of Phoenix, Maricopa County, the U.S. Postal Service, Mesa Public School, and Maricopa Community College—all in the top 25 employers—employ more than 62,000 people. Statewide, government employment is expected to grow by 2.5 percent to 3.5 percent next year.

In metro Phoenix, the State of Arizona leads the employment pack, with a payroll of 25,000 persons. Motorola is the county's second largest employer, followed by Allied Signal and America West Airlines which filed for bankruptcy in 1991.

Second to government, most Valley paychecks are written out of the service sector. In recent years, service has received a big boost as several credit card processing companies have relocated here. For years, American Express has maintained a regional headquarters for Travel and Financial Service in the city. In the short-range future, the strongest growth, statewide, in service industries is expected to occur in a narrowly defined area which includes health services, hotel and lodging employment and business services. More modest gains are anticipated in the transportation, communications and public utilities area, as well as finance, insurance and real estate. Since most service industries are located within the Phoenix metropolitan area, the Valley of the Sun stands to shine from a stronger service economy.

A young city, Phoenix emerged in the 1860s, nearly 100

years after the American Revolution. From the outset, it was an entrepreneurial paradise, a place where a bold newcomer like Jack Swilling could make a difference. In the 1850s Swilling saw remnants of prehistoric Hohokam Indian canals and with brash vision, imagined a new city rising along the banks of these old waterways. Jack Swilling is credited with starting what is today The Salt River Project, one of the state's larger employers and suppliers of power and water to both rural and metro areas.

Contemporary Phoenix remains a regional rather than corporate headquarters town, despite the city's efforts to lure headquarters operations to the desert. At present, Dial Corporation (formerly Greyhound) is headquartered here, and many major corporations have regional offices in Phoenix to capitalize on the good flying weather, hub location, and proximity to West Coast markets.

The capital of the state, Phoenix is a vast city of nearly 400 square miles. A fast growing but well-managed city, it was once considered mainly a tourist destination. Today, greater Phoenix boasts more four- and five-star resorts clustered in one urban area than any other city. Yet it has matured to become a major center of service, government, manufacturing and construction—with an ever-increasing population.

Traditionally, companies are attracted to Phoenix for its availability of land and absence of trade unions, plus the reasonable cost of building and maintaining real property, realities which, despite its growth, the city still enjoys.

In the last decade, Phoenix has decreased its dependence on manufacturing—particularly aerospace, electronic and semiconductor manufacturing—and concentrated more on growing the service sector of its economy. Still, according to the Arizona Occupational Profile on Manufacturing, 1991, the state's 5000 electrical and electronic engineers, the great proportion of whom live in metro Phoenix, makes this the third largest occupation in Arizona's manufacturing industry. Production managers and supervisors follow.

Leading the manufacturing employment pack are production and maintenance workers who account for more than half that industry's employment. One out of every four in that category are assemblers. Production and maintenance includes a wide range of occupations from assemblers, mechanics and repairers to truck drivers and craftsmen. Projections indicate that a variety of professional and technical occupations will open up in the future as manufacturing becomes increasingly more complex.

Despite the economic doldrums Phoenix has experienced for the last five years, 8000 new jobs were created in the city for last fiscal year. According to the Metro Phoenix Blue Chip Economic Forecast, only four large metropolitan areas (Denver, Seattle, Houston and Cincinnati) provided more new jobs over the same period of time.

Much of the explosive growth takes place in the East Valley (Mesa, Tempe, Chandler and Gilbert), an area of tremendous industrial and residential expansion for the past 10 years. Mesa's population stood at approximately 60,000 in the 1970s. Today that city is the size of Salt Lake City, Utah—and still growing fast. Nearby, the once sleepy farming community of Chandler blooms with industry: high tech to pharmaceuticals to plastics. Continental Medical Systems Inc. is planning two medical rehabilitation facilities in Arizona in 1992. One will be in Tucson; the other, a 56,000-square foot, $10 million building in Chandler.

As the service sector continues to expand, the immediate forecast predicts job losses in manufacturing. Like its sister California cities, Phoenix suffers when aerospace and defense-related production are weak. The scheduled closing of Williams Air Force Base in Chandler this year will affect the local economy. However, aerospace is still important to the Phoenix-Tucson economy.

Although commercial construction has slowed dramatically in the last five years, residential construction is showing renewed activity in Phoenix. In 1991, 12,000 housing permits were issued in Maricopa County, among the highest of any metropolitan area of the nation. In 1992, that number is expected to increase to 13,000.

SPOTLIGHT ON
TUCSON

Despite the struggling national economy, Tucson's forecast is for continued growth and low unemployment rates (less than 4 percent throughout 1991). According to Neil Shpritz, Director of Research for the Greater Tucson Economic Council, Tucson's appeal is more than sun and lush Sonoran desert. ''We also offer a small town with a more cosmopolitan atmosphere than Phoenix. Much of that can be attributed to the city's culture revolving around the University much more than it does in Phoenix,'' he adds.

The University of Arizona does make its presence felt in economic circles. Shpritz notes that the U of A has become one of the several centers for future development of fiber optics. In addition the University Medical Center houses one of the few heart transplant centers in the nation, and the cancer center is nationally recognized. The growth in health-related industries and businesses, such as biomedical research companies and the Muscular Dystrophy Association choosing Tucson for its new national headquarters, is a positive spin-off of the University's strong support.

In addition to a growing health sector, the city is a center for aircraft maintenance and refurbishment. Evergreen and Lockheed, long located in Tucson, are known leaders in this rapidly expanding field, and Bombardier (formerly Lear Jet) has enlarged its operational facility to handle refurbishment. As of February, 1992, Tucson (along with Phoenix) was on the short list for an aircraft rehabilitation facility for Alaska Airlines.

Supporting this emerging industry, Tucson's Pima Community College, the eighth-largest community college in the country, is teaching what is believed to be the first curriculum in the nation to focus on aircraft refurbishment.

A report for the Greater Tucson Economic Council (GTEC) notes that Tucson's manufacturing sector comes in at nearly 50 percent tech. Although IBM made news a few years ago for downsizing its Tucson facility, that company still employs 2500 people in Tucson. With a high tech base that includes IBM, GTEC expects the city to continue to attract state-of-the-art firms.

The job market in Tucson is selective, but overall quite good, especially for a well-educated person. Like Phoenix, Tucson is dependent upon the national economy for its overall economic health, yet recent statistics indicate a positive upswing. The vacancy rate in Greater Tucson for apartment buildings has dropped into the single digits and sales are strong, indicating a resurgence in building. At the same time, the glut on office space is showing signs of declining. Add to this the growing number of inquiries by companies considering relocating, and Tucson—with its moderate size (just over 500,000), livability, and cultural opportunities—appears well positioned for the near future.

Arkansas

Arkansas calls itself the "Land of Opportunity," and until recently this might have been taken to be irony of a very high order. After all, this is a very poor state, ranking 47th among the 50 in per capita personal income, and 48th in per pupil expenditures for education. It also remains one of the top ten states in terms of rural population, since only 40 percent of the people live in metropolitan areas.

But in fact Arkansas looks to be on the verge of a major economic growth period, one that will provide substantial job growth for most of the state. In 1991 Arkansas created 32,500 new jobs, about the same as Oregon and Colorado *combined*. More importantly 7,000 of those jobs were in the manufacturing sector, very close to the 10,000 created in services, bucking the national trend and showing the possibilities of a diversified economy.

Cheap, abundant labor and tax breaks for manufacturing firms have helped to make manufacturing the backbone of the Arkansas labor market. In the past 11 years, manufacturing failed to grow only twice. One of those years was 1982, during a statewide and national recession, said David Melugin of the Arkansas Employment Security Division. Thus while manufacturing is expected to decline nationwide by about 4.6 percent over the next decade, Arkansas projects manufacturing employment growth of more than 21 percent.

That trend is evident in the success of the state's largest manufacturing business, Tyson Foods. The Springdale-based chicken and processed food manufacturer has nearly doubled its number of Arkansas employees in the past five years, from 12,509 in 1986 to 22,428 in 1991. Two other Fortune 500 food processing corporations are located in Arkansas, Hudson Foods and Riceland Foods. Strong employment growth has been achieved by two large paper manufacturers, Georgia Pacific in Crossett, in the southeastern part of the state, employed just over 4,000 in 1986. Today its employees number more than 4,800. Meanwhile, International Paper grew by nearly 600 employees in 1991 alone, from 3,065 to 3,617.

Overall, the Arkansas labor market is expected to grow slightly faster than the national average through 2000. Arkansas employment stood at 962,410 in 1986, and is expected to jump 22.2 percent to 1,175,630 by the end of the decade. As is the case in most of the country, jobs in the service industry will increase at the expense of those in agriculture.

Agriculture, which currently makes up 4.6 percent of the labor market in Arkansas, will drop to just under 3.6 percent by the year 2000. The transportation and trade industries will pick up that slack, each posting growth of greater than 30 percent. Arkansas's transportation industries, which include U.S. Postal Service employees, will jump 31.53 percent, from 34,440 to 45,300 jobs, while the trade industries will increase from 184,760 workers in 1986 to a total of 48,720 in 2000, a rise of 34.62 percent. By the year 2000, three of every four jobs in the state will be in the service (34 percent), manufacturing (22 percent) or trade (21 percent) industries.

Slightly more than 20 percent of all employment will continue to be in Little Rock, the state's capital and largest city. The Little Rock area is expected to grow slightly faster than the state as a whole in almost all industries. It will even post a 35.5 percent increase in agriculture, forestry, and fisheries by the end of the decade, even though that industry is expected to decline statewide by more than 8 percent. Much of that increase will come from the burgeoning agricultural services segment, which includes soil preparation, crop services, veterinary services, farm management services, and landscape and horticultural services. Statewide, this segment of the agricultural industry is expected to grow from 3,330 to 5,290, or 59 percent, by the year 2000.

Service jobs will of course continue to grow for the rest of the decade. Retail sales jobs should increase by nearly 6,000 by the year 2000, making this one of the fastest growing jobs in the state, as well as the nation. Other fast-growing occupations will be the standard ones: cashiers, waiters and waitresses, and truck drivers.

The only caution that must be given about working in Arkansas is that wages are very low even compared to neighboring states such as Missouri and Tennessee.

California

National news stories about California are almost always about one disaster or another, earthquakes rattling major cities, massive brush fires devouring expensive homes, torrential rains that last for five days, and droughts that last for five years. But in the early months of 1992 the big news story was not about a natural disaster, but the fear of an economic one.

To be blunt, the news that came out of California had not been so bad since the devastating recession of the early 1980s sent unemployment rates soaring to 10 percent and beyond. After enjoying five years of unrelenting prosperity California has suddenly reversed course and created literally hundreds of thousands of newly unemployed workers. In 1990 the average unemployment rate was 5.6 percent but by December of 1991 it had climbed to 7.7 percent and it was rising faster than anyone had predicted. In fact by February 1992 California's 8.7 unemployment rate was significantly higher than that supposed paradigm of economic failure, Massachusetts, whose rate was 7.5 percent in the same month.

If this trend continues it will have a serious impact on the national economy and on the presidential election as well. The central importance of California to the health and well-being of the nation cannot easily be exaggerated; after all, one in eight Americans lives there. The dimensions of its economy are so enormous that they resemble those of a separate nation rather than one of the 50 states. The value of the goods and services produced there ranks California among the top ten economies of the *world* and its work force of over 13 million is greater than the population of all but three states.

California's ever-increasing population has always been one of the foundation stones of its enormous economic strength. It has been the most populous state since the 1960s and since then total population has doubled to over 30 million. During the 1980s California led the nation in population growth with another 6.1 million people added, a 25.7 percent increase. In the year following the 1990 census another 600,000 people were added, again the largest increase of any state.

But 1991 may prove to be the last boom year for strong population increases. Because that is when the troubles that had started in 1990 began to surface. In December of 1991, California had 158,000 fewer jobs than it did in December 1990. This steep decline occurred despite a strong *increase* of 85,000 jobs in the services area, meaning that the other sectors were hurt very badly: finance, insurance, and real estate declined by 11,000 jobs, construction by 43,000, wholesale and retail trade, 59,000, and manufacturing by a staggering 89,000, fully 20 percent of all the manufacturing jobs lost in the entire nation during that period.

Although employment in manufacturing has been declining since the 1970s it has remained a substantial part of California's economy, despite the contemporary white-collar/professional image of the state's prosperity. In 1972 manufacturers accounted for 27 percent of all jobs in the state, but by 1990 that figure was down to less than 20 percent and falling rapidly. The state office of employment development projects that it will continue to fall to as low as 16 percent by the year 2000. This may change, however, since the governor's office appears determined to take steps to reverse the trend that has sent manufacturing firms fleeing the state in droves for Utah, Nevada, and Idaho, where they can do business more cheaply, pay lower taxes, and avoid the bureaucratic red tape that has evolved over the years. Most analysts agree that like the nation as a whole, California must strengthen its manufacturing base.

One element in the manufacturing equation that is beyond the state's control is federal defense spending, one of the key factors in California's prosperity since the second World War. During the 1980s California became the center of aerospace research and development for all the military services; tens of thousands of jobs were created at major employers such as Lockheed and Douglas Aircraft. Between 1982 and 1986 the number of people employed in the aerospace/high tech industries increased by about 100,000 from 658,000 to 752,000. So many of these jobs, both blue- and white-collar, were high-paying that they had an immediate, palpable effect on the other elements of the economy, especially retail sales and construction. But the Cold War has ended and the binge spending on defense is about to go cold turkey. The chills this is sending through the California economy are severe, not the least of which has been the loss of 47,000 defense-related jobs during 1990 and 1991, with another 30,000 (at least) projected for 1992.

Several other areas of the California economy have fallen on hard times. The boom and bust cycle in housing construction entered a severe downslide after eight years of growth and price inflation for 1991, the number of building permits declined by 53 percent compared to a national decline of 15 percent. After a fall of that magnitude the only way is up, and most experts do see a strong upturn in housing permits of 20 to 30 percent in 1992. It should be noted, however, that the highly respected UCLA Business Forecasting Project decidedly disagrees and sees little growth in construction. It is highly doubtful in any case that employment in construction will stay at the 650,000 level, 100,000 more than it was in 1986.

The finance, insurance, and real estate sector held its own through most of 1991 despite the high-profile problems of one of the state's largest insurance companies, the continuing restructuring of the banking industry through several large mergers, and a weakening in home sales due to the recession. This sector only lost a few thousand jobs out of a total of more than 840,000 and the state authorities predict a 2.6 percent growth in 1992.

Wholesale and retail trade have also held up during the recession despite some severe weakening in retail sales even through the holidays. Retail sales, which employs over 2.2 million statewide, is projected to add a significant number of new jobs in 1992—but that prediction was made before all signs of recovery were wiped away in early 1992.

Services are projected to continue in a growth mode in 1992. Business and health services should lead the way, although the former is highly dependent on an economic recovery. This may not apply to legal services, which is growing rapidly throughout the state, nor to engineering, especially environmental engineering, and management consulting.

The state has predicted an increase of 154,000 jobs in services in 1992 which is probably very high (they had predicted 111,000 for 1991 and fell short by about 20 percent).

Now, a special word about the government sector in California. While in 1991 it added over 20,000 jobs to the slightly more than 2 million already there, its days as a growth sector may be over. With the state in serious financial disarray the present governor, Pete Wilson, is looking for every way possible to pare down the budget. Early in 1992, however, he surely went beyond the bounds of fair play by forcing government workers to take a pay cut, thereby placing blame on ordinary working people for the problems clearly created by the insatiable greed of developers, the overdependence of the state on federally funded jobs, and the lack of planning in the state house.

From these industry trends it's clear which jobs are going to be the most plentiful throughout California in the immediate future. Despite the recession state analysts believe that strong demand for legal services will create new openings for over 2,000 lawyers a year, almost 1,000 positions for paralegals (whose numbers have been doubling in recent years) and almost as many for legal secretaries. Nurses, physical therapists, home health aides, and medical technicians, as expected, will lead the way in health care services, but there will also be a continuing demand for physicians and surgeons despite the large number in the state already.

Other professional occupations, including teachers, computer systems analysts, and programmers, accountants, financial managers, mechanical and environmental engineers should all fare very well. Among the occupations employing large numbers of people (retail sales, secretaries, food preparation and service, truck drivers, etc.) the road ahead is bound to be a little more difficult to maneuver than during the good economic times, but as with any densely populated area the sheer number of jobs is so enormous that retirements, deaths, and separations create a tremendous level of turnover so jobs are opening up all the time. What remains uncertain is whether or not the recession will continue to severely hamper the creation of new jobs.

What should be kept in mind by anyone seeking a job in California is that the recession is hitting some areas much harder than others, as the following brief survey will reveal.

SPOTLIGHT ON
SAN FRANCISCO-OAKLAND

San Francisco's once-glamorous image has taken a beating recently from the 1989 earthquake, which caused $6 billion damage and left over 60 dead, and from last year's Oakland Hills fire that destroyed 4,000 homes. Stories on the beautiful Bay City's proliferating problems—drought, AIDS, homelessness, traffic jams, high housing costs—reached a lurid low in September 1991, when *Forbes* magazine accused San Francisco of "self-destructive lunacy" and "wacky economics" for piling on taxes and regulations that drove business (and jobs) away. But recession job-seekers should take a hint from millions of tourists, who have let neither bad ink nor bad times deter them from visiting the nation's most popular vacation spot. San Francisco remains an exciting place to live and work, as well as visit.

Seekers of the California dream can still find it in San Francisco. The nationwide recession arrived fashionably late in 1991, but unemployment topped 5 percent for only a month and ended the year at 4.7 percent. San Francisco's metropolitan area still has the nation's second-highest per capita income, a third higher than the U.S. average, and total income tops $150 billion a year. The stalled real estate market should resume its ferocious rise with lower interest rates in 1992. While other major western cities bristle with empty office buildings, a slow-growth ordinance approved by San Francisco voters in 1986 has kept the commercial vacancy rate around 12 percent—half the rate in Los Angeles. Massive defense cutbacks have scarcely rattled San Francisco, where the number one industry is tourism, followed by business services, and international trade. The metropolitan area added over 63,000 jobs a year throughout the 1980s and experts forecast another 55,000 jobs a year in the 1990s.

The best place to look for a job in San Francisco is probably outside the city itself. The greater Bay Area (pop. 6 million) encompasses nine counties, including the famous Silicon Valley. San Francisco (pop. 727,000) is across the bay from the booming counties of Alameda (1.3 million) and Contra Costa (800,000) where five-year job growth projections range from 13 to 15 percent. (San Francisco projects a more modest 3.4 percent.) Along the "580–680 Freeway Corridor" in Contra Costa and Alameda counties, east of Oakland, new offices and shopping malls have sprouted up alongside countless housing developments. Almost half of all new homes built in the Bay Area since 1985 have been in these two counties. And the "edge city" boom towns of Concord, Walnut Creek, Pleasant Hill, San Ramon, Dublin, Pleasanton, and Livermore have had the "Help Wanted" signs up for years.

Nurses, legal secretaries, computer programmers, and retail salespeople are already in high demand in the Alameda-Contra Costa region. Many more health care professionals will be needed as Kaiser Permanente plans extensive hospital expansions in the area. Thousands of openings for managers and office workers are expected as more businesses cross the bay from San Francisco, and the federal government is relocating 3,000 employees to Oakland in 1993. Job growth in business services, which already employs over 50,000 people in Alameda-Contra Costa, is projected at the phenomenal rate of 25 to 50 percent over five years. Suburban restaurants, bars, and auto dealers will employ nearly 80,000 workers here by 1993. Alameda-Contra Costa accounted for two out of five new jobs in the Bay Area in the 1980s, and that trend continues.

In San Francisco itself—where half the work force commutes daily from outside the city—tourism supports the service and retail sectors, which account for nearly half the city's 570,000 workers and all of its net job growth. By 1993, the city will add six new hotels, including a new Marriott, while major expansion of the Moscone Convention Center is expected to keep occupancy rates high. Supplying food and lodging is the livelihood of 60,000 San Franciscans and another 60,000 work in retail sales, so openings can be expected in these high-turnover fields. Nurses, sales personnel, janitors, and security guards are currently in short supply. But law is still the number-one growth industry in town, with heavy demand for lawyers, legal secretaries, and paralegals expected to continue in the 1990s. As in much of the United States, health care employment is increasing twice as fast as the population. Other growing service industries include temporary employment agencies; building maintenance and security; and marketing, advertising, and public relations. J. Walter Thompson recently announced it will relocate much of its advertising business from Los Angeles to San Francisco.

Employers in San Francisco's gleaming skyscrapers report a shortage of qualified managers, administrators, accountants, and engineers in their firms, but demand for typists and data entry clerks is slack. One in seven San Franciscans works in finance, insurance, and real estate, but the 77,000 jobs in this sector are shrinking fast. About 15,000 layoffs are expected to result from the largest bank merger in history between Bank of America and Security Pacific. Few new openings are expected among the 90,000 government jobs in San Francisco—and substantial losses will follow the closing of military bases at the Presidio and

Treasure Island. Construction jobs are disappearing in San Francisco thanks in part to severe regulations, but some work is available in specialty trades, especially building renovation. San Francisco boasts some new showcase warehouses and container shipping facilities, but overall the 70,000 workers in wholesale trade, transportation, and public utilities face shrinking job prospects. One exception: San Francisco and Oakland plan major airport expansions which could open 4,000 jobs for mechanics in the next few years. International trade is worth $50 billion a year in the Bay Area, and half is carried by air.

What about San Francisco's manufacturing sector? Barely 40,000 workers, or just 7.4 percent of the work force, are in manufacturing—and only 8,500 of them produce durable goods. Bay Area manufacturers weathered the last recession by concentrating in high-tech electronics, which has not fared as well in recent years, though Silicon Valley shows signs of revival. The few high-tech firms that prosper in the 1990s will probably not hire many new workers. The vast majority of manufacturing jobs in the city of San Francisco are in the declining or low-growth areas of food processing, apparel, and printing. A bright spot on the Bay Area's manufacturing horizon is the famous General Motors/Toyota NUMMI plant in Fremont, south of Oakland. Hundreds of new assembly workers will be hired when Toyota trucks start rolling off the line this year. Chemical plants and Standard Oil's refinery employ most of the manufacturing workers in Contra Costa county but scanty job growth is expected there.

Few places in the world can match San Francisco's charm and sophistication, but the vaunted quality of life is threatened by overcrowding and a growing gap between wages and housing costs. Median home prices exceed $250,000 in most suburbs, $300,000 in San Francisco, and $350,000 in Marin and San Mateo counties. Rent in the city approaches Manhattanesque levels. No wonder employers are shifting their operations to the suburbs or out of state. In the past five years, Bank of America, Wells Fargo, Chevron, and Pacific Gas & Electric have transferred 50,000 jobs out of San Francisco. Many firms complain they cannot afford to pay employees what it costs to live there, while special taxes and regulations make business a day-to-day nightmare. The ultimate insult came in January 1992, when the San Francisco Giants baseball team announced a move to San Jose. But the new pro-business Mayor Frank Jordan vows to halt the "self-destructive economics," so job prospects may improve in the 1990s.

SPOTLIGHT ON SAN JOSE

Although technically part of the San Francisco metropolitan area, this part of California has carved out a separate identity for itself. (Santa Clara county is the base area for the statistics compiled by the state.) The heart of the area, at the south end of the San Francisco Bay, is the city of San Jose, the third largest city on the west coast, the eleventh largest in the country. San Jose prides itself on being the "Capital of Silicon Valley," and with 1,500 of the 2,500 largest electronics firms in the nation located within a 30-mile radius of downtown, the claim is undisputed.

Silicon Valley covers much of the northern part of Santa Clara County. Many companies are located in Palo Alto (home of Stanford University), Mountain View, Cupertino, Sunnyvale, and Santa Clara. The area south of San Jose has maintained much of its agricultural base, although suburban sprawl grows closer every year as land becomes scarce in the northern part of the county. There has also been some movement up the east side of the Bay to the city of Fremont in Alameda County.

Despite all the setbacks in the computer industry due to foreign competition and industry restructuring, it is still a growing area. New markets that didn't exist 10–15 years ago are proliferating—workstations, networks, telecommunications, and perhaps the most promising of all (Wall Street certainly seems to think so): biotechnology.

Although some 13,000 jobs were lost in Santa Clara County in 1991, unemployment has remained relatively low (6.5 percent in January 1992, up from 5.2 in December). For the near future the area is expected to gain about 13,000 nonagricultural jobs per year. About three-fourths of new jobs will be in the services and trades sector.

Most of the services growth will be in business services, engineering and management services, health services, private education, and social services. Business services include temp employment agencies, data processing services, building services, and equipment rental. Many companies have turned to these specialized suppliers, contracting out previously in-house tasks. The growth of specialized programming, software development, research, and engineering services also reflects this trend.

Electronics manufacturing employment will grow more slowly than in the past (about 1000 jobs per year) mostly in computer manufacturing. Some of this slowdown is due to reclassification of positions to the business services sector mentioned above, but in an industry such as semiconductor manufacturing, international competition has taken a heavy toll. In the last few years, firms such as Cypress Semiconductor and Chips and Technology responded to this pressure by making special-purpose chips, avoiding the competition of mass-produced products.

Two of the Valley's larger employers, Lockheed and FMC Corp. (of Bradley fighting vehicle-Gulf War fame) could be hurt by defense spending cutbacks. FMC recently unveiled a modified version of the Bradley and the Army has ordered two for testing. FMC is looking for an order of several hundred from the Pentagon to avoid a 1994 planned shutdown of the San Jose Plant. Lockheed could fare better. With about 19,700 Bay area employees, it is one of the largest employers in the Valley and is working on many government programs. About 20 percent of the work force is attached to the fleet ballistic missile programs, mostly the Trident II, which survived President Bush's initial defense cuts. Other programs, such as the NASA advanced solid rocket motor and various work packages for the space shuttle, seem safe for now. If so, Lockheed plans to lose about 400 jobs during the year but through attrition. Retirements and normal turnover could lead to some hiring. Electronic optics engineering, electrical engineering, and aerospace would be the best areas to enter.

Most other industry divisions should see some growth. Electronics wholesaling will generate many of the new jobs in wholesale trade, while restaurants and bars will provide almost half of the additional jobs in retail trade. Construction will gain from housing and remodeling but the county's high vacancy rate in office and industrial space will slow commercial development. Transportation and public utilities will benefit from expansion of San Jose Airport, which American Airlines has recently designated as its west coast hub. Finance, insurance, and real estate will add a few jobs, while the government sector is crippled at every level by deficits.

SPOTLIGHT ON SACRAMENTO

About 100 miles east of San Francisco is the city of Sacramento, the capital of California and the magnet city in the Sacramento metropolitan area, which is made up of four counties: Yolo, El Dorado, Placer and Sacramento. During the 1980s this was one of the fastest growing areas as population increased about 35 percent to 1.5 million.

While the current recession has slowed economic expansion and 6,000 jobs were lost in 1991, unemployment has not been severe—at least not yet. Between December 1991 and January 1992 there was a sharp increase from 6.5 percent to 7.7 but some of this was seasonal in nature. Overall job growth is expected to resume in 1992 although the city of Sacramento must overcome the effects of the state's deficit problems and subsequent belt-tightening.

As the economy improves, the services, retail trade, wholesale trade, and construction industry divisions are expected to produce about 12–13,000 jobs per year for the rest of the decade. But this is very much dependent on the duration of California's growing recession. In early 1992, the only word for the job market was stagnant.

According to the state Office of Employment Development, services will provide more than half of all future openings with health care being the fastest-growing component. Business services will add about 1,000 jobs per year, reflecting the anticipated growth in new and expanding businesses and for new residents. Engineering, accounting, research and management services, social services and legal services are all expected to contribute to the services sector expansion.

Most of the projected 3000 new retail jobs will be added in restaurants and bars, with general merchandise and food stores also contributing significantly, followed by furniture and home furnishing retailers, and automotive dealers and service stations.

Within the wholesale trades, the distribution of durable goods is expected to produce the most growth with gains in such areas as hardware, plumbing and heating supplies, and industrial machinery equipment and supplies. In the nondurable goods category, smaller gains are anticipated in groceries, printing, and publishing.

Prior to the 1991 recession, employment in the construction industry had expanded rapidly due to population and economic growth, no doubt lured by the area's climate and favorable real estate prices. Construction is expected to return to its pre-recession pace when the area again becomes a relocation and expansion target.

Since Sacramento is the state capital, the government sector accounts for about 30 percent of all nonagricultural jobs in the area. Mather Air Force base and the Sacramento Army Depot are both expected to be closed by the federal government by the mid–90s. California's budget deficit has forced a hiring freeze and some state programs are being cut. These declines are partially offset by a shift of some state programs to local agencies and by the increase in demand for public services that will follow the population growth.

Recently the insurance industry has provided the most jobs in the finance, insurance and real estate division. Sacramento has become the regional headquarters for several large insurance companies. The finance area is much less stable, due to the lingering effects of the savings and loan problems and even more so to the current trend towards consolidation among the state's major banks. Again, population growth will have some ameliorating effect in this area.

Moderate growth is expected in manufacturing, transportation, and public utilities employment, while the small mining sector should remain stable. The long-term outlook for employment in agriculture continues to be unfavorable.

SPOTLIGHT ON
LOS ANGELES—LONG BEACH

The economy of Los Angeles resembles a Hollywood starlet, glitzy, sexy, and appealing to look at, but fragile, skittish, and unpredictable at the core. Vulnerability may be a positive commodity for an aspiring movie star but in the real world of working people it causes only problems and pain.

The recession hit this area very hard in late 1991 and early 1992, as the unemployment rate jumped from 6.6 percent in early 1990 to 8.3 percent in December 1991 and then rocketed to 9.9 percent by February 1992, the highest it had been since February 1983 when it stood at 11.5 percent. In December 1991 there were 61,000 fewer jobs than in the same period the year before.

Over 4.5 million people work in the Los Angeles-Long Beach area, which encompasses an area of 4,080 square miles containing 86 incorporated cities, 10 of which have populations greater than 100,000. The city of Long Beach is the 32nd largest city in the nation (pop. 430,000), and Los Angeles is the second largest (pop. 3.5 million). Both of these cities rank in the top 10 of all U.S. ports and together handle over 100 million tons of commercial goods annually. Los Angeles is the center for financial, business, and legal services and for tourism, with much of the attraction coming from its Hollywood connection. Long Beach is more industrialized with major manufacturing units in aviation (McDonnell Douglas and Hughes Aircraft are both there) and shipbuilding at the world-famous naval shipyard.

The work force in the region reflects this diversity with 7 percent in finance, insurance, and real estate, 12.5 percent in government, 15 percent in retail sales, 20 percent employed in manufacturing and 29 percent in services. Manufacturing is struggling the most. With the decline in defense spending, jobs in aerospace have plummeted, but there are some signs that other opportunities will open up as the region as well as the nation retools for peace. Lockheed, for example, is opening a repair and modification center in San Bernadino, and Hughes Aircraft will be producing components for GM's electric car in a plant in Torrance.

But as the recession deepened toward the end of 1991 all aspects of the economy were affected even the growth of health services slowed down. Retailing, in the words of the LA Economic Development Corporation, "fell off a cliff in 1991, posting a stunning 5.8 percent decline . . . it seemed that almost every furniture chain in the area was going out of business." A slight upward trend is forecast for 1992 in part spurred by the entry of Wal-Mart and Ikea into the region.

Tourism, too, should post a small gain in 1992 after the number of visitors actually declined by 2 percent in 1991. The impact of the decline on the hotal industry was fairly dramatic as occupancy rates fell to 63.5 percent. Some analysts fear that the "negative image" of L.A. will prevent a quick recovery.

The making of movies, of course, is an important industry here and employs over 77,000 people. In recent years the drop in ticket sales and the movement away from made-for-TV movies to save money has hurt the employment situation very badly. As many as 25,000 more people could be employed when the recovery sets in.

All of these negative factors have cast a shadow over two of Los Angeles' best known industries, construction and real estate. With office vacancy rates topping 20 percent in most of southern California hardly any commercial space is being built. On the residential side the number of housing unit permits dropped by almost 40 percent. However, low interest rates and a low level of inventory are expected to ignite a gain of almost 20 percent in housing permits, bringing the total to just over 50,000, and bringing some construction workers back from the unemployed.

In general the Los Angeles area's job market is obviously going to be tough throughout 1992. Most forecasts that we've seen are even hedging about 1993. Massive funds from the national transportation bill will help and a slight rise in international trade and tourism can take some of the edge off, but the truth is that the area's leaders must find a way to keep manufacturers here, and create jobs to replace the defense-related ones that have been lost forever.

If those things happen then the generally optimistic trend predicted for professional and service workers will continue. Early in 1991 the state's Employment Development Department issued its projections for job growth between 1988 and 1993 in the Los Angeles-Long Beach area. In a telephone interview in March of 1992 a department spokesperson said that basically the projections remained on target for most of the state but perhaps the demand for electronic

Fastest Growing Jobs—
Professional and Technical Occupations

Paralegals
Tax preparers
Law clerks
Computer programmers
Lawyers
Medical records technicians
Landscape architects
Financial and credit analysts
Preschool and kindergarten teachers

Occupations with Largest Job Growth—
Professional and Technical

Occupation	New Jobs (Avg. Annual Growth)
General managers, top executives	3,000
Accountants and auditors	1,600
Registered nurses	1,550
Computer programmers (incl. aides)	1,100
Lawyers	1,000
Computer systems analysts	800
Financial managers	660
Marketing, advertising, publicity managers	425
Teachers—elementary	400
Physicians and surgeons	350

engineers would decline, but that's as specific as they would be. With that in mind here are selected lists of some of the fastest growing jobs and jobs with the greatest projected increase by numerical growth. There are no surprises. But note well that these projections are for new jobs only and do not include the large number of openings that occur through replacement needs. In the Los Angeles area replacements total over 140,000 a year.

Occupations with Largest Job Growth— Service Occupations

Occupation	New Jobs (Avg. Annual Growth)
Salespersons—retail	3,575
General office clerks	2,200
Waiters and waitresses	2,100
Guards and watch guards	1,550
Cashiers	1,400
Receptionists, information clerks	1,350
Sales reps, non-scientific	1,230
Secretaries	960
Food preparation workers	900
Bookkeeping, accounting clerks	890
Combined food preparation and service	870
Janitors, cleaners	870
Dining room attendants	830
Legal secretaries	815
Cooks—restaurant	815

SPOTLIGHT ON
SAN DIEGO

Best known in years gone by as the home of a major U.S. Naval Base with a large contingent of Marines, this once sleepy seaport exploded during the 1980s and now ranks as the sixth largest city in the nation. Its 1.1 million people— 27 percent more than in 1980—make up about half of the population of the metropolitan area that surrounds the city. During the 1980s San Diego was also one of the fastest growing metropolitan areas in the nation, with a population expansion of over 600,000, a 34 percent increase, to 2.5 million.

As with so many regions of California this kind of growth created many new jobs, most of them in construction, retail trade, and services. Health services was and remains especially strong because of the presence of the world-famous Scripps Clinic and Research Foundation, the Jonas Salk Institute, the University Medical Center, a large VA Hospital, and Sharp Health Care, which includes 5 hospitals, 14 clinics, and employs about 9,500. Health services remains the most active sector of employment, with five of the 10 fastest growing jobs, including physical and occupational therapists, as well as medical and radiologic technicians; new jobs for registered nurses are also opening by the hundreds each year.

According to Kelly Cunningham, an economist at the Greater San Diego Chamber of Commerce, the region's strength in medical research has led to the first stirrings of success in the biotechnology field. Mycogen and Hybritech are two of the many burgeoning companies Mr. Cunningham cited as actively seeking to hire new employees.

With beautiful beaches, a paradisiacal climate, and an extraordinary, well-publicized zoo, tourism naturally became an essential part of San Diego's economy. Today it employs 15,000 people directly and 125,000 in so-called tourism-related jobs such as those in hotels, restaurants, etc. The America's Cup in May 1992 should help in the short run. Tourism is expected to remain a very good field especially for young people, although the recent disastrous break in the city's only sewage line that caused raw sewage to pour into the ocean not too far offshore has left a residue of fear that people will choose other areas for vacations.

Most of the other sectors of San Diego's economy are stagnant at best. Banking, however, has been through very difficult times and employment levels have dropped without much chance of recovering. In general, though, with population growth continuing at 2 percent a year, no one anticipates serious problems or a spiralling economy.

The employment rate in the San Diego area has been lower than the LA-Long Beach rate, only occasionally rising to 6.5 percent during 1991. There was a net loss of about 17,000 jobs in 1991 made up mainly of small losses in several areas including construction, retail trade, and government, but 5,000 were lost in manufacturing. More than half of those losses were defense-related and although San Diego is not as vulnerable as its northern neighbors in this field, defense does account for 20 percent of all employment.

There have been defense cuts here and doubtless there will be more. They will surely have an impact on some of the largest employers in the region including General Dynamics and Rolm Industries, both of which have begun meaningful employee layoffs. Ironically the military base itself with over 130,000 active duty personnel will probably be strengthened not reduced. As one of the primary bases on the west coast it is a reasonable assumption that more people will be sent here from the smaller facilities that will be closing. According to Mr. Cunningham, the San Diego economist, this should help both the retail sales and the construction sectors; in fact a slight housing shortage is foreseen over the next few years (although commercial real estate is already very overbuilt).

Like much of southern California, San Diego seems to

be waiting for something bad to happen, not an earthquake but the end of the era of unbridled growth, which could cause more aftershocks than anyone is predicting just yet.

Colorado

While the rest of the country was reeling in a recession during 1991 and early 1992, Colorado was holding its own economically. Job opportunities were expanding and unemployment rates remained well below the national average. People have been moving to Colorado from all across the country because of its expanding job market and comparatively low cost of living.

According to Tucker Adams, an economist with Central Banks of Colorado, Denver, "Growth in Colorado is gaining momentum. People involved with real estate and construction are particularly upbeat. Housing sales in metropolitan Denver reached a six-year high in 1991. There is a serious shortage of construction workers and, people are pouring back into the state after a five-year out-migration."

Colorado has diversified its economy since the mid–1980s when the state basically depended on four major industries: oil and gas production, tourism, high-tech industries, and mining. While those industries remain important, they no longer play the dominant role in the economy they did ten years ago.

The 1980s saw Colorado go full circle in the economic cycle, from a boom area in the early '80s to the bust and near depression of 1986 and 1987. State financial analysts say the economy "bottomed out" about 1988.

In 1989 renewed growth was reported in several key areas. The state for example saw an increase in jobs in 1989 and 1990 of 46,200 and 35,900 openings respectively. Even during the 1991 recession Colorado added over 17,000 nonagricultural jobs, only four states added more. Over 12,000 of those jobs were in the Denver area. This growth trend is expected to continue over the next five years, according to the Colorado Department of Labor and Employment.

The services industries, a broad market which includes business, health care, educational and food services, generated the most jobs in 1991, followed by state and local government, according to the state Department of Labor and Employment. Jobs in wholesale and retail trade saw the third largest instance of growth.

"Services and trade have been for the last five years the fastest growing industries statewide. I think that will continue," said Ben Garcia Jr., an economic forecaster with the state Department of Labor and Employment.

Garcia cited business services, including all of the computer fields, and data and information processing, among the fastest growing areas within the wide-open services field. Several large companies opened branch offices in Colorado, including Merrill Lynch and American Express.

Another services-related field expected to see marked growth in the next several years is janitor and maintenance jobs at apartment complexes and office buildings.

The aerospace industry in the Boulder area has also seen a significant expansion. And a reemphasis has been placed on agriculture, which some state financial analysts believe was neglected during the oil boom of the early 1980s.

The public sector, which includes federal, state, and local government workers, currently employs nearly 300,000 people, or about 15 percent of the total work force in Colorado. The majority of public sector employees (165,300) work at the local levels of government, with 91,600 in education. More than 72,000 people are employed at the state level, including 48,000 in education. The federal government employs 56,900 Coloradoans.

According to the Department of Labor and Employment, government will be one of the largest generators of jobs during the next five years. Over half of those jobs are expected to be created at the local level.

Tourism is a Colorado industry that, despite the economic downturn of the late '80s, grew steadily throughout the decade, said Don Merrion, a research manager for the Colorado Board of Tourism. In 1991, an estimated 104,600, or 4.3 percent of Colorado's work force, was employed in tourism and travel. The largest proportion of those jobs, nearly 30,000, were in food services, followed closely by lodging accommodations.

Contrary to the image of a busy ski season as the peak time for visitors, two-thirds of the state's tourists come in the summertime. Merrion said summer tourism also provides jobs in restaurants and hotels.

For those who fantasize about working the winter in Aspen or Vail, skiing in their spare time, the reality is that there are plenty of seasonal jobs in ski areas. Some resorts even run radio ads seeking workers. "One of the big issues in Colorado, especially in the winter months, is that there are labor shortages in the ski towns," Merrion said. "The demand for workers has grown, but the population of people who generally work in those areas, mostly college-aged people, has declined."

SPOTLIGHT ON DENVER

The Denver metropolitan area covers a six-county region including the cities of Aurora and Boulder, and has a total work force of just over one million people. The largest percentage of those workers, one-third, are employed in services. State economists predict that the percentage will expand during the next five years as employment opportunities grow along with the population.

Ben Lewis, president of the Aurora Chamber of Commerce (Aurora, which borders Denver to the east and is the third largest city in Colorado, is a bedroom community of more than 200,000 that is directly linked to the success or failure of the Denver economy.), said his office receives as many as 20 phone calls each day from people from around the country who are planning to move to the Denver metropolitan area.

"Even though we had been in a recession here in Denver up until about the summer of '89, we're now in better shape than either coast," Lewis said. "We're far better off than the rest of the country. We have less unemployment, fewer foreclosures, bankruptcies, etc., all of the things that go with an economic downswing."

The Denver-metro area's economy mirrored that of all of Colorado's during the 1980s. Considered a "boom town" in the early '80s, the city slipped into a deep recession towards the end of the decade. The area has since bounced back and Denver has seen growth in virtually every important economic category.

"We've been on a recovery track since 1988," said Patricia Silverstein, chief economist for the Greater Denver Chamber of Commerce.

The sectors expected to see the most expansion in the Denver metro area are business and health care services, with especially good opportunities for legal secretaries and administrative assistants, nurses aides, physical therapists, and medical and dental assistants.

Construction has provided jobs for thousands of Denverites in the last four years. The majority of these jobs resulted from public works projects, according to Ms. Silverstein. The Denver Chamber of Commerce economist said that trend is expected to continue into the '90s due in large part to public projects which are either underway or about to begin. These include the building of a new airport, a baseball stadium, and continued repairs of area roads and highways.

"We've been investing in our future by improving the city's infrastructure. And that's starting to pay off," said Ms. Silverstein.

The state Department of Labor and Employment cites

three reasons for Denver's recovery and continued growth: the strength of the construction sector, Denver's location and relatively low cost of living, and the continuing strength of the services industries.

Richard Wobbekind, director of the Business Research Division at the University of Colorado at Boulder, was more cautious in his optimism over Denver's economic growth.

"The economy is expanding," he said, "but not as rapidly as we had hoped as a result of the [national] recession. We expect an overall growth in the job market of about 2 percent for 1991. That's mainly as a result of growth in the services industries. But we are losing jobs in manufacturing, as you can read in the paper almost any day."

While there is no question that the jobs are out there, the competition for those jobs is stiff. Highly skilled, white collar jobs are harder to obtain than lower level office and retail work because most high skills jobs are filled by word of mouth.

"I can honestly say that the vast majority of white collar jobs [in Denver] are filled through networking. But in the other fields, if you're the first person at the door and you have the proper background, you'll get the job," says Ben Lewis.

Small businesses, or those with less than 10 employees, provide jobs for more than half of the state's work force. This is also true of the Denver-metro area. A common opinion held throughout Denver's business community is that there are more entrepreneurs in Colorado than in any other state. Denver's business climate, they say, is very attractive to someone starting a small enterprise because of the availability of labor.

Denver's largest private employer is US West Communications. The telecommunications firm employs 17,000 workers statewide, 12,000 in the Denver-Boulder metro area. A spokesman for US West said the company is "always hiring." "We are mostly looking for engineers, computer programmers and systems analysts, and sales marketers and telemarketers," he said.

Connecticut

A convergence of downturns in several industry cycles, coupled with a drastic reduction in U.S. Defense spending have combined to create one of the worst economic disasters in Connecticut's history. Since 1989, the state has lost more than 100,000 jobs, ranking the Nutmeg State second only to Massachusetts in greatest job decline in 1991.

By share of gross state product, manufacturing is Connecticut's major industry. Connecticut is the sixth most industrialized state in the union. The second largest industry is what's called the FIRE sector, comprising finance, insurance and real estate. Manufacturing experienced a decline of 4.5 percent over the year. FIRE, in response to bank and insurance company consolidations and reorganizations, suffered a 3.1 percent drop in jobs.

Many jobs lost in manufacturing resulted from Connecticut's historical reliance on defense spending. About 70 percent of all manufacturing in the state is defense-oriented. Until last year, the state, nicknamed "the arsenal of the nation" during the American revolution, was number one in defense spending per capita, with about $1800 of federal funds per person. In 1991, however, defense spending in Connecticut dropped to under $1300 per person, putting the state second to Massachusetts. Hard times are expected to continue, as Pratt & Whitney, the jet engine maker, and General Dynamics have announced a total of more than 16,000 layoffs over the next six years.

As elsewhere in the country, health care professionals are surviving well in the recession. So too are medical-related industries such as the Norwalk-based United States Surgical Corporation, which increased its staff by 60 percent in 1991. "We're hiring like crazy," said Catherine Wrenn, manager of media and community relations for the world's largest manufacturer of surgical staples. Overall, the health services professions expanded by more than 2100 jobs, an increase of 1.5 percent in 1991 alone.

Legal and professional services (which grew 0.4 percent) provided additional jobs. But overall the services sector, Connecticut's third largest industry, was down 1.5 percent, with the largest decline occurring in the hotel/lodging field (down 7.1 percent) and business services (down 6.8 percent).

In retail trade, Connecticut's fourth largest industry, jobs fell by 3.4 percent (9300 jobs) with the largest losses in general merchandise and food stores. It was the same story in the transportation/utilities sector (2100 jobs lost) and wholesale trade (4100 jobs lost). Even government employment was off by 1 percent, a drop of 2200 jobs!

The focus of Connecticut's Department of Economic Development has recently been that of retaining current employment and preventing further losses. Two main initiatives recently have been loan guarantees (to assist business hurt by tight credit) and help for defense-related industries to develop new products and new markets. In addition, Governor Weicker's State of the State message on February 5, 1992, promised tax breaks for manufacturers and a lessening of the burden of workers' compensation expenses for businesses generally.

It is doubtful that any measures will help Connecticut's job market improve in the short run. Nor has anyone dared to predict the long-term outlook for the economy if those high-paying manufacturing jobs are not replaced. Connecticut is not the place to plan a career even if it still ranks first among the states in per capita personal income.

Delaware

Nowhere does the beleagured banking industry show up on top 10 lists of promising job markets.

Except in Delaware.

Back in 1983, Delaware issued a tempting invitation, known as the Financial Center Development Act, designed to lure banks, credit card companies and the like to incorporate in the state. The finance industry has responded enthusiastically ever since to the tax and financial incentives provided by the act, and while state economists say the growth in that sector may level off, they don't expect it to stagnate.

In fact, Bob Schulz, a labor market analyst for the Delaware department of labor, predicts that the financial industry, along with insurance and real estate, will lead the state's job growth in coming months. Schulz' department expects those three industries to provide 9 percent of the state's jobs by the year 2000. Despite the continued economic doldrums, Schulz said those industries are ahead of schedule in meeting the goal set for them by state prognosticators.

J.T. Walbert, of the Delaware Private Industry Council, Inc., concurs. Walbert, whose office coordinates training and placement for unskilled workers in the state, said the majority of job seekers trained by the industry council continue to find clerical jobs in banking and law.

Banking is not as fertile a job territory as it was even three years ago, Walbert said, but he said clerical jobs overall continue to be in demand in Delaware, in defiance of a national trend.

Indeed, many of the unhappy economic trends sweeping the rest of the nation seem to have bypassed this tiny Atlantic-coast state. Unemployment has been rising here, to a rate of 5.4 percent as of December, 1991. But that was far below unemployment in neighboring states, and well short of the national rate of 6.8 percent.

Not only are banks holding their own here, but manufacturing, too, has managed to avoid the downward slide that sector is enduring in surrounding states.

But Schulz calls manufacturing's comparatively favorable numbers "sort of phony" because they include employment figures for Delaware's mammoth chemical companies. Companies such as DuPont, the state's leading employer, are lumped into the manufacturing segment, although a large number of their jobs are white-collar, management positions, or research jobs held by highly trained scientists, Schulz points out.

Delaware may be faring better than many of its East Coast neighbors, but the state is not insulated against hard times.

Some 4,000 workers at Chrysler and General Motors plants here face uncertain futures. The food processing industry in the state's southern end sees trouble ahead. Construction already has been hit hard. Even the behemoth DuPont company has announced plans to eliminate 3,500 jobs here, mostly through attrition and early retirement incentives.

So where can such workers turn in Delaware if the axe does fall?

Where else—the health care industry.

Schulz said he expects that segment of the state's economy to employ 28,187 people by the year 2000, a 34 percent net gain over 1987. In all, the service sector, which includes most health services jobs, will provide 46 percent of all jobs in the state, up from 34.8 percent in 1987. Other high-demand jobs in the services category include waiters and waitresses, cooks and food providers, retail sales, flight attendants and janitors.

Delaware may be a small state but it still ranks eleventh in per capita personal income. With only 345,000 nonfarm workers job growth will never be enormous but what jobs are here seem solidly in place. Slow, steady growth looks assured with very good opportunities for the well-educated white-collar worker.

Florida

Florida has been one of the fastest growing states in every national census since 1950. During the 1980s, however, its population growth exploded with such intensity that the impact will be felt for decades to come. Ranked seventh among the states in total population in 1980 with 9.7 million people, Florida added another 3.2 million in one decade and leaped to fourth position overall with almost 13 million; by 1992 the total state population had reached 13.2 million.

Moreover, according to the 1990 census, eight of the ten fastest growing metropolitan areas in the U.S. were in Florida, and six of those had extraordinary growth rates of 50 percent or better: West Palm Beach-Boca Raton-Delray Beach (50 percent), Orlando (53 percent), Ocala (59 percent), Fort Myers-Cape Coral (63 percent), Fort Pierce (66 percent), and Naples (77 percent).

Out of such unheard-of statistics comes the image of Florida as a virtual job-creation machine. As the people came, so too did the need for homes, buildings, stores, and the boom in the construction industry. Obviously that phase of Florida's growth had to level off and it finally has after literally decades of unprecedented expansion. Every other segment of the state's economy has had or will soon have the same experience as population growth assumes closer to normal levels especially in the major metropolitan areas.

But don't be misled, Florida will still have greater population growth during the 1990s than any other major state. Over the next decade two areas for very strong job growth are traditional ones in Florida, health care and tourism.

Many people believe that tourism started in Florida twenty

years ago with the arrival of Disney. Although these theme parks are the number one attraction today, the selling of surf, sand, and sunshine started 70 years ago in the 1920s. "Twenty years ago when Disney first opened its gates there were about 23 million people a year coming to Florida. Today we have over 41 million visitors, and less than one-quarter of them come to visit Disney," said John Evans, president of the Florida Tourism Association.

In 1990, the Florida Department of Revenue reported tourism/recreation sales of $27.69 billion, 20 percent of all taxable income. While 1992's tourism growth is estimated at only 0.6 percent, over 81,000 new direct tourism-related jobs (amusement and recreation services, hotels and motels) and over 164,000 new food services jobs are projected for the year 2000.

New, so-called indirect tourism jobs (jobs in enterprises that derive even a small portion of their revenue from tourist dollars) are harder to calculate, although the Florida Tourism Commission is proposing "45 types of business deemed to be tourist related, ranging from supermarkets, bookstores, florists and other retailers, to doctors, lawyers, hair dressers and newspapers." The state estimates a need for 4,900 taxi drivers, a 67 percent increase, and over 5,000 travel agents, a 51 percent increase, by the end of the decade.

Throughout the country, the demand for medical professionals continues strong but in the state with the highest number of older people it is beyond any ordinary adjectival description. The state estimates an increase of over 214,000 new health service jobs by the end of the century, a 50 percent increase, the requirements for registered nurses (47,000), nursing aides and orderlies (23,000), and licensed practical nurses (18,000) accounting for 42 percent of the growth.

In addition, because Florida is the number one retirement location in the U.S. its retirement and nursing health care needs are also the greatest in the country. Although there will be an estimated 16 percent decrease in retirees during the '90s, one of the state's largest population groups will still be people over 75.

In 1990, Florida recognized its leadership position in this area by creating the Department of Elder Affairs. Eventually, everything having to do with senior or elder citizens will be handled by this government agency. The state already projects new jobs for over 10,000 home health care and personal home care aides.

SPOTLIGHT ON ORLANDO/ORANGE COUNTY— CENTRAL FLORIDA

Despite the recession, Orlando's economy continues to thrive. With a 27 percent population increase, Orlando proper will lead the state's metro areas during the 1990s. During the 1980s, population increased 53 percent to over 1 million. Neighboring Orange County's 6.8 percent growth rate over the next two years will be Florida's fastest.

Tourism drives the Orlando economy and Disney is at its heart. A local study found recently that 26 percent of all jobs in central Florida would disappear without tourism and there would be an $87 million annual revenue shortfall. By the year 2000, over 32,000 new direct tourism jobs, 39 percent of the state's total increase, are projected. Also over 20,000 new jobs in the food service and drinking places will be created. The presence of Disney World creates special needs. For example, over 2,200 amusement and recreation attendants will be needed, along with over 700 producers, directors, actors, entertainers, dancers, and choreographers, all by the year 2000.

Since Orlando is the center of the tourism, it is not surprising that the service and hospitality industries are projecting fast growth. But the Florida Department of Labor predicts that social services, printing and publishing, health services, real estate, and special trade contracting will also have fast job growth.

In the defense sector Orlando's Martin Marietta had contracts totalling $985 million in 1990 for R&D of missiles, aircraft accessories and components. The future should be good despite defense budget cutbacks since the company has diversified into night-vision and electro-optics technology.

SPOTLIGHT ON TAMPA BAY

The Tampa Bay region (Hillsborough, Pinellas, Pasco, and Hernando Counties) is the largest and richest metropolitan area in the state, with a population of over two million residents. Population growth for the 1990s is expected to be 20 percent according to the University of Florida, and the area will remain number one in the year 2000 with a population of 2.5 million, more than half a million more than the Miami area.

Tampa Bay is the leading metro area in Florida in terms of the number of people employed in the construction, retail trade, and manufacturing. About one in five of Florida's manufacturing employees works in Tampa Bay. The Port of Tampa is the state's largest (ranging 7th in the U.S. in total annual tonnage) and handled 52 million tons in 1990.

The largest employment sector in the Tampa Bay area is the services industry (business, legal, educational services, etc.), accounting for 32 percent of the work force. Some analysts predict that Tampa Bay will lead the state in job creation, adding more than 230,000 new jobs by the year 2000. Over 118,000, or 51 percent of these jobs will be in services.

The New York Times Publishing Co. recently relocated

other service departments to Tampa Bay, after the successful initial move of their Customer Service Department. And Salomon Brothers is currently moving its service operations to Tampa Bay. The state predicts that there will be over 43,000 new jobs in the business services sector alone by the end of the decade.

The state also predicts that over 20 percent of new jobs (43,000) in Florida's health services will be in the Tampa Bay area. This is a reflection of both the total population and the high percentage of elder or senior citizens that lives in the area.

Tourism in Tampa Bay is centered on the Bush Gardens Theme Park and the more placid beaches of Florida's Gulf coast, which appeals to both older and European vacationers. The state's Labor Department expects a 36 percent increase in tourism-related jobs by 2000.

In defense, the large Pinellas County contractors will hold their own. *Florida Trend* magazine reported that Olin Corporation, an ammunition manufacturer, "is expanding its operations . . . to include unexploded ordnance removal, explosive waste remediation and other environmental projects." And Honeywell Inc. "will continue to benefit from development of smart-bomb weaponry." The only problem area will be the scheduled realignment and partial closing of McDill Air Force Base. That effect has not been fully calculated.

SPOTLIGHT ON JACKSONVILLE

Jacksonville is the financial services, insurance, and corporate headquarters capital of Florida. The University of Florida predicts that the city's population of 672,000 will increase by 19.6 percent by the end of the decade.

Financial services giants, such as American Express Travel Related Services, AT&T, and Merrill Lynch have both longstanding operations and expanding presences. Many insurance companies: American Heritage, Prudential, Independent Life, Acordia Benefits of Florida, and Blue Cross/Blue Shield of Florida have major corporate centers in Jacksonville. And The Haskell Company, CSX, and Winn-Dixie are some of the major companies with corporate headquarters in the metro area.

The largest employment sector is of course in services, employing over 27 percent of the work force. The state predicts an increase of over 13,000 new jobs in the business services sector by the year 2000. In health services, *Florida Trend* magazine reported that "The Mayo Clinic is one of the jewels in Jacksonville's burgeoning medical community." When it opened in 1986, it was the first ever satellite of the famous Rochester, Minnesota medical facility. In five years, the doctor staff has tripled, support staff increased to 700, physical plant doubled to 300,000 square feet, and in 1992 a new $15 million research will be started. The State of Florida predicts that new jobs in the health services sector will increase by over 11,000 in Jacksonville by the end of the decade.

SPOTLIGHT ON
MIAMI

Miami was the one employment area of Florida that was not healthy early in 1992. Unemployment was at 9.5 percent. Miami's problems were the result of the massive layoffs caused by the shutdown of Eastern Airlines and Pan American and the collapse of Southeast Bank, Centrust, and Amerifirst. Over 46,000 jobs were lost in 1991 alone. The federal government is now contributing additional funding for specialized retraining efforts.

Prospects for the future, however, are positive. The population for the Miami metropolitan area is projected to be over 2.1 million by the year 2000, a 12 percent increase. Although this will be small by Florida standards, the Miami area will still account for 25 percent of all new jobs in Florida by the end of the decade.

Miami's culture is a blend of Anglo/Latin, and Miami is the gateway for business activity with Latin America. The business services sector will be one of the fastest growing industries. Almost 30 percent of all new jobs in business services will be in the Miami metropolitan area.

SPOTLIGHT ON THE PANHANDLE

The Florida Panhandle includes both the state capital at Tallahassee and the Pensacola metropolitan area. Normally, government centers are sources of jobs. But, due to severe economic conditions and ongoing negotiations between the Florida governor and legislature about reducing the size of state government, no significant increase in jobs is anticipated in the Tallahassee area for the immediate future.

In Pensacola, heavily dependent on military installation, things are different. Steady growth is anticipated, but not the rapid growth of the '80s. In February 1992, the U.S.S. Forrestal, a training aircraft carrier, will arrive. Also Pensacola Naval Air Station is the contracting agent for the three new Gulf Coast bases (Texas, Mississippi, and Alabama). These requirements will provide quite a boost for local and regional maintenance and support subcontractors. As a result the state Labor Department predicts a significant increase in new jobs in the wholesale and retail trades.

Georgia

Growth in Georgia nonagricultural employment has resumed following the state's worst recession since 1974. Dr. Donald Ratajczak, director of the Georgia State University Economic Forecasting Center, predicts the Georgia economy will create 34,000 new jobs in 1992 for a 1.1 percent gain in total nonagricultural employment.

"Most 1992 growth will be concentrated in just two sectors," explains Ratajczak. "Services, which will account for 15,000–18,000 new jobs; and retail trade, which will generate another 10,000. Nondurable goods manufacturing and transportation will also produce several thousand new jobs apiece."

Georgia has two distinct economies: Atlanta, a diversified regional service center that is home to approximately half of the state's 3 million jobs with a per capita income 15 percent above the national average; and the rest of the state, which depends primarily on government and basic industry with a per capita income less than 80 percent of the national average. After creating jobs at twice the national average in the 1980s, Georgia underperformed the U.S. as a whole in the recession, with metro Atlanta uncharacteristically underperforming the state. In 1991 the Georgia Department of Labor reports Georgia lost 54,000 jobs—with Atlanta responsible for more than half of the decline.

The disappearance of Atlanta's Eastern Airlines hub, serious overbuilding of luxury office space and housing, the acquisition of five Georgia-based *Fortune* 500 companies by outside interests in 1990–91, all contributed to a depression in banking, construction, and real estate. The shutdown of one of two General Motors Atlanta auto assembly plants and the threatened closure of the second did not help.

Nevertheless, a multitude of factors points to a recovery beginning in 1992: the severity and length of the recent recession in Georgia; low interest rates, a stimulative federal monetary policy; accelerating corporate transfers; rebounding international investment and trade; and increasing migration to Georgia.

SPOTLIGHT ON ATLANTA

More than most cities, Atlanta relies on attracting new facilities for much of its employment growth. According to a recent survey of 340 chief executive officers conducted by Impulse Research of Los Angeles, more than half of all U.S. national companies plan to transfer a major operation during the next five years. Fortunately, metro Atlanta remains a favorite destination for relocation companies. Last fall, 600 U.S. executives named Atlanta the best place to do business in a poll conducted by relocation consultants Moran Stahl & Boyer for *Fortune* magazine. The respondents said they like Atlanta's moderate costs (it is the 15th least expensive city in the sample, with an average office lease rate of $23.50 per square foot); its pro-business attitude (it is home to 22 Georgia-based Fortune companies, with another 700 doing business there); and its access (Hartsfield airport ranks third in the world in passenger loadings).

This sentiment is shared by most people, who have continued to migrate to Atlanta in large numbers even during the recession. During the 1980s, Atlanta grew faster than any other metro area in the Southeast, posting an annual average population gain of 2.9 percent per year, four times the national average. (Other Georgia average percentage growth rates were as follows: Augusta 1.4, Savannah 1.0, Macon 0.6, Columbus 0.2.) Seventy thousand people moved to Atlanta in 1991 alone, as the metro area led the nation in housing permits and starts for the second consecutive year.

At least four companies—United Parcel Service of America Inc. (U.P.S.), Holiday Inn Worldwide, GE Capital Services Corp., and Saab Cars USA—announced plans to shift their corporate headquarters to Atlanta during 1991.

U.P.S. moved 625 people from its former Greenwich, Conn. headquarters and created 150 additional jobs after the transfer was announced in May, 1991. Total headquarters employment will reach 1,000 when three temporary offices are consolidated at a permanent 36-acre site in suburban Sandy Springs in 1994. A new parcel delivery center in suburban Clayton County will employ another 300 people.

Holiday Inn Worldwide has also transferred its corporate headquarters and data center from Memphis to Sandy Springs, creating approximately 1,140 Georgia jobs. GE Capital Services and SAAB USA will bring 250 and 200 new jobs to the city, respectively.

Other major announcements included Hewlett-Packard's consolidation of all regional operations in DeKalb County (1,300 jobs); a new Equifax credit reporting and customer service center in Cobb County (500 jobs); and a new Mindis International recycling center at the site of the GM Lakewood auto assembly plant (500 jobs).

After falling 1.5 percent in 1991, Ratajczak predicts total Atlanta employment will grow by less than 1 percent in 1992. So although news that the 1996 Olympics will be held here helped to buoy spirits, the hard truth is that Atlanta's great period of rapid growth is over. All job seekers must therefore regard the outlook as mixed at best.

OTHER METRO AREAS

Augusta Gains in Augusta non-durables manufacturing have been more than offset by President Bush's decision to discontinue weapons production at the Savannah River nuclear plant. Employment will be flat this year, following a 0.5 percent decline in 1991.

Columbus Total Systems Services, a successful bank service company, and Aflac, an insurance firm with strong penetration in Japan, are expected to be major contributors to Columbus' 1.5 percent employment growth in 1992. Metro employment fell slightly in 1991.

Macon-Warner Robins Macons faces continued reduction in government payrolls as defense spending winds down. Recovery in construction, trade and manufacturing will account for nearly all of the 1992 metro employment growth of less than 1 percent, which follows an approximate 1 percent decline in 1991.

Savannah In-migration of retirees and expanding export trade through the Port will more than balance cutbacks in nearby military installations. Employment will grow by 1.5 percent in 1992, following a 0.5 percent gain in 1991.

Fastest Growing Occupations in the 1990s

(Average annual gain in total employment in percent, 1990–2000)

Medical assistants	4.5%
Radiology technicians	4.3
Operations research analysts	3.6
Computer programmers	3.3
Corrections officers	2.9
Temporary help	2.8
Personnel consultants	2.8
Precision assemblers	2.5
Management analysts	2.4
Insurance underwriters	2.4

Source: *U.S. Bureau of Labor Statistics*

New Job Sites in Georgia 1991

Company	Type	County	Jobs
Hewlett-Packard	Headquarters	DeKalb	1,300
United Parcel Service	Headquarters	Fulton	1,000
Holiday Inn Worldwide	Headquarters	DeKalb	900
Dillard Dept. Stores	Distribution Ctr.	Lowndes	500
Equifax	Data Center	Cobb	500
Mindis International	Headquarters	Fulton	500
Ritz Instrument	Plant	Burke	500
Ebasco Services	Office	Richmond	400
J.H. Harvey Grocery	Distribution Ctr.	Crisp	400
Five Rubber	Plant	Spalding	350
Matsushita	Plant	Muscogee	340
MBNA Marketing Svcs.	Headquarters	DeKalb	325
Quad Graphics	Plant	Upson	400
Bel-Tronics Ltd.	Plant	Newton	300
The Travelers	Data Center	Gwinnett	300
United Parcel Service	Distribution Ctr.	Clayton	300
Whirlpool Corp.	Distribution Ctr.	Clayton	300
Winn-Dixie Stores	Plant	Ben Hill	300

Source: *Georgia Dept. of Industry, Trade & Tourism*

Hawaii

If you want an indication of just how deeply the recent recession has affected American confidence, talk to people here on the edge of paradise. Despite low unemployment—during the last months of 1991 and into early 1992 unemployment rates remained below 4 percent, sometimes running as low as half the national rate—Hawaiian economists and business people are quite worried about the future.

This concern stems from the fact that Hawaii's is a fragile economy, built in good part on the sun and sand of tourism and so exceedingly vulnerable to the rapidly shifting winds of economic change. So when unemployment grew from 2.9 percent in October 1991 to 3.6 percent in January 1992, the alarms went off around state offices.

Economists here concede that even the latest figures represent negligible unemployment rates compared with most mainland states. But they fear the trend may signal an oncoming wave of trouble. Just as the state is a few time zones behind the mainland, they say, it may be a couple of quarters late in feeling the recession's punch.

The number of visitors to Hawaii dropped about 3 percent in 1991, to an estimated 6.8 million. Accordingly, hotel occupancy fell by about 6.5 percent and scores of other ancillary industries endured slight declines as well. The numbers could well have been more grim were it not for the steady influx of Japanese and other Asian visitors, who, on a per capita basis, outspent their western counterparts by about five-to-one. Economists at the Bank of Hawaii, however, expect tourism to bounce back in 1992, and by year's end, they anticipate a 7.5 percent increase in the number of visitors landing on Hawaiian shores. That economic shot in the arm means the state probably will sustain in 1992 the 4.6 average annual rate of hotel-industry job growth state Department of Labor and Industrial Relations predicted back in 1998.

State forecasters have pinned job-growth promises to a host of other tourism-related industries as well. Travel agents lead the list of the 40 projected fastest-growing occupations, with an estimated 57 percent increase in the number of practitioners in that field between 1988 and 1993. Also on the list of growing tourism-related occupations are taxi drivers, reservation and ticket agents, waiters and waitresses, bartenders and maids.

In all, Hawaii will have gained over 70,000 new jobs between 1988 and 1993. Not all of those jobs, of course, will be tourism related. Also on a list of 40 fast-growing occupations in the state are retail salespersons, secretaries and office clerks, registered nurses, accountants and auditors, cooks, nurses aides, carpenters, managers and top executives, electricians, legal secretaries, social workers and elementary school teachers.

Only a few of these growing occupations will be in two sectors that drove Hawaii's economy in past years, defense and agriculture. Anticipated cuts in federal defense spending will affect nearly every corner of the nation, but Daniel Kinoshita, of the Labor Department's Commission on Employment and Human Resources, said the cuts probably won't mean a tremendous jolt for Hawaiians.

"Defense 30 or 40 years ago was our number-one industry. But the decreases in defense spending in Hawaii have been occurring gradually over time," thereby lessening their impact, Kinoshita said. He also indicated that the state's large military bases would remain open.

State forecasters have tracked similar declines over time in agriculture. The Department of Labor foresees only 2,640 new agriculture jobs during the five-year projection period, and most of those will be for gardeners and groundskeepers. More and more sugar and pineapple fields are being plowed under, replaced by hotels and by homes, which still are in short supply in this growing state.

Between 1980 and 1990, Hawaii's population grew by 1.7 percent annually. That rate is expected to flatten during the current decade, but population growth combined with tourism growth is expected to drive the construction industry. Although construction sagged in 1991, most economists here expect it to stage a comeback this year.

Overall, the economic news, like the weather, is mostly good in Hawaii. And Hawaii continues to push toward establishing itself as a Pacific Rim trading hub, in order to guarantee that job and economic growth remain steady in coming years.

Idaho

In recent years, Idaho's job market has not been able to keep pace with the state's sudden surge in population growth. More than 33,000 people migrated to Idaho between 1990 and 1991, a 3.2 percent increase that makes the state third in population growth, behind only Nevada and Alaska. (Compare this to the 63,000 people who moved to Idaho in the entire decade between 1981 and 1990.)

"We've seen a great deal of migration from California, Washington, and Oregon," said Cathy Bonner, a research analyst for the Idaho Department of Employment. "But when the people get here, they find that the job situation is not that good." After increasing by 54.9 percent between 1973 and 1987, total employment in Idaho grew by only 1.5 percent, or 7,000 jobs, in 1991. Although the state's total 6.1 percent unemployment rate was nearly a percentage point lower than the national average, unemployment ran as high as 14 percent in rural areas.

A decline in silver prices was responsible for a nearly 19 percent decrease in mining employment. The Idaho Department of Employment attributes an 8 percent decrease in timber industry employment to the recession, which brought a slowdown in new residential construction in California, and to proposed federal legislation to save the woods inhabited by the spotted owl, which will continue to threaten timber cutting throughout the Northwest.

All of Idaho's other industries, however, experienced fairly solid growth. The influx of new people was particularly good news for the construction and service industries, which grew by 2.9 and 3.7 percent respectively. Within the service industries, jobs in state education grew by nearly 12 percent, while amusement and recreational services skyrocketed by 20 percent. The state's trade and tourism industries, fueled primarily by the state's ski resorts, remain robust.

Like many northwest states, Idaho faces a shift in its economy away from the historically dominant industries in rural areas to service-related fields in the big cities. The state Department of Employment expects agriculture to remain constant at about 2.8 percent (with potatoes still being the dominant crop) while it projects more than 20 percent growth in jobs in the service, transportation, and manufacturing industries over the next decade with about 3,000 or more openings for retail salespersons, truck drivers, and elementary and secondary school teachers; also there will be over 2,000 openings for registered nurses, as well as for general managers and top executives.

Total employment in the state, which hovered around the half-million mark for much of 1991, is expected to continue growing at about the same 1.5 percent per year, to a total of about 568,000 by the year 2000.

Most economic growth has occurred in the metropolitan area around Boise City, Idaho's capital and largest city; about 20 percent of Idaho's 504,800-strong labor force works in Ada County, Boise City's seat. That number is up more than 2 percent from the year before.

Although Idaho has been adding jobs every year recently, remember that the total number of new jobs will remain small because the population is not that large. In 1991 just over 10,000 jobs were added, about 4,000 of them in Boise City.

Illinois

Illinois is by population the nation's sixth-largest state, and historically it has been dominated by Chicago, where over 65 percent of the state's work force is employed. "Downstate," the term used for the balance of Illinois, is 80 percent farmland. Yet many people have been carving out solid careers in Illinois' downstate cities, which boast small-town atmosphere and big-city opportunities. The state is home to 48 Fortune 500 companies—26 of which are outside of Chicago.

"The financial headaches Illinois has now are really in Chicago. There are a lot of positive things in downstate Illinois," said Diane Swonk, a regional economist at the First National Bank in Chicago.

Manufacturing continues to be a major employer (300,000 downstate and over 600,000 in Chicago), but Illinois has mirrored national trends as the proportion of manufacturing employment has declined. "Most new jobs in the Illinois economy are in the trade, services and finance, insurance and real estate sectors," according to a spokesperson for the Illinois Department of Commerce and Community Affairs.

The top industry in the state, based on average annual new jobs being created, is business services with 10,338, reports the Illinois Department of Employment Security. Annual openings of over 3,500 are expected for accountants and auditors; another growing sector is securities and financial service sales, with average annual openings of 1,146. Other top industries in new job creation are: health services (4,700); eating and drinking places (4,583); education (2,746); and retail stores (2,162).

Despite the existence of stereotypical white-collar, information-society jobs, not all growing employment fields require extensive education or training. Helpers, laborers and material moving and handling workers rank first in total employment in Illinois, followed by secretaries, sales and related workers, retail salespersons and office clerks, according to the Department of Employment Security. Total average annual openings of 17,000 for sales workers, 12,000 for janitors, cleaners and maids, 11,600 for retail salespersons, 9,000 for office clerks, and 8,000 for secretaries are projected. Those jobs also are leaders in the number of openings that are due to growth. Illinois also projects average annual openings of 6,600 for protective service workers—a jump of 37 percent in the field between 1986 and 2000.

Downstate economic regions with vigorous growth include the Bloomington-Normal area, which has been stimulated by a new automobile assembly plant built by Mitsubishi and Chrysler (since bought out). Since 1985 Bloomington-Normal, home to State Farm Insurance, has logged more than $1 billion in new business projects and thousands of new jobs. And economist Swonk said Mitsubishi will increasingly use domestic suppliers, benefitting downstate auto parts suppliers, machinery makers and business services companies.

Lake County, north of Chicago near the Wisconsin border, has boomed—setting growth records in 1991—as firms and commuters have sought out less expensive real estate. The area is home to huge medical supply firms Baxter International and Abbott Laboratories. The list of Illinois' big employers also includes: Motorola, in Schaumburg; John Deere in Moline and East Moline; and engine parts maker Woodward Governor Co. in Rockford.

Clouding the employment picture for downstate Illinois in early 1992 was a United Auto Workers strike that shut down the mammoth Caterpillar Co. in October 1991. At publication more than 8,000 people remained out of work. The strike hit hard in Decatur and Peoria and had a chain reaction on Caterpillar's suppliers in the state. The problems were not blamed on the recession, and Caterpillar—with 55 percent of its sales in a strong international market—is considered a company that will rebound quickly.

"Illinois will probably end up chugging along in 1992 and 1993 at about the national average," Swonk said. "It will not be a star performer, but it will come out of the current problems."

Although the state lost jobs in 1991, the number was very small (16,000) considering the size of the work force (5.3 million). Still, until the recovery kicks in strongly no one can be certain that the state's optimistic job projections will materialize. Recent developments in Chicago, however, may help considerably.

SPOTLIGHT ON CHICAGO

While not as economically nimble as some smaller cities, Chicago has a historic position as a center of commerce, as well as a critical mass of businesses and services, that will continue to make the city a Midwestern and national employment leader. Chicago's labor force is drawn from a population of 4 million in Cook County, with an additional 4 million living in the five "collar counties" of DuPage, Kane, Lake, McHenry and Will that constitute the Chicago metropolitan area.

Chicago financial analysts like to say, "As goes the nation, so goes Chicago." The phrase implies—rightly—that Chicago went through the nation's much-publicized late 1980s streamlining of white-collar management and then was hit by the recession. The city actually performed a little better than the nation as a whole in the recession because it is a major export center, said Robert Dieli, vice president and economist for Chicago's Northern Trust Company. Traditional exports include capital goods, such as punch presses and computers. But an array of consumer products made in Chicago are sold overseas.

Chicago's strength as a financial center can be seen in

the fact that 80 percent of the world's commodities are traded through three of the city's five legendary exchanges. Chicago leads the nation in the trading of commodities, stock options, currency and interest rate futures. Chicago's financial exchanges employ more than 33,000 people directly and an additional 110,000 work in related services jobs. The city has 130 domestic banks and 70 foreign banks; more than 10 of the institutions have assets of over $1 billion. The First National Bank of Chicago, the city's largest, has assets of around $35 billion.

"Chicago is as vulnerable to the national trends in financial services and business services as any place else," Dieli said. "The downsizing and 'lean and mean' stuff has been going on here, maybe not quite as pronounced as on the coasts." The result is that growth in white-collar jobs has been slow, and the metropolitan area's 8.6 percent unemployment rate (December 1991) is distributed evenly through all employment sectors. (Cook County's rate was 9 percent.) "As far as white-collar goes, it isn't The End of the World Part III," Dieli added, "but in the next five or 10 years growth will be relatively modest."

However, a major economic stimulant—and creator of thousands of jobs, especially blue collar—will result from construction of a new, third airport on Chicago's southeast side that is estimated to cost $10.8 billion. Job estimates for construction at the Lake Calumet site have been placed at 40,000, and city officials have estimated permanent jobs at 200,000. "There are some people who are going to get fabulously wealthy off this construction," said Dieli, noting that the new airport will continue to sweeten the economy once built: "Do you know what it's like to get the hot dog concession at O'Hare?" The new airport, to be under construction by the mid–1990s and open in 2010, will supplement Midway Airport and O'Hare International Airport, which handles 60 million passengers a year as the world's busiest airport.

Another major construction project is a $1 billion addition

planned to begin in 1993 on McCormick Place, the largest convention center in the country. In 1986 McCormick Place underwent expansion that brought its size to 1.6 million square feet; plans now call for adding a new hall, public square, and galleria, plus thorough renovation. The city estimates that expansion will create 11,600 permanent jobs and have an annual economic growth impact of $1.6 billion. Construction also was scheduled for Spring 1992 on the new Chicago Stadium.

Chicago's busy, burgeoning airports and the never-ending additions to McCormick Place underscore the city's role as a national and international transportation hub. Transportation plays a key role in the city's economy. Chicago is the nation's leader in air freight, and over 20 major domestic and foreign airlines offer direct, nonstop service to Europe and Asia.

A web of highways converges on Chicago, enabling trucks to carry 50 million tons of freight in and out of the city each year. With more than 200 truck terminals, Chicago is the nation's largest trucking center. Chicago also remains a major railroad center, with 37 routes radiating from the region. More than 50 Amtrak trains enter Union Station each day, while the Santa Fe Railway loads up to 3,000 freight containers daily for shipment across the nation. Chicago is a leading port city, with access to the Great Lakes, the Mississippi River and the St. Lawrence Seaway. Lake Calumet Harbor, with direct access to the expressway system, handles the most cargo (1.7 million short tons in 1990). Each day, 850,000 workers commute into the central city via highways, commuter trains and rapid transit.

Some 2.2 million people work in Cook County, home of Chicago, with an additional 800,000 working in the surrounding metropolitan area that includes DuPage, Kane, Lake, McHenry and Will counties, according to the Illinois Department of Employment Security. A breakdown of the metropolitan area in 1990 showed that manufacturing remains the area's single-largest employment sector, with

653,000 jobs. "Chicago is a great center of metal-bending, making all sorts of gizmos and flanges, and now plastics," says economist Dieli. He points out that the manufacturing sector is quite broad. While headliners such as Pullman and International Harvester have moved on, many machine shops, tool-and-die operations and speciality manufacturers have remained. "There are a lot of semi-large companies that are not Fortune 500, but they would easily be Fortune 1,000." Despite the historic strength of manufacturing, city leaders like to emphasize Chicago's economic diversity, on the theory that diversity makes the region more "recession proof."

Job sectors that are forecast for the most rapid growth tend to reflect a national trend toward information processing, as well as Chicago's position as a center of trade. In an analysis by the Department of Employment Security of employment expectations from 1986 to 2000, the fastest-growing field in the Chicago metropolitan area is business services, which will grow by 59.4 percent and employ 338,727 people in 2000. The next-fastest growing field is retail sales of building materials, garden supplies and mobile homes, a sector employing 30,220 people in 2000, reflecting job growth of 56 percent.

Credit agencies other than banks were next, with over 15,000 jobs expected to be added—a 51.4 percent change—as the field grows to 45,700 jobs by 2000. Social services—day care counseling for families, etc.—will be strong, growing by 50.6 percent in the period and employing 53,000 in 2000.

Other job fields with fast rates of growth expected in the Chicago metropolitan area include: security and commodity brokers (48 percent); legal services (39.4 percent); hotels and other lodging (39 percent); miscellaneous services (38.6 percent); furniture and home furnishing stores (34 percent); general building contractors (33 percent); miscellaneous repair services (31.7 percent); and auto repair services and garages (31.5 percent). Wholesale and retail trade are forecast to grow by 22.7 percent in Chicago, employing 1 million people in 2000.

Despite the prospects of continuing high unemployment rates, Chicago has not been losing jobs recently and there are signs of renewed vigor especially in the construction sector. By 1993, the job market should be very promising.

Indiana

Indiana likes to call itself the "Crossroads of America," emphasizing its location and the seven interstate highways, the cluster of rail routes, three major ports and an international airport that link the state to the nation and to the global marketplace. The phrase resonates with Indiana's historic pride in job opportunity and affordable housing that put the American dream within reach of most Hoosiers.

Yet with national confidence shaken by recession, Indiana's pitch may seem suspect. However, Indiana will recover from the recession sooner than most of the nation, predicts Morton J. Marcus, a research economist at Indiana University and director of the Indiana Business Research Center. He attributes Indiana's resiliency in part to a lack of massive amounts of empty housing and retail space to fill.

In 1991, 15,000 new jobs were added, not overwhelming in a work force of 2.6 million but certainly promising in a serious recession. And there continue to be jobs available.

"Job opportunities in Indiana are mostly in the largest cities—Indianapolis, Fort Wayne, South Bend, Evansville—with additional growth available in Bloomington and Lafayette (home of Indiana and Purdue universities respectively)," says Marcus. In particular, he says job seekers will find good prospects in health care and insurance. A rebounding economy will open opportunities in medium-sized cities, such as Richmond, Terre Haute, Marion, and

Michigan City, where businesses provide services to companies in the larger cities.

Marcus expects low interest rates to stimulate car sales nationally—a boon to Indiana where many of the largest employers and many smaller businesses serve the auto industry directly or indirectly. "There will be opportunities not only for production workers but also for designers, engineers and office personnel, such as accountants," he says.

Unlike some states that are overshadowed by a single major city, Indiana's employment is distributed evenly throughout the state, with three-fourths of jobs outside Indianapolis. Five of Indiana's top ten businesses in earnings are outside the capital city, including: Delco Electronics, in Kokomo; Cummins Engine Company and Arvin Industries, in Columbus; and the Ball Corp., based in Muncie.

The state has been trying for a decade to diversify its historic manufacturing base. Recently the Indiana Department of Commerce commissioned a study that targeted the high-growth fields of pharmaceuticals, data processing, plastics products, periodicals publishing, industrial machinery and business support as being particularly suited to the state.

Manufacturing, which accounted for 40 percent of jobs in the 1960s, employed 25 percent of Hoosiers in 1988 (still above the 1988 national average of 18 percent). Indiana's largest number of jobs will remain in the broad area of manufacturing and mechanical trades. Opportunities for mechanics and installers are good, but most jobs will arise from replacement needs rather than from expansion, the Indiana Department of Employment and Training Services reports. "Workers with flexible skills and adaptability to new technologies will be in demand."

Services are the fastest-growing employment area. More than half of Indiana's jobs by 1995 will be in public education and health care, according to the state. But business services and legal services are the fastest-growing job categories within the services sector. "Rapid growth is anticipated for medical assistants, flight attendants and social welfare service aides,'' predicts the state employment and training department. ''These three occupations are at the top of the listing of 20 fastest-growing occupations.''

Indiana restaurants and bars are increasing in numbers and so too are the jobs—an estimated 32,730 new jobs (for managers, cooks, servers, cleaners) are forecast between 1984 and 1995, an increase in employment of 25 percent for the field.

In professional and technical occupations, nurses, accountants and auditors are among the 20 occupations with the greatest number of job openings in the state. In administrative support, computer operators are among Indiana's top 20, with strong need for insurance adjusters, examiners and investigators. Marketing and sales jobs are also projected for strong growth, with jobs abounding for retail salespersons. Fast-growing jobs in the marketing field include travel agents and securities and financial sales workers.

SPOTLIGHT ON INDIANAPOLIS

In the past two decades Indianapolis's economic and social rebirth has been featured in *Time, Fortune, USA Today* and *The Wall Street Journal*. Gone is a slumbering Dullsville surrounded by cornfields that awoke once each year with the Indianapolis 500 automobile race. The city's slumber may have been a legacy of the days when river traffic—not trucking, railroads or air routes—was the dominant mover of goods and services. Modern technology and the state capital's central location means it is perfectly placed to serve both coasts.

Yet just 20 years ago the Indianapolis downtown was dying. An alarmed business community made a successful bipartisan push in 1967 to elect Republican Mayor Richard Lugar (now U.S. Senator) with a mandate to revitalize the downtown. Lugar helped usher in Unigov, which merged the city and county in 1970. Government was streamlined, the tax base greatly expanded, and the city's land area was quadrupled to over 300 square miles. Overnight, Indianapolis joined the list of major U.S. cities and today is 12th largest by population. Groups of influential citizens, foundations, and progressive businesses—led by the civic-minded Eli Lilly & Co.—united with city leaders to plan, build and promote the new Indianapolis. When the Indianapolis Hilton opened in 1970, it was the first hotel built downtown in 40 years. But within the next 15 years, 10 new hotels, including the $50 million Embassy Suites, had sprung up. In 1991 construction began downtown on the $300-million first phase of Circle Centre Mall, the largest construction project in Indiana history.

United Airlines recently announced plans to build a $1 billion maintenance facility in the city. The project, scheduled for completion in 1994, is expected to add at least 6,300 jobs. The Indianapolis International Airport, a USAir hub for connecting flights, scored another coup when the U.S. Postal Service chose the city for its new Eagle Air hub. When the $62 million center is opened in late 1992 express and priority mail for much of the U.S. will be sorted there.

Eli Lilly, a Fortune 500 international pharmaceutical firm, is the city's financial leader, with annual sales volume in 1991 of $5 billion, according to Dunn and Bradstreet. Lilly employs 8,500. The company has announced plans to invest $1 billion in new facilities and add more than 1,000 new jobs by the end of the decade. Thomson Consumer Electronics, makers of GE and RCA products, is another of the state's top firms based in Indianapolis, with $2.8 billion in annual sales and 1,900 employees. After two years of scrutinizing new sites, Thomson announced in January 1992 that it would build its new American headquarters in Indianapolis and occupy the facility in 1993. The headquarters will consist of an administrative building and a research and development center.

Indianapolis draws on a total labor force of 1.2 million workers within an hour's commute. Wholesale and retail trade account for 26 percent of the city's jobs, followed by services at 23.5 percent, manufacturing with 16.6 percent, government with 14 percent, and financial, insurance and real estate firms with 7.5 percent. Indianapolis is a regional health care center, a financial and insurance center, a distribution hub and a business telecommunications leader. Among the service firms that make Indianapolis a convenient location for businesses are data processing, health services, auto parts, management consulting, public relations, janitorial contractors and personnel supply houses.

Opportunities in Indianapolis for starting new businesses are considered good because of support services, helpful government, and the city's diversified economy. In a June 1991 study by *INC* magazine, Indianapolis was named the top city in the Midwest and as one of the top 10 cities in the nation for growing a new business. The magazine's analysis was based on population growth, the number of new jobs, new companies and high-growth companies. The city's economy has been growing faster than most cities as well, ranking second among 15 Midwestern cities and 11th among the nation's top 75 cities, according to the Bureau of Economic Research at the University of Louisville.

Manufacturing still employs the largest number of the city's workers. General Motors has some 21,700 making transmissions and turbines in four locations; another 5,000 are employed nearby in Anderson. Another auto giant, Ford, employs 3,000 workers in Indianapolis. Two hospitals, Methodist and St. Vincent, are big employers with 5,900 and 4,200 respectively. Other large companies in the city include Associated Insurance Companies, American States Insurance, Bindley Western Industries and Inland Container Corp. Indianapolis is a headquarters for American United

Life, the Mayflower Group moving company, and Boehringer Mannheim, maker of medical devices and diagnostic equipment.

Professional and amateur sports have become major contributors to economic diversity, quality of life, and a favorable national image for Indianapolis. Like the other aspects of the city's regeneration, becoming a sporting center was no accident. In the late 1960s and early 1970s city leaders decided to use sports as an economic and community development tool. To date the city has built more than $168 million worth of sports facilities, including the Hoosier Dome and Market Square Arena, and has attracted the headquarters of more than 20 sports organizations.

The result of the aggressive pro-sports strategy is that the city is a three-ring circus of sporting activity. Indianapolis is home to the NFL Indianapolis Colts and the NBA Indiana Pacers. More significantly, Indianapolis has re-invented itself as the "Amateur Sports Capital of the World." The city, host for the 1991 NCAA Final Four basketball tournament, also was the site for the 1987 Pan American Games, the world's a second-largest multisport event. In 1988 more pre-Olympic competitions were held in Indianapolis than any city in the U.S. The city is being reviewed for permanent status as a U.S. Olympics training center.

Iowa

In the recent hit movie, *Field of Dreams,* the spirit of baseball immortal "Shoeless" Joe Jackson stands in the middle of a baseball diamond carved out of a cornfield and asks the owner, "Is this heaven?"

"No," answers the young farmer, "it's Iowa."

In the midst of a deep national recession, Iowa's brilliant success story makes it easy to understand how the two might be confused. With its stable, increasingly diversified economy, low unemployment rate (under 5 percent), record-level housing starts, and steadily increasing land values, Iowa has risen from the ashes of the mid—1980s farm collapse to become the envy and perhaps the model for the region.

Like all redemptions Iowa's extracted a heavy sacrifice, mainly from its agriculture sector, which dominates the state's economy. The 1990 census revealed that Iowa's population actually declined by almost 5 percent during the 1980s and over 15,000 farms were lost or, more accurately, absorbed into larger ones. As a result the number of farmers and farmworkers declined, a trend that will continue at least into the next century. By 1996 only about 100,000 of Iowa's work force of about 1.5 million will be employed in agriculture even though the state will still rank third (behind only gigantic California and Texas) in the value of its farm products.

Although the name Iowa will remain synonymous with an agricultural abundance drawn from the richest soil on earth, the experience of the last decade foreshadows some major changes in the way its people will earn a living. Fortunately there are elements already in place that are making the transition possible. Between 1992 and 1996 total non-agricultural job growth is projected to be 4.6 percent, about 66,000 new jobs.

These figures may turn out to be conservative since they were generated before the latest population survey that showed Iowa's population actually growing again between April 1990 and July 1991 by about 18,000 or 0.7 percent.

But even the unrevised figures show an economy on the rebound. About 17 percent of the state's work force is employed in the manufacturing sector, which is not surprising, since Iowa has long been home to such well-known corporations as John Deere, Maytag, Bandag, and Winnebago. While the rest of the nation has seen a decade-long decline of 5 percent in manufacturing jobs, Iowa's number has remained virtually unchanged and it is expected to grow by more than 6 percent (almost 15,000 jobs) by 1996.

Construction, too, will grow in Iowa (over 8 percent, 3,300 jobs) as will the other sectors that follow a healthy economy: retail trade will add 15,000 new jobs, and services about 26,000 (7,000 in the health care sector alone).

In addition to these new jobs the Iowa Department of Employment Services is also projecting over 310,000 job openings over the next four years mainly because of retirements. Iowa has one of the oldest populations in the country; only Florida, for example, has a higher percentage of people over 65 (18 percent vs. 15 percent in Iowa and 12.5 percent in the U.S.).

Most job opportunities will of course be in metropolitan areas such as Cedar Rapids—Iowa City (home of the state university and its internationally known medical center which employs 7,000) and Des Moines, the state's largest and most prosperous area. During the 1980s while the state was losing population the Des Moines metro grew by about 7 percent and created a large number of jobs in several key sectors including almost 100,000 in finance and insurance (The Principal Financial Group and Central Life Assurance are headquartered here). Des Moines is also home to Meredith publishing, one of the most successful magazine groups in the country.

Continued population growth in Des Moines will create many job openings (through 1996) especially in construction and maintenance (4,600), services (3,200), and retail sales (2,400).

Kansas

A small monument near Lebanon in the north-central portion of Kansas marks the historical geographic center of the 48 contiguous states. Kansas may be the heart of Middle America but fortunately—like some other states in the Midwest—it was spared the devastation of the 1991–92 recession. It was affected, to be sure, but not as much as the nation as a whole, and it certainly escaped the ravages that visited the Northeast and California.

If anything, Kansas achieved a soft landing in the recession. Statewide, Kansas added jobs, growing a bit less than 1 percent in 1991. With a relatively small work force of 1.3-million persons, its unemployment rate was 4.2 percent in November 1991, more than two percentage points below the national average. A year earlier, the jobless rate had been 4.3 percent. The Kansas employment economy rose through 1991, with a 5.3 percent unemployment rate in the year's first quarter and 4.6 percent in the April-through-June quarter.

Economists at Wichita State University have noted that Kansas indeed does not follow the patterns of the nation, and that has benefited the state in the most recent recession. Its steady growth can be attributed to a diversified economy with strong manufacturing and agribusiness components that had survived stormy times in the 1970s and 1980s. Their strengths tend to cushion the losses in struggling industries such as oil exploration, whose depression continued into the 1990s.

For the decade ending in 1995, Kansas is projected to have slow job growth, adding about 1.1 percent annually to its employment total. The rate would be significantly higher if agricultural employment, which was projected to lose 17,000 jobs over the decade, were excluded. In July 1991, 60,300 Kansas workers were employed in agriculture, down 9.3 percent from a year earlier. Still, Kansas is projected to have 650 openings a year for farm managers.

While Kansas continues to be a part of America's bread basket—albeit with fewer people engaged in agriculture—it also is a significant participant in America's productive machinery. More than 185,000 workers were involved in manufacturing at the end of 1991, and the category that includes manufacturing and construction was projected to grow more than 1.1 percent a year through 1995. Through most of 1991, manufacturing employment was essentially unchanged.

As elsewhere, Kansas' growth will be concentrated in service industries and retailing to the middle of the decade. Among better-paying jobs, the Kansas economy is projected to need more than 1,800 truck drivers a year, and more than a third of those openings will be new positions. With major medical facilities in Kansas City (which is regarded as a part of the Kansas City, Missouri, metropolitan area), Wichita and Topeka, the state's requirement for registered nurses is projected at 570 a year, with growth producing somewhat less than half of those jobs slots. Other health professions do not fare as well in the mid-decade projections, however; Kansas is projected to have fewer jobs for doctors and dentists.

Among the fastest-growing jobs will be travel agents, whose positions are projected to grow by more than 4 percent a year, and insurance sales workers, a category that will add almost 140 positions annually. Computer systems analysts will be in demand, with their positions growing by an average 3.7 percent annually, and job prospects are projected to be good for mechanical and electrical engineers.

SPOTLIGHT ON WICHITA

In its earliest days, Wichita was one of the jumping-off points for travel to the West, and it subsequently was a rowdy, raucous cow town. Today, Wichita is a pleasant and prosperous city that has taken wing in the 1990s on the strength of its aviation manufacturing. Three of the nation's largest manufacturers of private aircraft—Beech Aircraft, Cessna Aircraft and Learjet—have major operations in Wichita, and the region's largest employer is Boeing Co., which assembles jetliners and other aircraft with a work force of about 22,500. Aircraft-manufacturing employment in the region is roughly 40,000.

Manufacturing accounts for one of every four jobs in the Wichita region, which is above the national average and most likely accounts for the region's relative prosperity. The average manufacturing wage exceeds $13 an hour. But Wichita is not a one-industry town—it learned some painful lessons about relying on a few industries through cycles of boom and bust in the 1970s and 1980s—and has developed a well-diversified economic base. The city has a large health-care industry, employing more than 20,000 workers, and it also is the world headquarters of Pizza Hut, Inc., which was founded in 1958 by two Wichita brothers.

For a recessionary year, Wichita had a very good 1991, although the manufacturing sector began to soften in the last months of the year. The unemployment rate stood at 4 percent of the Wichita region's 261,200-member work force in November 1991, the same rate as November 1990. Because of the manufacturing softness—down by 400 jobs in 1991's third quarter and largely attributed to structural changes in the aircraft companies' suppliers—the 1992 rate is expected to edge up. Because a significant part of Wichita's economy is based on exports, the recession may come to Wichita in early 1992, but the local economy is expected to resume its growth in the last half of the year.

Nonetheless, prospects in the aircraft industry looked strong through mid-decade. Carlene Hill Forrest, director of the Center for Economic Development and Business Research at Wichita State University, noted that demand for new aircraft is "long-term and worldwide. Existing orders for both commercial aircraft and business and general aviation crafts will keep the bulk of our manufacturing sector in full production well into the mid–1990s."

The backlog of Boeing 737 aircraft stood at 800 planes in November 1991, and the company announced plans to add 700 new permanent workers to build its new 777 aircraft in Wichita. Boeing Wichita builds 75 percent of the 737 airframe and major subassemblies for other Boeing commercial aircraft.

The general-aircraft business, which went through a major slump in the 1980s, has recovered. Shipments were up in 1991 at both Cessna and Beech, and Learjet shipped two fewer craft than in 1990. Cessna announced plans to hire 900 engineers to work on its CitationJet and Citation X programs. The company has orders for 100 CitationJets and has indicated that it plans to build 1,000 of them over the next decade. An additional 300 assembly workers are to be hired to produce CitationJets.

Beech Aircraft announced plans to add workers in 1992 to build its 1900D regional airliner. Learjet has a backlog of some 50 aircraft extending through mid–1993. Among subcontractors, the German firm Buderus Sell GmbH announced plans to build airliner food galleys in a 29,000-square-foot Wichita plant with 100 workers initially. Over five years, the company plans to increase employment to 500. The area is projected to have strong growth for electrical engineers, with 120 job openings annually, and electrical-electronic technicians, with a projected 30 annual openings.

Employment in the region's health industry also will be increasing. A major employer is HCA Wesley Medical Center, which is constructing a 60-bed rehabilitation hospital that will employ 200 workers. In addition, the Rehabilitation Hospital of Wichita was scheduled to employ 170 persons when it opened. St. Francis Regional Medical Center, another major employer, also is expanding. The region is projected to need 150 registered nurses and 50 licensed practical nurses each year.

With the manufacturing economy in good health, Wichita's retailers also have been doing well. Wichita's State's 12th annual Business and Economic Conference developed a consensus of 3.6 percent growth in retail sales for 1992. In addition to a projected 590 annual jobs openings for retail salespersons, the Wichita area also is projected to have 100 annual openings for insurance sales workers and 170 for sales representatives.

SPOTLIGHT ON TOPEKA

Located 65 miles west of Kansas City, Topeka is Kansas' capital city and has a diversified economy with a moderate amount of manufacturing and heavy employment by government and service industries. The city also is equidistant between the state's largest educational institutions, the University of Kansas in Lawrence and Kansas State University in Manhattan. Although it had a higher unemployment rate than either Wichita or the state as a whole—Topeka's jobless rate was 4.5 percent of its 90,886-member work force in November 1991, down from 4.9 percent a year earlier—Topeka appeared to have weathered the recession's storm with little long-term damage. The region lost less than 1,000 nonseasonal jobs in the year ended November 1991, with a 200-job decline in manufacturing and a 600-job loss in trade.

The region's largest employer, by far, is the state, with a payroll of 12,100 in October 1991. The largest private employer is Goodyear Tire and Rubber Co., which employs 2,125 workers at a plant that manufactures many sizes of tires, including those for large tractors and heavy equipment. Topeka also is the major shop for the Atchison, Topeka, & Santa Fe Railway Co., which employs almost 1,800.

Also near the top of Topeka's employers are two hospitals, Stormont-Vail Regional Medical Center, which employs 1,800, and St. Francis Hospital and Medical Center, with 1,700 employees. Topeka also is the location of the world-renowned Menninger mental-health center, a research and treatment facility that employs 1,200. The region is projected to need about 120 registered nurses a year as well as 50 licensed practical nurses.

A significant share of Topeka's job growth to mid-decade is projected to be in low-paying food-service positions. Food workers for restaurants, fast-food and institutions account for the top six fast-growing occupations in the Topeka area. The region also is projected to have nearly 500 openings a year for retail salespersons.

Kentucky

Kentucky is one of those Midwest states that ducked much of the 1991–92 recession's impact because it was still recovering from the virtual collapse of its industrial base in the 1970s and early 1980s. For the job seeker in the early 1990s, the Louisville area and a few others offer some opportunities because they have not been ravaged by the national recession and, after a slight slowdown, are likely to continue moderate economic expansion.

As a result, Kentucky's job growth—projected at more than 5,000 positions a year to the end of the decade has not been seriously affected by the recession. Job openings, including both new jobs and vacancies, are expected to total more than 20,000 a year. By late in the decade, that growth very well could exceed the gains in the state's work force, which stood at 1.74 million in 1989.

The job opportunities will most likely parallel those of the national economy. The greatest need will be for health-industry workers in every classification from physicians to orderlies and janitors. Service industries and financial services will continue to grow.

The state's Cabinet for Human Resources, which conducts annual labor-market planning surveys, also found that a heavy demand exists for managers. Some of those managers surely will be recruited from outside the state because of Kentucky's generally low education levels. Statewide, only slightly more than half of the adult population graduated from high school, one of the lowest percentages in the nation. The state has undertaken a massive rebuilding of its education program, but budget shortfalls may slow the progress into the mid–1990s. When it is implemented, the educational restructuring should provide additional opportunities in secondary and primary education.

Kentucky's existing and future jobs will be concentrated in three areas—Louisville, Lexington and the Covington area across the Ohio River from Cincinnati. While these three cities form a triangle approximately 80 miles on each side, to call it the Golden Triangle is a misnomer. The jobs are within a short radius of each city, and beyond them are the state's declining agricultural areas. While opportunities exist in other areas, such as Ashland in the east, Bowling Green in the south-central part of the state and the western cities of Paducah and Henderson, the remainder of Kentucky is lightly populated, undereducated and, by national standards, poorly paid. In 1990, the average Kentucky annual paycheck was $19,000, compared with a national average of more than $22,500.

Still, some special factors will be in Kentucky's favor for the next few years. A particular strength is auto manufacturing. Toyota, which built a highly automated and efficient plant in Georgetown, north of Lexington in the state's center, plans to double the size of the plant in the next few years. Louisville has two Ford plants, one building heavy trucks and the other turning out the popular Explorer sport-utility vehicles and the Ranger light trucks. Bowling Green is the home of Chevrolet's only Corvette plant, although its fate will depend on the extent of General Motors's restructuring and any model realignments.

SPOTLIGHT ON LOUISVILLE

Of the 20,000 job openings in Kentucky each year, approximately one in three will be in the Louisville area. The region is projected to have about 7,100 job openings each year, and approximately 30% will be new positions rather than replacements. Although the industrial base has stabilized, almost all of the growth in the Louisville economy will be in service occupations.

When the Rust Belt virtually turned to dust in the early 1980s, no area of Kentucky sustained a heavier hit to its economy than Louisville. In 1980, manufacturing accounted for more than one in every four jobs in the Louisville region, which also includes the southernmost portion of Indiana. By the end of the decade, manufacturing accounted for fewer than one job in every five. In all, the manufacturing sector lost more than 14,000 jobs in the 1980s.

The Ford plants are two examples of Louisville manufacturers that are highly competitive in the global market. In addition, General Electric has a large appliance-manufacturing operation in Louisville and is the area's largest private employer with more than 12,000 jobs.

Louisville itself has a growth industry in United Parcel Service, which has more than 7,000 full-time and part-time workers in the area. Louisville's Standiford Field serves as the hub for UPS, which accounts for a substantial portion of the air traffic into and out of the airport. The airport will soon begin a major expansion that should add construction jobs through 1994 and the possibility for other air-related enterprises after the project's completion.

The brightest employment picture in Kentucky is in health care, and both Louisville and Kentucky generally can expect gains beyond those occurring nationally. Most of those gains will be concentrated in the Louisville area, although both Lexington and Covington are projected to have robust growth in health-related employment throughout the decade.

Louisville is the corporate home of Humana Inc., the nation's largest for-profit health provider. In both Louisville and Lexington, Humana has stiff competition from traditional private health providers. Humana's health-insurance and health-maintenance organization business has been growing, and it is likely to bolster the Louisville area's employment through the 1990s.

The Louisville region is projected to need more than 360 registered nurses each year, and more than half will be new positions. Similarly, the region is projected to need 169 doctors a year, 163 licensed practical nurses, 445 nurses aides and orderlies, and more than 100 health-services administrators annually.

In all, Kentucky will require 1,200 registered nurses a year to the end of the decade. The state will need almost as many new doctors, 504, as it will licensed practical nurses, 550, each year. For the doctors, 147 of those projected jobs are new positions, and 270 new LPN positions are projected to be created each year. In addition, Kentucky is projected to need more than 1,400 orderlies and nursing aides, 200 medical assistants, and 181 medical secretaries each year. In addition, Kentucky will require more than 300 medical and health-services managers annually, with almost half of them new positions.

Strong growth also will occur in the area of management services. Demand for general managers will be strong, with more than 3,000 openings a year statewide and roughly one-third of them in the Louisville region. Although the general-manager positions can range from heading a major corporation to a machine shop, the annual growth is almost equal to the state's and region's requirement for retail salespersons, which is generally an entry-level position. Demand for managers of food-service operations and lodgings also will be strong, with almost 500 openings annually.

In areas of business services, public relations and marketing are growth industries in Kentucky, projected to provide 280 openings a year, and demand also will be strong for accountants, with nearly half of 550 annual openings representing new positions. Almost 200 of the accounting positions will be in the Louisville area. In sales, state officials project strength in business-services sales, which will add approximately 130 jobs a year across the commonwealth.

Computer services will be a growth area in Louisville,

as elsewhere. Altogether, this category will add nearly 100 jobs a year in Louisville, with almost half of them new positions.

Among the trades, Kentucky will have almost 2,000 openings a year for truck drivers, with more than one-third of them new positions. Again, about one in three of those jobs will be in the Louisville area. The state also is projected to need more than 600 carpenters each year, with about one-quarter of them new positions.

The Louisville economy is not totally immune from recession or aging plants and technologies. In February, 1992, a large printing operation, Standard Gravure, closed its doors. Other potential negatives over the long haul relate to alcohol and tobacco. Louisville has several distilleries, and Philip Morris USA has a cigarette manufacturing plant there with more than 3,000 employees. Barley remains Kentucky's chief agricultural crop, ahead of thoroughbred horses, a major but economically depressed industry in the Bluegrass area around Lexington.

SPOTLIGHT ON LEXINGTON

Much more than Kentucky generally, Lexington reflects the national economy, and that was bad news in 1991 and early 1992. The recession and corporate downsizing both affected the Central Kentucky economy. Still, the Lexington area will account for roughly one in every four Kentucky job openings each year.

The region is bucking the trend of fewer production jobs, though, because of Toyota and its Georgetown plant, which now produces about 213,000 Camrys a year. In large part because of Toyota and related operations that have developed in all of the areas around Lexington, production-worker employment in the Bluegrass will grow by more than 1 percent a year through the decade, compared with a statewide annual average of 0.7 percent.

Toyota's doubling of its production capacity—a new engine plant already is in operation and further assembly capacity will be added in the early 1990s—will raise employment to 5,400, making it the region's largest employer. It is not the easiest place to obtain employment, however. With a large pool of potential workers to draw upon, Toyota has been very exacting in its hiring. For Toyota, being picky paid off; the plant is efficient and produces a quality product.

When it reaches its peak employment, Toyota will surpass International Business Machines and Lexmart, the company to which IBM sold its low-technology operation in 1991. When a restructuring is completed, IBM is expected to have about 1,000 employees in Lexington, and Lexmart will have 2,800, which will be down from about 3,400 when the sale took place. Lexmart, which reduced its payroll through liberal buyouts, manufactures such IBM-label products as electric typewriters and a laser printer that has been favorably reviewed by computer magazines.

Hughes Aircraft is scheduled to build a facility for manufacturing a video tube used in aircraft trainers. The operation should create 235 high-tech manufacturing jobs. The tube was developed by a University of Kentucky professor, and the facility will be built in the university's Coldstream Research Campus. A major pharmaceutical project is to be installed at the Coldstream center, and development officials are working to attract other high-tech manufacturers to the center. UPS has a major ground-transporation depot in Lexington, but its staffing is principally part-time workers.

SPOTLIGHT ON
COVINGTON

The Northern Kentucky area will have almost 2,000 job openings each year, while one-third of those openings will be new positions. The next largest growth area is the Bowling Green area, which extends down to the Tennessee border and the Nashville area. It is projected to have 1,200 job openings, many concentrated in the production trades, and about one-quarter of the openings will be entirely new jobs.

Earl Turley Jr., Kentucky's supervisor of occupational statistics and reports, said his 1987 projections for Kentucky's job growth through the year 2000 have been accurate so far with the exception of the Northern Kentucky area around Covington. Greater Cincinnati International Airport is located in Florence, Ky., and Delta Air Lines threw off his projections when it located a mini-hub at the airport and added new jobs. Before Delta came in, Turley nonetheless had been projecting healthy growth for the local Northern Kentucky economy.

The state also has its share of potential negatives. The biggest one is its highest paid industry, mining. Kentucky mining is a receding industry, down a projected 15 percent by the year 2000. Still, with the aid of United Mine Workers contracts, it is the highest paid wage-earning job in Kentucky, more than $600 a week vs. about $250 in the state's robustly expanding retail trade. In 1989, the state's average wage was $362.03 a week.

State officials foresee nothing on the horizon to change the outlook for growth in the major urban areas and minor job gains elsewhere. One future growth area will be the counties north of Lexington, on the Interstate 75 corridor that runs through central Kentucky to Cincinnati. Another is the far western corner of the state. Although coal mining will become less of a factor in the Paducah area's economy, the region has a strong transportation system and therefore would be suited for manufacturing operations.

Louisiana

The worst is over for Louisiana.

In the mid–1980s, while the rest of the country was booming, the Bayou state's most powerful economic engine, the oil industry, went bust. The result was a localized recession more crippling than anything the '90s have wrought in most other states. In 1986, the nadir for the state's economy, unemployment soared to 13.1 percent, nearly double the nationwide rate at the end of 1991.

Just as Louisiana may have been the first to suffer, it may be among the first to recover, as years of efforts to attract new, non-oil industry and diversify the state's economy begin to pay off.

By the end of 1991, unemployment in the state had dropped to 6.4 percent, according to Louisiana Department of Employment and Training figures. And optimism abounds, even among the economists. Dr. Timothy Ryan, director of the business and economic research division of the University of New Orleans, can talk for 10 or 15 minutes on segments of the Louisiana economy he expects to grow. And when Ryan talks about growth, he doesn't mean five or 10 years down the road. He's referring to this year. At the end of 1991, Louisiana had more jobs than at the beginning.

The growth fields in Louisiana ring familiar when compared with much of the nation. The Louisiana Department of Employment and Training, in its employment projections through 1995, expects opportunities to be most plentiful for retail sales clerks, registered nurses, truck drivers, general managers and executives, janitors, cashiers, elementary school teachers, secretaries, office clerks, and welders.

Like virtually every corner of the nation, Louisiana expects its greatest job opportunities will come in the medical field. But in Louisiana, medical employers' needs will be particularly acute because the state hasn't been producing nurses, technicians, records keepers, physical therapists, and home-care practitioners fast enough to meet demand.

"You'd think with high unemployment, if you had a sector with a lot of available jobs, that people would gear up and train workers for those jobs. But you'd be wrong," Ryan said.

Among those who might have the most difficulty finding jobs in Louisiana are industrial heavy equipment operators, data entry operators, photographers, bank tellers, and accounting clerks.

Overall employment in the state is projected to increase 10.17 percent over 1986 levels, to 1.73 million by 1995. Economists here are even bullish on agriculture, which is declining in much of the nation. Here, farm income grew by almost 50 percent—the nation's largest hike—in 1990.

And, remarkably, Louisiana economists foresee modest gains in manufacturing, a segment that is stagnant if not decimated in many parts of the nation.

Shreveport, the manufacturing hub of a state not traditionally noted for its heavy industry, may soon become home to a video-phone manufacturing plant, and possibly to a new McDonnell Douglas aircraft refurbishing facility. That plant would help the state recoup thousands of jobs lost in the '80s, when Boeing shut down a similar facility in Lake Charles.

Lake Charles is dotted with industry, much of it struggling to hold on in a turbulent economy. But here, too, local analysts are optimistic that new industrial blood may pour in. An airline and a defense contractor are among the companies that have expressed interest in bringing their operations—and thousands of jobs—to the region.

Baton Rouge, the state's capital, may be slightly hurt by

an expected decline in government jobs, but that could be offset by gains in construction, retail, insurance, and tourism.

SPOTLIGHT ON
NEW ORLEANS

In metropolitan New Orleans, not surprisingly, tourism is the big story. That industry has grown by about 10 percent annually in recent years, according to Kathleen Timmons, manager of the Jefferson Parish Economic Development Commission in suburban New Orleans.

The area is sprucing up its waterfront, and recently opened the Aquarium of the Americas, as part of an effort to lure more families to the city noted for its adult diversions. And when a new phase of construction is completed, the Louisiana Convention Center in New Orleans will be the nation's largest such facility.

All this means job opportunities for hotel workers and managers, waiters, waitresses, and, "if you listen to our governor, we're going to need croupiers and dealers," Ryan said, referring to Gov. Edwin Edwards' proposal to legalize gambling on land. The state already has legalized riverboat gambling.

In this city where cooks made blackened redfish so popular that the redfish no longer can be harvested in Louisiana, the search is on for additional chefs. In addition, experts foresee a growing need for those who offer professional services—lawyers, accountants, doctors and the like. The New Orleans area's accessibility to land, air, and water transportation make it a natural distribution hub.

The influx of distributors has brought with it a number of light-manufacturing firms that refine or upgrade the products arriving in the New Orleans area. Such ventures should become more plentiful as entrepreneurs take advantage of both New Orleans' accessibility to a growing Latin American market, and its undeveloped, inexpensive land.

Maine

The Pine Tree State is typical of most states in the New England area in that it ranked at or near the bottom in almost all job growth categories. Maine ranked 46th in total non-agricultural job growth in 1991, dropping 3.17 percent from the year before. The state's labor market fell from 530,000 jobs to under 514,000. Maine also ranked 47th in trade job growth, 43rd in manufacturing job growth, and 45th in construction job growth. Unemployment reached 7.5 percent in 1991, third-highest in New England behind Massachusetts and Rhode Island.

What growth there will be in Maine will most likely come in the country's typical high-growth service areas, such as health care personnel and paralegals. Rising school enrollments—the result of fairly steady if small population growth through the 1980s—and an unusually large number of retirements will also create a need for schoolteachers of all levels in the mid 1990s. Tourism, expecially in summer on the coastal areas, remains one of the fastest-growing segments of Maine's labor market. In addition to vacationers seeking to beat the heat in states further south, Maine benefits from Canadian shoppers looking to avoid Canada's value-added tax.

Maryland

"Maryland is America in miniature," goes an old local saying. And it's easy to see why in a state where the December (1991) unemployment rate stood at 6.8 percent, exactly the same as the national rate. Steel and the feisty blue crab were once signs of prosperity, but today these industries employ a tiny percentage of the state's 2.4 million workers, and analysts aren't counting on a revival. Maryland lost more than 45,000 manufacturing jobs in the past 15 years, over 6,000 in 1991 alone.

These days the state's top employers include the Baltimore-based Johns Hopkins University, weighing in with a combined full- and part-time work force of 24,500, and Giant Foods, Inc., with 18,000 workers. Like many states, Maryland's service sector—health, legal, education, etc.—expanded greatly in the 1980s, a whopping 75.3 percent. Services accounted for a solid 29 percent of total payrolls, generating over half of all new jobs in such places as Baltimore hospitals, suburban Washington offices, and labs in the high-tech Washington-Baltimore corridor.

Unfortunately the recession hasn't spared even the most stable employers of the 80s. In 1991 the state lost over 51,000 jobs, as funding shortfalls in state and local governments resulted in layoffs and furloughs. In Montgomery County, just outside of Washington, D.C., officials say a $185 million budget gap has prompted the elimination of 500 jobs. What's more, U.S. Defense Department cuts are expected to be felt most painfully by hardware suppliers located near Baltimore.

Still, the long-term job outlook is not all gloom and doom. Predictably, the shake-out in middle management of the past two years has run a nasty course in the services, but not all white-collar jobs are in jeopardy. Research and testing is also likely to show continued strength, spurred on in part by the location of over 60 federal laboratories in Maryland.

Still the recession has taken a heavy toll here and strong job growth isn't likely in 1992, even for health care workers. Unless you have a job waiting Maryland is not presently a place conducive to launching a career.

SPOTLIGHT ON BALTIMORE

Producing half of the state's goods and services, the six-county Baltimore area is still the engine of the state economy. The region's long-term prospects remain good, in large part because of a strong base in health services and a diverse employment picture. Health services, which in the Baltimore area has expanded just above the national average, remains on the upswing. The demand for nurses, technicians, and administrators will continue to expand. And analysts say the growth in health services will spur purchases of real estate, financial services, and insurance.

With 15,014 businesses, including giants such as USF&G (insurance), Alex Brown (financial), and Piper and Marbury (legal), the city of Baltimore still employs more workers than any jurisdiction in the state. The city counts more than a third of the state's jobs in finance, insurance, and real estate. And while manufacturing jobs are on the downturn, services is the leading jobs producer, weighing in with 33 percent of city employment.

Jobs are gradually moving from the city itself to the Washington-Baltimore corridor. With major employers such as Martin Marietta and Bethlehem Steel, for example, Baltimore County has replaced the city as the state's leading manufacturing center.

Located thirty-four miles southwest of Baltimore, Montgomery County boasts high-tech jobs in biotechnology and telecommunications and counts Vitro Laboratories and Comsat among its major employers.

It is a similar story in Anne Arundel County, located on the Chesapeake Bay and the home of Annapolis, the state capital. The county has experienced rapid growth in high-technology and regional headquarters. During the past five years, some 11 million square feet of commercial space have been built around Annapolis and the Baltimore-Washington International Airport. Major employers include USAir and Westinghouse Electronic Systems Group.

At the same time, employers such as Johns Hopkins University and other health-related concerns are likely to ensure that the city maintains a vibrant employment base. Baltimore has a distinguished history of civic pride and pumping money into downtown development. Whether that kind of commitment can make a difference here again is not very certain.

Massachusetts

By now it is no secret that Massachusetts is just about the worst place in America to look for a job. The so-called Massachusetts Miracle that helped Michael Dukakis secure the Democratic nomination for president in 1988 has turned to economic disaster. Massachusetts, ranked among the worst five states for growth in every segment of the labor market in 1991, placing dead last overall, as well as in construction, wholesale and retail trade, and government. Massachusetts lost more than 138,000 jobs in 1991 alone, declining more than 4.6 percent, from 2.95 million to 2.81 million. The state's 1991 unemployment rate of 8.8 percent was the highest in New England and one of the highest in the country.

But while the outlook in the Bay State is not rosy for the immediate future, neither is it catastrophic. Massachusetts is still one of the wealthiest states in the country, third only to Connecticut and New Jersey in personal income per capita, according to the U.S. Census Bureau. The state also has more doctors per capita than any state except Maryland. And though they have diminished in number, the computer and electronic research companies that ring Boston on Route 128 are still employers of national importance in that industry.

Some professional opportunities are actually growing in Massachusetts, particularly those in the health care industry, and especially in the Boston metropolitan area. Not only is this region home to several of the finest medical institutions in the world (Massachusetts General Hospital, Brigham and Women's Hospital, and the Dana-Farber Institute), these hospitals have one of the highest occupancy rates in the country. This means that there is a chronic shortage of certified medical technologists, X-ray technicians, physical therapists, dental hygienists, and some medical specialists including gynecologists and internists. Some major HMOs, including the Harvard Community Health Plan, have been hiring steadily, though lower turnover rates have sharpened the competition for jobs. The Harvard HMO, which runs 14 health centers in Massachusetts, hired an average of 90 people each month in 1991.

Some biotechnology and communications technology firms have also weathered the recession well. The Cambridge-based Biogen corporation, which discoverd the alpha-Interferon drug used to treat AIDS and cancer patients, increased its staff by nearly a quarter last year, and is expected to do so again this year. State officials also expect some growth in repair technologies, waste management, water treatment, and other ecologically oriented companies.

But basically the job market here is on hold, and that's putting an optimistic spin on all the available information. Economic recovery is due by the end of 1992 but no one in the Bay State is counting on it. Cynicism dies hard when strong promises and miracles prove false.

Michigan

"The Big Three" . . . "Motown" . . . "Motor City": Michigan's identity has been tied in to the automotive industry for most of this century. Cities like Detroit, Flint, Ypsilanti, and Saginaw conjured up images of smoke-spewing plants and assembly lines at Ford, GM and Chrysler. But with the steady decline in sales of American-made cars over the past decade, the employment reality was much different from the reputation.

Auto industry employment in Michigan peaked at 490,000 in 1978, and has been steadily declining since 1985 when about 341,000 workers were employed in motor vehicle manufacturing. With the latest round of cuts announced in early 1992 by GM, the number of auto workers in Michigan will hover around 250,000 very soon. The erosion of the auto industry was further evidenced in 1989 when it lost its position as the single largest employer in the state, pushed aside by the rapidly growing health services industry with 294,700 doctors, nurses, therapists, technicians, aides and other medical workers.

The auto industry slump helped push Michigan's unemployment rate to a high of 11 percent in March 1991. Although the rate dropped to 8.9 percent in early 1992, it will remain among the highest in the country for the foreseeable future. The auto industry accounts for about 7.1 percent of the state's manufacturing jobs and 14 percent of the state's earnings. Other manufacturing areas such as fabricated metals (3 percent) and industrial machines and computer equipment (2.9 percent) are directly linked to the auto industry. Even when the economy recovers, the forecast is not good for auto industry jobs, with the Michigan Employment Security Commission predicting a dismal outlook for assembly line workers, machinists, manufacturing painters and welders. Gone forever are the days when workers with minimal skills could earn a decent income on a car assembly line. The commission warns that today's auto workers need ''basic reading, writing and math skills,'' adding that many will need ''retraining programs to help them master new production processes.''

All types of manufacturing account for over 26 percent of Michigan's workers and the state predicts that overall employment in these occupations is expected to decrease, except at smaller manufacturers.

The growth in Michigan over the last decade has been in the service-producing industries, including 18.9 percent in wholesale and retail trades, with the largest group employed in food service occupations. *Michigan 2000,* an employment forecast compiled by several state bureaus, predicts that both areas will continue to grow. In sales, for example, demand will continue to be high for cashiers (2,200 openings annually), retail salespeople (1,120 openings) retail sales managers (2,600 openings) and wholesale sales representative (3,310 openings).

In the services category two areas stand out as good employment prospects: food service and health. The food industry will benefit from the national trend of more Americans eating out or purchasing takeout food, as well as from the increased demand in schools, hospitals, institutions and hotels. Job prospects are good for cooks and chefs (2,040 openings annually), food counter workers (1,860 openings), food preparation workers (1,730 openings) and food service managers (1,080 openings).

The health care industry in Michigan, as in the rest of the country, benefits from an aging population and advanced medical technology. According to a state employment forecast for 1988–2000, the health care area will see a tremendous growth rate. Six of the top ten jobs on the growth list are in the medical fields, including home health aides, with a projected 69.6 increase in available positions; surgical technicians, increasing by 54.4 percent; medical records technicians, increasing by 51.8 percent; medical assistants, increasing by 47.4 percent; radiological technicians, increasing by 46.4 percent; and occupational therapists, increasing by 45.7 percent. The state also predicts that demand will remain high for health administrators (240 openings annually), licensed practical nurses (1,050 openings) and registered nurses (3,050 openings).

Business and office workers account for more than 26 percent of the state's total employment. Demand for these workers will be particularly strong in insurance companies, manufacturing firms, and professional service organizations, according to *Michigan 2000*. Jobs as varied as accountants (1,270 openings annually), insurance adjusters (130 openings) and receptionists (1,660 openings) are expected to expand much faster than the average for all jobs in Michigan. Paralegals are expected to see a 70 percent increase in demand for their services because until recently, Michigan lawyers did not rely as heavily on paralegals as did lawyers in other parts of the country.

While traditionally a large number of engineers have worked in the auto industry and continue to do so, a significant number of openings are available in smaller companies drawn to Michigan, especially Detroit, by the highly skilled labor pool. Electrical engineers (650 openings) and mechanical engineers (1,010 openings) will find jobs, especially if they are able to ''retool'' for nonautomotive work. Firms are also attracted to the state because of the labor pools graduated from two nationally recognized universities, the University of Michigan and Michigan State.

Two bright spots in employment have been the growth of high tech companies in Ann Arbor and in Oakland County, both of which are in the Detroit metro area.

SPOTLIGHT ON DETROIT—ANN ARBOR

Detroit, once a booming manufacturing city, has endured race riots, a bleeding auto industry and losing half its population since 1950. Despite its problems, the city is slowly rebuilding a new economy based on high technology and growing international trade. Because of its concentration of skilled engineers and other technicians, Detroit has become attractive to companies specializing in research and development and high tech. *Site Selection* magazine named Detroit the number one metro area in 1991 for new and expanded research and development companies. The big growth has been in small companies specializing in development of products for air pollution and environmental control, according to Jack Steiner, a research director with the Detroit Chamber of Commerce. Other new companies concentrate on the design and engineering of medical apparatus and biotech products. One of the fastest growing employers has been EDS, with more than 20,000 workers doing product development in the telecommunications and medical records fields.

Foreign companies have also been attracted to the city. 650 foreign companies, employing 57,000 people, have moved into the area in the last six years. The companies, subsidiaries of German, Japanese, Canadian, and British corporations, manufacture products ranging from auto parts to thermal plastics. The reason for the growth is the educated work force, says Steiner, explaining, "Detroit has the largest engineering society in the world. It started with the auto industry need for designers and engineers. Engineering schools followed. Now the engineers are working in other industries."

Michigan 2000 cites the continuing need for highly trained technicians and engineers, citing demand in Detriot and surrounding Oakland County for computer programmers (660 openings), computer systems analysts (680 openings) and electrical engineers (650 openings), and industrial engineers (240 openings).

Detroit also benefits from the free trade agreement with Canada. Detroit is the mid-point between Toronto and Chicago, and there could well be an upswing in jobs in wholesale and distribution as the agreement goes into full effect. The city is joined to Windsor, Ontario, by three tunnels and two bridges over Lake Erie. A new railroad tunnel to handle the anticipated increase in transportation needs is under study, according to Steiner.

Northwest Airlines opened a hub in Detroit two years ago and it projects continued growth. This is reflected in the state's employment outlook, which predicts a 45.7 percent increase in jobs for flight attendants and 37.7 percent increase for pilots and flight engineers.

Another bright spot for the area has been the increase in retail outlets, exemplified by the upscale Neiman Marcus opening a department store in the area. "Detroit is finally being recognized as a good market," says Steiner. "We are the fifth wealthiest metro area in the nation."

With its medical centers, high-tech companies, universities and booming service industry, Ann Arbor is the economic exception to the rule in Michigan. The unemployment rate for Washtenaw County, where Ann Arbor is located, has been well below the state average through the past ten years because 56 percent of the work force are white collar workers in recession-proof jobs. While blue-collar workers constitute 28.5 percent of the work force, they are balanced by 15.5 percent in service jobs. What also makes the Ann Arbor workers an anomaly in Michigan is that they are young, with a median age of 26.6, and well-educated, with more than 36 percent with college degrees and more than 90 percent with high school diplomas.

Ford and GM have plants in neighboring Ypsilanti but are overshadowed by the major Ann Arbor employers in higher education and health care. The University of Michigan, Eastern Michigan University and Washtenaw Community College combined have almost 19,000 employees. Health care centers at the University of Michigan, Catherine McAuley, and the Veterans Administration Hospital employ more than 14,000 people. Other major employers include five high-tech/research and development firms, four printing/publishing companies, and three bio-medical companies. Warner Lambert/Parke Davis alone employs close to 1,200 in Ann Arbor.

Projections for the rest of the decade call for the county to continue to increase industry job growth at almost double the statewide rate. The service, sales, managerial and technical fields are all expected to grow by more than 20 percent by 1995.

Minnesota

Minnesota is a state of mind.

To outsiders it's a cold and forbidding land with wind-chills of Siberian magnitude that force people to stay indoors and to keep their car batteries charged all through the night. To the natives it's the land of 10,000 lakes, a magnet for outdoorsmen, and home to hardworking, well-educated folks who have built a special place for themselves in this country.

Almost in defiance of its location Minnesota has played an influential and at times central role in the life of the nation. In politics it is the home state of Eugene McCarthy, in the arts of F. Scott Fitzgerald and Sinclair Lewis, in entertainment of Judy Garland and Charles Schulz, and in medicine, Charles and William Mayo, founders of the world-famous Mayo Clinic. It was the home of Richard Sears of Sears & Roebuck fame and the birthplace of a dozen or more *Fortune* 500 companies. Today 18 companies from that prestigious list are located in Minnesota, including such well-known companies as General Mills, 3M, and Honeywell.

During the 1980s Minnesota continued to defy geographical expectations. While its neighbors lost population or remained virtually unchanged, Minnesota added 300,000, a 7.3 percent increase. In addition, new employers, especially high-tech companies, began to move here helping to swell the work rolls. As a result, in 1991, as much of the nation sank under the weight of the recession, Minnesota's work force grew by over 16,000, mostly in the Twin Cities of Minneapolis and St. Paul.

The state's 2.3 million-person work force is spread across an array of industries that makes Minnesota more resistant to economic potholes than the United States as a whole. Unemployment in Minnesota consistently averages 1.5 percentage points below the national average, a trend that has continued during the current recession: In November 1991, the U.S. unemployment rate stood at 6.6 percent, while in Minnesota the rate was 5.0 percent. Minnesota's economic expansion compares favorably with that of surrounding states, as it received 40.8 percent of the employment growth experienced in the region consisting of Iowa, North Dakota, South Dakota, and Wisconsin.

Minnesota can be divided into three primary regional economies: the north central and northeast part of the state has strong forestry, mining, and tourism industries (those based on natural resources), the Twin Cities constitute the main manufacturing and service-producing area, and the western part of the state has an agriculturally based economy. Because of the disparity among these types of economies, all regions of the state do not fare equally well. The areas of the state dependent on farming continue to lose jobs, while the more economically diverse Minneapolis/St. Paul area attracts both jobs and people. While the seven-county Twin City metro area gained over 200,000 people during the 1980s, the rest of the state added only about 35,000 residents.

Minnesota's economy is heavily weighted toward service-producing industries, which provide about 75 percent of total employment statewide; goods-producing sectors account for only about one quarter of the state's jobs. From 1979 to 1988, services grew from 19.2 percent of the state's employment to 23.6 percent. Over the same period, finance and insurance grew from 5.3 percent to 6.0 percent. These were the only two cohorts to experience increases in percentage of total jobs. Trade dropped from 26.1 percent to 25.8 percent; manufacturing from 22.3 percent to 20.0 percent; government from 15.6 percent to 14.7 percent; transportation and utilities from 5.0 to 4.8 percent; and agriculture, forestry, fishing, and mining from a combined 1.7 percent to 1.2 percent.

High-tech firms employed 126,000 Minnesotans in 1988,

with electronics, scientific instruments, computing equipment and computer/research services accounting for the bulk of these jobs. Although possessing only 2 percent of all U.S. wage and salary positions, Minnesota has a disproportionate share of the country's employment in high-tech industries, resulting primarily from the fact that the state claims more than 4 percent of all scientific instrument jobs and almost 9 percent of all computing equipment jobs nationwide. Another major employer is the wood and paper products industry (including printing and publishing, lumber, furniture, and paper/allied jobs), which accounted for more than 100,000 jobs statewide.

The Department of Jobs and Training predicts that retail salespeople will be the fastest growing occupation from 1986 to 1993, adding nearly 14,000 jobs over the period. Other professions that will experience job growth are waitpersons and janitors/cleaners/maids (7,000 more jobs each); general managers/top executives and cashiers (an additional 6,000 jobs each); registered nurses, secretaries, general office clerks, and truck drivers (approximately 5,000 more jobs each); computer programmers (4,000 new jobs); nursing aides/orderlies, accountants/auditors, and elementary/kindergarten/preschool teachers (3,500 each); and food sales, computer systems analysts, stock clerks/sales floor jobs, receptionists/information clerks, hairdressers/cosmetologists, food preparation workers, and blue collar worker supervisors (each predicted to grow by more than 2,000 jobs). Most of these jobs will be added in the Twin Cities area described below.

Outside of the Twin Cities, however, there are many major employers whose presence must be acknowledged. The largest is Marvin Lumber and Cedar Co., in Warroad, which provides jobs for 3,000 people. Others include Potlach Corporation (Cloquet), which employs 2,600 people in making coated printing/business paper; L T V Steel Mining in Hoyt Lakes (1,600 employees); U.S. Steel-MN Ore Operations in Mountain Iron (1,600); Minnesota Power in

Duluth (1,600); St. Luke's Hospital in Duluth (1,450); Boise Cascade Corporation-White Paper Division in International Falls (1,420); and Cold Spring Granite Company (1,200).

SPOTLIGHT ON
MINNEAPOLIS—ST. PAUL—ROCHESTER

It's no secret that winters come early and hard to this part of the country but in 1991 a "Halloween Blizzard" caught even Twin City natives by surprise. As always the people remained serene and this time perhaps even a little amused because as the temperature tumbled so too did the unemployment rate. In defiance of a national and statewide trend, and despite increased layoffs in construction, the Minneapolis/St. Paul area unemployment rate dropped from 4.6 percent to 4.4 percent.

While this figure is up a full percentage point over November 1990 this region has not felt anything like the pain of the coastal recessions. In fact it had 10,000 more jobs at the end of 1991 than at the beginning ranking behind only Houston, Seattle, and Denver in actual job growth.

More than half (approximately 2.1 million) of Minnesota's four million people reside in the seven-county Twin Cities metro area. As such, its economic health is responsible in large part for the well-being of Minnesota as a whole. Five of the state's six fastest-growing counties in population are in the Twin Cities region, and employment in the area has increased by 20 percent since 1979. Many of these positions are filled by commuters from the suburbs and even places as far away as St. Cloud and Rochester. Commuters also head for jobs in the suburban counties outside of Minneapolis and St. Paul. More than 200,000 people migrated to the Twin Cities during the 1980s.

The metro area is surrounded by a fringe region that includes 26 counties (with another million people) and radiates 100 miles in all directions from the urban hub, providing commercial interaction and workers for Minneapolis and St. Paul. Population here grew by over 6 percent between 1980 and 1990 and employment expanded by over 52,000 jobs. This region includes Rochester, officially a separate metropolitan area (pop. 106,000), but generally considered part of the Twin City job market.

All of Minnesota's 40 largest employers are situated within the Twin Cities and the fringe region. Minnesota Mining and Manufacturing (3M), located in St. Paul, provides 23,000 jobs, and Dayton Hudson Corporation in Minneapolis operates a chain of retail department and specialty stores employing 21,650 people. Northwest Airlines, headquartered in Eagan, provides 17,500 jobs. Other companies employing more than 10 thousand workers include the Mayo Foundation (Rochester) and Health One Corporation (Minneapolis), both health-care providers, and Honeywell Inc. (Minneapolis), maker of aerospace and defense systems. Rounding out the top ten are IBM Corporation in Rochester (9,300 employees); Lifespan Inc. of Minneapolis, another health-care provider, providing 8,800 jobs; Norwest Corporation (8,151), which offers a variety of banking, trust, venture capital, and leasing services; and Unisys Corporation, a computer equipment firm that provides 8,000 jobs.

Mississippi

Things change slowly in the Magnolia State, of that you can be certain. Since 1950 while the nation's population grew by about 40 percent, Mississippi's increased by only 15 percent (its neighbors, Alabama and Louisiana, grew by 25 percent and 36 percent respectively). And Mississippi remains a poor state, ranking dead last in per capita personal income in 1990 as it has for most of the century. One major reason for this is that over 36 percent of the population is black—the highest percentage of any state—and a large number still live in rural areas.

But change is coming.

In Mississippi, as in the rest of the United States, services are up and agriculture is down. "Agriculture is becoming more and more mechanized, needing less and less labor," said Raiford Crews, Chief of the Labor Market Information Department. "Farm workers, many of whom were elementary school dropouts, have to be retrained. The only types of jobs they can get are low-skilled repetitive jobs in manufacturing or low-paying jobs in the service industry, like day care workers."

The Mississippi labor force was just over a million people in 1989, and is expected to post a modest 12.9 percent gain by the year 2000, according to the Mississippi Employment Security Commission. Sparking that growth is a projected 20.6 percent increase in the services industry. Agricultural employment, which in 1989 stood at 28,090, is expected to fall 4.8 percent to 26,740 by the end of the decade. It is the only sector of the Mississippi labor market that is projected to contract over this time period.

Considering the economic climate, job growth during 1991 was strong with over 8,300 jobs being added. Almost 3,000 were in manufacturing and 2,700 in services. Mississippi's two metropolitan areas, Jackson and Biloxi-Gulfport, have been leading the way in employment growth. The two areas are currently responsible for employing more than 27 percent of the state's work force and that number will increase slightly by the year 2000. Biloxi-Gulfport is expected to grow at about the same rate as the state, while Jackson should see employment growth of close to 16 percent by the end of the decade.

But even rural areas are adapting to the changing job market without high levels of unemployment. Except for the Mississippi Delta, most of the state's terrain doesn't lend itself to large row farms, so many small farmers have already made the transition from agriculture to manufacturing, said Crews. And even on the Delta, where huge plantations once dominated, the number of jobs has been increasing steadily since 1960, even though the population has been declining. Today, the service industries provide nearly three times the number of jobs in the Delta as agriculture.

Not surprisingly the biggest winners in Mississippi will be retail salespersons, registered nurses, and cashiers. All three occupations are expected to grow by more than 4,000 jobs over the next decade. Truck drivers, general managers, nursing aides, and waiters and watresses will also see growth in their fields.

Paralegal personnel will see their employment pool grow the most, as the need for legal services in Mississippi is projected to increase dramatically. Jobs in the health service industries will also be plentiful.

While it's doubtful that Mississippi will ever become a major employment center for all kinds of workers, there is change in the air and plenty of job opportunities for those who seek a southern style of life.

Missouri

Job prospects in Missouri are a tale of two cities. One city, Kansas City and its Missouri-Kansas metro area, avoided much of the agony of the 1991–1992 recession until the first months of 1992. The employment market in the western part of Missouri reflected the situation throughout the state: With some pockets of weakness and some problems on the horizon, the economy continued to grow at a slow pace.

The second city, of course, is St. Louis, which has a Missouri-Illinois metro area. Its employment outlook was slammed badly by a sudden decline in two major industries: automobiles and aerospace. The automotive layoffs were a result of the recession and the latent effects of an American auto industry that allowed its factories to become outdated and inefficient. The aerospace weakness can be traced to problems in the airline industry and the reduction in defense orders following the Soviet Union's dismemberment.

As a whole, Missouri entered 1992 in fairly good condition economically. To be sure, its agricultural heartland, located to the north of the Missouri River, was still reeling from the farming depression that struck in the late 1980s. Some countries in the state's northern section have lost 10 percent of their population since the early 1980s.

At the end of 1991, Missouri's nonagricultural work force totaled 2,706,888 persons, with an unemployment rate of 5.9 percent. A year earlier, the work force totaled 2,487,093, and the jobless rate was 6.0 percent. Over the year, the Missouri economy added 58,812 jobs, and the jobless total declined by 2,141. At the end of 1991, more than half of the state's jobless were located within the St. Louis metro area.

Outside of the major cities, Missouri fared reasonably well in the recession despite some major setbacks. In the southwest, near the state's border with Oklahoma and Arkansas, Springfield was growing, as was Joplin despite the loss of a Zenith assembly plant. The food industry in the southwest corner of the state grew with the construction of poultry-processing plants that added 7,000 jobs. That growth partly offset earlier losses in Missouri's packing industry.

In the state's southeast section, the area north of Cape Girardeau had retained its employment base. The region has experienced growth in its wood-products industry, particularly around West Plains. Although residential furniture sales nationally have been depressed by the recession, the Missouri furniture industry has not been heavily affected because of its concentration on office furniture and specialty products. O'Sullivan, a large mass-market manufacturer of office furniture, has operations in Missouri. Central Missouri, which includes the state capital of Jefferson City and the University of Missouri main campus in Columbia, largely was spared recessionary damage in an economy that traditionally has had a low unemployment rate.

Through the end of the decade, Missouri's employment is projected to grow an average of 1.47 percent annually, with most of the expansion in service-producing industries. Manufacturing industries are projected to add about 0.38 percent a year, although the shaky state of automobile and defense manufacturing may stunt growth in this area. One of the growth areas will be construction, with annual job growth averaging 1,400 positions. The recession slugged St. Louis's construction industry in particular. In November 1991, it had lost 5,500 jobs from a year earlier. Gains elsewhere in the state—including 200 new jobs in Kansas City—reduced the statewide loss to 2,300 jobs.

As in other areas of the nation, Missouri will experience strong growth in low-paying retail and service jobs and in jobs that require more education, such as registered nurses and general managers. Missouri is projected to have 8,000 openings a year for retail salespersons, 3,500 for cashiers and 4,400 for janitors and cleaners. Fast food also will be a growth industry, adding an average of about 2 percent to employment a year. The state is projected to need 2,200 registered nurses annually, with half of them new positions, and almost 3,600 workers to fill general manager positions, the category that covers the managers for most small businesses.

Missouri is clearly one of those states where you have to pick and choose before you can be certain there will be jobs in a given area. At the beginning of 1992, it was safe to say that Kansas City was clearly the best bet.

SPOTLIGHT ON KANSAS CITY

According to the lyric in the Rodgers and Hammerstein song, ''everything's up to date in Kansas City.'' Indeed, Kansas City's diverse and up-to-date economy insulated it from the initial effects of the 1991–92 recession. It has plenty of manufacturing, but that base is complemented by agribusiness, trade, banking and finance. *Fortune* magazine ranked it fourth among 50 American cities for its business climate, and rated it first in access to quality labor. At the end of 1991, the two-state region—encompassing both Kansas Citys—had a labor force of 872,872, up from 855,830 a year earlier. Unemployment declined slightly to 4.8 percent at year's end, and the region added 16,705 jobs over the year.

The Kansas City metro area's employment is projected to grow by 1.45 percent annually to the end of the decade, or some 10,000 jobs a year. Service-producing industries will grow the fastest, to the point where they will account for four of every five jobs in Kansas City by the end of the decade. Durable-goods manufacturing is projected to lose more than 100 jobs a year, while nondurable manufacturing will be buoyed by printing and chemicals, expanding employment by an average of 1.3 percent a year. Employment in agricultural chemicals is projected to grow vigorously, adding almost 60 new positions a year.

The region's diversity will be its defense against changes that will occur in the 1990s and beyond. Some of its major employers will be under pressure from changes in the American economy and auto-industry competition. As 1992 began, Kansas City began to experience its first major setbacks from the recession. Allied-Signal Aerospace Corp., a major defense contractor, announced an 830-job cutback at its Kansas City, Mo., operation. That cut represented a 10 percent work force reduction by the region's third-largest nongovernmental employer. However, the plant is high on the U.S. Energy Department's list of preferred sites for continued production of non-nuclear weapons, so new jobs may surface soon.

The region's largest private employer is Hallmark Cards, whose Kansas City job force numbered 8,000 in 1991. According to statistics compiled by the Kansas City *Business Journal*, Hallmark added more than 1,000 jobs in the year that ended in September 1991. The greeting card company reflected strength in the region's printing industry, which is projected to add an average of almost 100 jobs a year.

After AT&T, which reduced its Kansas City-area employment in 1991 to 6,000, the region's next largest employers are health-care providers, the University of Kansas Medical Center (5,500 jobs) and Research Health Services System (5,000 jobs). Unlike other areas of the country, health services are not a booming industry in Kansas City. Growth in all health-services jobs is projected at less than 2 percent through the 1990s, and hospital employment will grow by an average of 0.25 percent. Demand for registered nurses will be approximately 565 positions a year.

The next largest employer is Ford Motor Co., with a September 1991 work force of 9,100 at its Claycomo, Mo., assembly plant. Despite a $2-billion loss in 1991, Ford is probably the healthiest of America's automakers, and it opened a new paint shop in 1991 at the plant, which manufactures the Ford SuperCab F-Series truck, the Mercury Topaz and the Ford Tempo.

General Motors has a Kansas City, Kan., plant, where it employed 3,800 workers in 1991. In 1992, the plant reduced its employment significantly when it eliminated a second shift. With GM's continuing efforts to reorganize itself into an efficient corporation, many of its plants must be regarded as expendable.

Despite the 1991 increase in construction jobs, Kansas City's building-industry prospects appeared to have been turning downward in the final months of the national recession. In late 1991, the value of nonresidential construction was down almost 13 percent for the year. Residential construction—Kansas City is regarded as a very affordable city for housing—climbed 0.6 percent through November 1991, the Greater Kansas City Chamber of Commerce reported.

One construction project, a 15-story office building for Twentieth Century Companies Inc., was to begin in 1992 for completion in 1994. The company is a fast-growing mutual fund manager that employs 1,000 in Kansas City and planned to add another 300 positions. Employment in finance, insurance and real estate was projected to increase by an average of more than 1,000 jobs annually through the decade.

Retail sales were up 10 percent for the year in a region where demand for sales workers is strong. Kansas City is a lively market for sales representatives, with projected annual openings of 261 jobs for scientific-products salespeople and almost 800 for other sales reps.

Kansas City's second largest private employer is Trans World Airlines, which filed for protection under Chapter 11 of the U.S. Bankruptcy Act in early 1992. TWA has major operations in Missouri, including a St. Louis hub, and they were at risk after principal owner Carl Icahn's filing, which had been arranged in consultation with the company's largest creditors. Some observers questioned whether TWA would survive in the airline industry's highly competitive market. TWA employed more than 6,500 workers in 1991, and it indicated that it needed aircraft maintenance workers and employee-relations workers in the Kansas City area. Air transportation in the region is projected to have modest growth to the end of the decade, adding fewer than 40 new positions a year.

SPOTLIGHT ON
ST. LOUIS

Despite some body blows to its employment levels, St. Louis' work force grew in 1991 and totaled 1.2 million. Unemployment continued to rise through the year but was still below the national average for the period, averaging 6.4 percent. The largest shock came from McDonnell Douglas Corp., a manufacturer of commercial aircraft and a major defense contractor. Both sectors took major hits in 1991, and McDonnell Douglas laid off 11,000 of its 37,000 St. Louis-area workers.

Another large employer is TWA, with 7,700 employees. Two other major employers are GM and Chrysler Corp., with more than 5,000 workers each. In early 1992, Chrysler announced that it was temporarily closing one of its two plants and laying off 3,700 workers. At the same time, the smallest of the U.S. automakers was adding employment at the adjacent plant that manufactures minivans.

Nonetheless, St. Louis retains some manufacturing strength, which is projected to employ 23 of every 100 workers in the region by the end of the decade. Monsanto Co., a St. Louis-based chemicals company, employs 6,350, and Anheuser-Busch, the nation's largest brewer, has both its corporate headquarters and 5,600 employees in St. Louis. May Department Stores Co., one of the nation's most successful retailers, also has its headquarters in St. Louis, where it employs 6,400.

St. Louis is projected to have strongest growth in business services, health services, and retailing. Personnel supply services are projected to undergo explosive growth, averaging 4.5 percent a year—or 1,200 jobs. Demand for workers in computer and data-processing services will expand by about 3 percent a year, with the St. Louis region needing an average of 222 data-processing analysts and 122 programmers annually for vacancies and new positions.

In other professional positions, demand will be strong for engineers, with the area requiring almost 1,000 a year to fill openings. Demand will be strongest for electrical and mechanical engineers. With a stabilizing school population, demand for elementary and secondary teachers will be relatively thin, with the prospect that the state's university system will provide the 675 teachers that the region will require annually.

St. Louis's demand for health workers will be strong, particularly when compared with the modest employment expansion in Kansas City. Hospital employment is projected to grow by 2 percent a year through the decade, while nursing-home and extended care employment will expand by greater than 4 percent annually. In all, health-care employment is projected to exceed 130,000 by the end of the decade.

As elsewhere, registered nurses can practically write their own ticket; the region is projected to need more than 1,150 RNs a year, with a majority taking newly created positions. The area also will need a projected 400 licensed practical nurses, 900 nurses aides-orderlies, and almost 100 medical-services managers to fill vacancies and new jobs.

Sales will be another growth area. In addition to the modestly paid retail positions, St. Louis will—like Kansas City—have strong demand for sales representatives. On average, the area will need 1,200 sales reps a year.

Montana

It must say something about the changing nature of American life that this state, the birthplace of Gary Cooper and Myrna Loy, has been in the news recently more because of the breakup of Julia Roberts and Kiefer Sutherland than for any other reason. So perhaps it is not surprising that tourism has replaced mining as a leading industry in what's called "Big Sky Country" just a bit too often to keep its authenticity.

Only a decade ago, much of the state's economy was based on the manufacture of wood products and the mining of coal and other natural resources. In recent years, Montana's jobs have shifted from the mines and the forests to urban centers around Billings and Butte.

Most of these newly developed jobs are in the service sector. The state Department of Labor and Industry anticipates some 3,560 new jobs annually, with about 3,100 in the service-producing industries. By the year 2000, 87 percent of the state's four million salaried workers will be employed in service-producing jobs.

The largest concentrations of service jobs are in education, health care, and the food service industry. More than 30,000 people are employed in the state's secondary schools, six state universities and two private colleges. In the next decade, the biggest single employment opportunity will be in elementary education for regular and special education teachers and teachers' aides. The growth is associated with the echo of the baby boom—adult baby boomers now having their own children. Elementary school teachers are number four on the state list of high growth careers. The state also predicts an increased demand for licensed day care center workers as more and more women enter the labor force.

Health services are the single largest growth area of the business/consumer service jobs. Registered and licensed practical nurses, medical technicians, especially in radiology and medical laboratory science, as well as physicians and surgeons are all in continued demand. One reason for the large number of health care workers is the large, specialized medical centers in Billings, Great Falls, Missoula, and Helena, according to Tom Cawley, a research specialist with the state department of Labor and Industry.

While the entire retail sector, including all types of stores, is expected to expand, by far the fastest growth will be for food markets and bars and restaurants. Over the rest of the decade, state projections indicate that food stores alone will experience a growth of more than 2,000 new jobs and that restaurants and similar businesses will develop almost 5,500 new jobs. In fact, after registered nurses, the number two and three jobs on the state's high growth list are cashiers and waiters/waitresses. Much of the growth, according to Cawley, can be attributed to the state's booming tourism industry. About six million tourists spent $760 million to view the state's scenic beauty in 1990, an increase of 600,000 tourists over 1988.

Those tourists will find better highways to travel along in the coming years thanks to a federal highways bill that will pour millions of dollars into the state for road and bridge repair. As a result, construction jobs are expected to grow by 22 percent, largely in highway repair crews.

While Montana has become a fashionable area for the Hollywood crowd it will assuredly remain a small state in terms of population. There will be job growth but because of the state's location very few new jobs will be high-paying professional or technical occupations.

Nebraska

From an easterner's point of view, the two most exciting things that happen in Nebraska on a recurring basis are a victory by its powerhouse university football team and the monthly release of the state's unemployment statistics. While the nation slogs through a recession with unemployment levels rising to 7 or 8 percent, Nebraska's work force of almost 860,000 has seen rates consistently below 3 percent, a remarkable feat that seems likely to continue for the foreseeable future.

A study done by Arizona State University's Economic

Outlook Center ranks Nebraska second only to Texas in the creation of new jobs from October of 1990 to October of 1991. Nebraska's 43,900 *new* jobs represent a 5.9 percent increase, putting it first in the country (up from sixth the previous year). The same study ranked Nebraska's job growth as improving in all sectors of the economy it measured: construction (up 16 percent); manufacturing (4.2 percent); transportation, communication, and public utilities (0.6 percent); trade (3.2 percent); finance, insurance, and real estate (2.6 percent); and services (7.9 percent).

Residential construction accounted for most of the construction employment growth (6,000 jobs) in 1991 while nonresidential construction declined.

Manufacturing added 4,000 jobs and increased from 11.4 percent of total nonfarm employment in 1986 to just over 13.0 percent in 1991. Employment in this sector is almost equally divided between the production of durable and nondurable goods. Employment in nondurable manufacturing increased over 4.2 percent over 1990 employment and in plants producing durable goods it increased by 3.4 percent.

The state's food processing industry has been especially resistant to economic cycles and is the state's largest nondurable manufacturing segment. Meat product processing employment jumped nearly 13 percent in a year's time making it the state's fastest growing area of nondurable manufacturing. Printing and publishing, another industry that is relatively resistant to economic downturns, is the state's second fastest growing nondurable goods producer.

The service sector is typically less buffeted in recessions than other parts of the economy. Service jobs account for approximately 25 percent of the state's nonagricultural employment. During the 1980s Nebraska experienced significant growth in telecommunications and data processing, most of it in the two metropolitan areas.

Of course agriculture still plays a vital part in the economy of the Cornhusker state (amounting to over 13 percent of gross product), but today only 9.5 percent of the work force is employed in this sector. So while the state proudly boasts that it's still number one when it comes to feeding cattle and marketing calves it has worked very hard to diversify and to build a "recession resistant economy" that now employs 784,000 nonagricultural workers. Nebraska's Dept. of Economic Development asserts that the combination of agriculture, manufacturing, and services provides a safety net against the extreme fluctuations of the national economy.

Speculation on why Nebraska has shown growth centers on the Employment and Investment Growth Act and the Employment Expansion and Investment Incentive Act, two bills passed by its unicameral legislature in the 1980s giving tax breaks not only to large businesses who come to the state, but also to Nebraska businesses who expand their employment rolls. Another reason for job creation may center on wages. According to figures from the state's Department of Labor, Nebraska's average weekly pay ranked in the bottom ten states in 1990.

Nebraska has been receiving a great deal of attention in the national media because of its recent economic success. But, job seekers must always be cautious when considering an area with such a small total population (1.6 million) and with jobs heavily concentrated in one area. It is always hard to predict that growth will continue in places such as this, but in early 1992 the outlook was very positive indeed, especially in Omaha.

SPOTLIGHT ON
METROPOLITAN NEBRASKA

Omaha is Nebraska's largest metropolitan area and its 335,000 jobs account for 45 percent of the state's employment. Approximately a one-hour drive away is Lincoln, the state's capital (and second largest city) where approximately

126,000 people are employed. The two metropolitan areas at the eastern end of the state employ 59 percent of the state's nonagricultural workers.

Omaha prides itself on its diverse business base and its accompanying economic stability. No industry sector accounts for more than 30 percent of total employment. Manufacturing represents just over 17 percent of the metropolitan area employment and the two largest sectors, service and trade, account for just over 54 percent of the employment. Since 1980 the fastest growing sectors of the metropolitan economy are services, trade, and finance, insurance and real estate. Major Omaha employers include: ATT Network Systems, First Data Resources, Integrated Marketing Services, Mutual of Omaha, U.S. West Communications, and Union Pacific Railroad, all employing over 2,500 people each.

The fastest growing parts of Omaha's economy according to a study done by the University of Louisville comparing the first two quarters of 1991 with the same time period a year earlier were construction, manufacturing, and services. Omaha's service sector grew 7.5 percent over the previous year. The three largest components of that sector in job growth are: health care, business services, and educational services.

The most spectacular growth in recent years has been in telemarketing and, for related reasons, in airline reservation centers. Omaha's telemarketing and reservation service firms together employ over 10,000 people during peak periods and handle over 100 million calls a year.

Omaha is the nation's telemarketing capital primarily because of the region's sophisticated telecommunications systems. This system was originally set up to serve the Strategic Air Command. One employer who relocated to Omaha from New York City also credits Nebraskans with having friendlier phone manners and a neutral accent ''that can be understood by callers everywhere.''

The large and efficient telecommunications systems not only have attracted telecommunications companies, but also information processing services. First Data Resources, an Omaha subsidiary of American Express, employs over 2,500 people and handles over 800 million credit card transactions a year.

Nevada

The population of Nevada exploded in the last decade, growing by more than 50 percent. In 1970 the state listed a population of 489,000 people. Ten years later, that number climbed to 800,000, and by 1991, the population topped 1.2 million. No surprise that in the period April 1990 until July 1991, Nevada, which grew by 82,000 people or 6.8 percent, was the fastest-growing state in the nation.

In recent months, the hot growth has cooled. Still, in the Nevada desert, cool is relative. This is a state which has been widely praised for its positive business climate, low taxes including no state income tax, and quality of life. In 1989 *Inc.* magazine noted that Nevada moved from 10th to the number one entrepreneurial state in the U.S. in just 2 years. *Money* magazine called it one of the five "tax havens in the United States" in January 1990. And the *Job Growth Update,* published by Arizona State University Economic Outlook Center cited Nevada as the national leader in job growth among states in 1990. That Nevada fell to 18th in job growth (behind Utah, 3; Arizona, 8; Colorado, 9; and New Mexico, up to 12th from 28th) in 1991 indicates how quickly economies can change.

By 1990, Nevada had led the nation for four consecutive years in the creation of new jobs. In 1991, its rate of job growth dropped to 4.1 percent but despite that hitch, by comparison to other states and cities, both Nevada and Las Vegas still look golden.

Consider that construction here is touted to be unusually slow. Yet in Las Vegas, alone, the MGM Grand has broken ground on a $1 billion mega-resort, and Steven Wynn, owner of the Mirage and Golden Nugget, has announced plans to build a $300 million Treasure Island, a destination theme resort; in addition Circus Circus Enterprises has a $290 million project on the books and the Hard Rock Cafe will be adding a hotel/casino next to their property.

As Las Vegas goes, so does Nevada, since most people in the state live in either the Las Vegas or Reno regions. Las Vegas accounts for nearly 800,000 people. Consequently, when job growth skids there from double digit to low single numbers, as it did in the last six months of 1991, the whole state feels the blow.

Fortunately, Las Vegas has a glitzy cushion of comfort. More than 15,000 people work in gaming, an industry that continues to stay on a strong roll. The largest employment sector, which includes the hotel and gaming and recreation industries, accounts for the paychecks of 64 percent of Las Vegas residents.

According to the "Las Vegas Perspective, 1991," the job climate in Las Vegas is expected to brighten in 1992. Gaming will grow slowly, but construction and government will improve. It was predicted in 1991 that employment would reach 410,400 people in Las Vegas, a gain of 34,400 jobs or a 9 percent increase.

Statewide government also shows strong growth. In 1992 Nevada anticipates a 10.1 percent expansion in that sector. The state is a major landlord (the federal government owns 81 percent of the land in the state) as well as a big employer. Nellis Air Force Base employs more than 12,000 military and civilian personnel and pumps about $800 million into the region's coffers annually.

Growth also is occurring at the local school level. It is projected that the need for teachers will increase as local governments try to keep pace with the enormous population growth. The Clark County School System, for instance, recently opened 18 more schools to meet the needs of the area.

In an attempt to keep its economy diversified and on track,

Nevada aggressively pursues foreign investment. The State's International Office markets reverse investment and exporting opportunities in Japan, Korea and Taiwan. The state also maintains a Washington, D.C. office, the only state entity to establish an office to focus on trade and economic development in the nation's capital. And, Las Vegas, which is a designated foreign trade zone, enjoys a reputation for being among the largest world centers for trade conventions and exhibitions. All this international marketing activity is paying off. During 1990–91 more than 75 foreign firms—from Hong Kong to Japan, Europe to the Middle East—have located in the Las Vegas area.

Despite recent growth and job deceleration, Nevada remains a goldmine of future opportunity. Today gaming and construction lead the economy, but the state is trying hard to spread its domestic industrial wings. During this last year, Las Vegas landed many new firms which have provided new employment opportunities. In the first quarter of 1990, 14,697 firms were listed in the area. A year later that number had jumped to 15,653, an increase of 956 companies. The Finance, Insurance, and Real Estate industries recorded the biggest gains, and even construction, while registering a loss of overall jobs, came in at significantly above the national average.

What's ahead? The Nevada Employment Security Department forecasts job gains in the Las Vegas MSA to increase by 5.5 percent in 1992 as more new companies come to town. And despite the temporary effects of the national recession, good growth is anticipated in the transportation/communications /public utilities, trade and service sectors. State economists predict increases in the 5 percent range in 1991/92. Construction, an industry that experienced "astronomical job growth during the past few years," won't hit its previous stride, but permit numbers are ahead of last year's levels, so signs are encouraging. As housing picks up and hotel casino projects progress, construction jobs are expected to increase by 3 percent.

The manufacturing picture is less impressive. Nevertheless, small projected losses in 1991 should be recouped and new firms such as Mojava Manufacturing, Super Brands Inc., and Drill International will come on line. Statewide, mining promises the biggest jackpot for the 15,000 people employed in this sector. Gold and silver is big business in rural Nevada and this industry pays the highest average wage.

Looking beyond Las Vegas, business is robust in Reno/ Sparks. Kenneth Lynn, executive director of the Economic Development Authority of Western Nevada (EDAWN), reports 1991 was the best year ever for the Reno area's attracting new business. Five years ago, if 25 companies committed to his area, he says, it was cause for rejoicing. In 1991, 43 companies signed into Reno, an all time record.

In contrast to the gaming/tourism world of Las Vegas, Reno is mostly business. Located just ten miles from California, it profits from its proximity. It is a natural for the distribution industry and an easy alternative to the high cost of California living. Located on the main highway from San Francisco to New York and Los Angeles to Washington, the Reno/Sparks region is ideally located for companies wanting to do business in California, the West Coast or across the country. Recently, Reno significantly increased its manufacturing base. Says Lynn, "We see this as a positive as these jobs are higher paying and higher skilled."

Statewide, Nevada maintains a strong national advantage. Unlike many other western states, per capita income here is above that of the U.S. During the 1970s and 1980s, per capita income in the State ran 12 to 20 percent higher than the nation. In recent years, that advantage has narrowed, some. The 1990 figures show Nevada's per capita income at 2 percent above the national average. Still, in tough times the numbers are impressive.

Like Arizona, Nevada is showing signs of pulling out of its doldrums. Economists warn not to expect a quick return to the old boom days when jobs were going begging. Preliminary estimates for 1992 predict growth in the 2.0–2.5 percent range, slow by Nevada standards but still remarkably healthy in an ailing economy. Taken in context, Nevada's overall performance, while painfully slow by its own standards, keeps it far ahead of the national pack.

Still, Nevada is definitely a question-mark area for the immediate future. Many of the projections have been made on premises that may not hold up, especially if recovery is slow.

New Hampshire

During the 1980s, New Hampshire was one of the fastest-growing states in the country, adding 200,000 people for a net gain of over 20 percent. More importantly, it was attracting people with money and good jobs who helped to boost the state's per capita personal income so dramatically that by the end of the decade, it ranked 8th in this category, up from 23rd in 1980.

But as the candidates for president—and the rest of America—recently discovered, New Hampshire has been mired in one of the worst economic recessions in its history for several years. The state ranked 47th in total nonagricultural job growth in 1991, declining 3.2 percent, losing more than 16,000 jobs in a labor market of less than a half-million workers. Unemployment in February, 1992 reached 7.8 percent, the highest rate since 1982. Bankruptcy rates more than tripled between 1989 and 1991. And in this fiercely independent state, the number of people on welfare has doubled since 1988.

The trouble was that so much of the state's economy simply mirrored that of its neighbor, Massachusetts. In the 1980s, businesses and residents flocked to New Hampshire because of its proximity to Boston's research and educational establishments, and, more importantly, because of the lack of a state income or sales tax. Much of this growth came in the two southern cities of Manchester and Nashua, which are less than an hour from Boston.

But when the Massachusetts Miracle dried up in the late 1980s, so did New Hampshire's growth. Cutbacks in defense spending and increased competition in the microcomputer field crippled New Hampshire's high-tech industries, and in quick succession, the construction, real estate, tourist and retail trade industries collapsed, sending the state into a recession nearly two years before the rest of the nation.

With little economic base of its own, New Hampshire will have to wait for a recovery in the Boston area before things ease up in the Granite State. In the past year, only the service industry has shown any signs of growth, and even that was a modest 800 jobs. Retail trade showed some signs of recovery toward the end of 1991, posting growth of 300 jobs in October, 1991. That offset a decrease of more than 7000 jobs over the entire year, and a loss of 200 jobs in wholesale trade over the same month. Government jobs also increased by 1,200 in October 1991 after declining by 2,300 jobs in the 11 previous months.

The future of New Hampshire's economy is hard to predict; so hard, in fact, that no one in the state's Department of Employment had any helpful information to offer on that topic. Suffice it to say that some signs of change have begun to appear. Between April 1990 and July 1991, this once rapidly growing state witnessed a population decline of 4,000 people. Doubtless there will be many more defections in the years ahead.

New Jersey

Ever since Ben Franklin referred to New Jersey as the turnpike between Philadelphia and New York, the Garden State has never received full recognition as the economic powerhouse it actually is. Although New Jersey ranks 46th among the states in land area it is the ninth largest in population and holds the eighth position in Gross State Product. In the crucial category of per capita personal income, New

Jersey ranks second among all the states; four of its counties are among the richest in the nation.

New Jersey's work force grew dramatically in the 1980s. Several times during the decade the state added about 100,000 jobs annually and the unemployment rate dipped to half the national average. A large part of those new jobs was created by the boom in corporations moving to the state. New Jersey ranks third nationally in the number of corporate and division headquarters. Such well-known companies as American Cyanamid, Revlon, and Nabisco are headquartered here.

But it's no secret that the recession hit hard here and it will take some time to recover. The state lost about 95,000 jobs in 1991; 42,000 of those jobs were in manufacturing, but virtually every sector of the economy was adversely affected. Coupled with this came an ill-advised tax package from a new governor that actually got the normally quiet middle class protesting in the streets with the result that New Jersey's confidence was severely shaken. In the beginning of 1992, however, visible signs of optimism returned because the economic foundations of New Jersey are so strong and likely to get stronger.

In 1991 alone a total of 103 companies—among them such diverse and successful establishments as Nestlè, Sumitomo Bank, Fine Arts Graphics, and Canon North America—announced plans to move to New Jersey from New York, Pennsylvania, and five foreign countries. About one-third were manufacturing businesses, while the remaining two-thirds were distributed among general services, transportation, finance/insurance, and wholesale trade. The state expects as many as 10,000 new jobs to result just from these relocations. All together the state Department of Labor believes that several hundred thousand jobs will be created before the end of the century, and as many as 100,000 replacement openings will also occur.

One area of continued growth has been among high-tech and research and development companies. With more than 140,000 scientists, technicians, and engineers, and more than 11 percent of all government and industry R&D funds, the state is known as the home of such internationally famous technology centers as AT&T's Bell Laboratories.

In the service sector, both health and business—two of the state's largest industries in recent times—are expected to increase by 65 percent and 46 percent respectively and create over 250,000 new jobs in the next decade.

The health field follows the national trend, but also reflects the longtime existence of pharmaceutical and medical establishments such as Becton-Dickinson, Johnson & Johnson, and Merck. Business services will present opportunities in the computer and data processing fields; some estimates suggest that one in every five new jobs will be in this field.

Other areas that will grow in the next decade are restaurants (37.1 percent), wholesale trade (36.2 percent), and the retail grocery trade (17.7 percent).

Among professional workers, strong job growth is anticipated for physicians, nurses, accountants, technicians, engineers, administrators, and sales personnel. For blue collar workers, the best opportunities will be found by mechanics, repairers, and installers—particularly those who can perform multiple maintenance skills, with significant openings as well for plumbers, carpenters, electricians, drivers of trucks, buses, and taxis.

Unfortunately another significant growth area in the state is envisioned in protective services, with the most jobs foreseen for guards and corrections officers.

The area of the state most expected to thrive is the Atlantic/Cape section—with an anticipated 2.1 percent annual employment increase. New Jersey's southern tip has always depended on tourism, but strong job growth also reflects the advent of casino gambling in the late 1970s. Most of the jobs are in the hotels and casinos themselves, while other positions are in restaurants and bars, health services, trade construction, and retail.

At the other end of the spectrum, the Essex-Hudson region—which comprises Newark, New Jersey's largest city—will show the slowest anticipated employment growth in the state, with an annual employment growth foreseen at 0.9 percent. Jobs in this area will dwindle in the manufacturing industries, but are expected to rise slightly in business and health services. Many of the business jobs here are centered at Newark International Airport and at the corporate headquarters for large communications and utilities companies.

So the outlook for the job market in New Jersey is generally very good for the long term but questionable over the 1992-93 period.

New Mexico

As New Mexico heads toward the year 2000, look for trade, services and government to carry the state. These three industries will continue to create the majority of employment opportunities. In 1990, they accounted for more than 75 percent of all new jobs created.

According to the "New Mexico Occupational Outlook 2000" prepared by the New Mexico Department of Labor, by the turn of the century the service sector will swell by 32 percent. Many new employment opportunities will open in tourism, which traditionally is an important contributor to New Mexico's economy, pumping $2.2 billion into the state annually. But it is health-care that will push services into the limelight. Growth in large part will result from the state's aging population. Like much of the nation, New Mexico is aging fast. By the year 2000, a 51 percent increase is projected for the 65 and over age group. As a result, New Mexico expects to need more outpatient care facilities and nursing homes, which in turn will dramatically increase the need for more RNs and home health care workers.

Government has long played a dominate role in this southwestern state's economy. The state has been the site of many pioneering efforts for both atomic research and space flight. The federal government supports two major research laboratories, Sandia National Labs in Albuquerque and Los Alamos National Lab in Los Alamos. In addition to existing federal research and military installations, many private firms operate as government contractors. Honeywell's Defense Avionics Systems Division and BDM International, Inc., both in Albuquerque, are private defense contractors who, between them, employ 3,300 workers. Nearly 8,000 other private defense contractor employees work on defense installations around the state.

While government will continue to be a leading player, expect slower growth here due to cutbacks in budgets on the state and federal levels.

New Mexico's manufacturing base is small. It accounted for only 43,100 jobs in 1990, but the computer and electronics industry will be an increasingly important player. Looking ahead to the year 2000, the state expects electronics manufacturing to add a good jolt to the economy. By then, this sector will increase by 40 percent as new jobs are created for engineers, technicians and other personnel related to this industry.

How important is the electronics industry to New Mexico's future? Here's what the New Mexico Occupational Outlook 2000 predicts. "The single greatest number of new jobs will occur in professional and technical occupations as technological innovations accelerate the demand for highly-trained workers in a variety of fields." The demand for engineers, alone, is expected jump 70 percent by the year 2000. In Albuquerque job openings for engineers is anticipated to grow by 240 jobs a year through the end of this decade. Statewide, New Mexico projects 530 new engineering jobs a year created by the end of this decade.

Industrial machinery and equipment manufacturing is also predicted to expand for the rest of this century. Much of this growth will occur in computer and office equipment manufacturing where more than 700 new jobs will open by the year 2000.

As more businesses relocate to New Mexico by the year 2000, personal incomes should rise, and if air fares decrease it is anticipated that travel agents will be one of the fastest-growing occupations in the state in terms of sales opportunities. Both travel agents and insurance sales workers jobs are expected to increase by 40 percent.

Statewide, employment projections indicate that by the year 2000, New Mexico will generate nearly 111,000 new jobs. Most will occur in more traditional career paths, such as service sector, electronics-related opportunities, healthcare workers and ancillary personnel needed to provide clerical and administrative support. New Mexico's labor analysis also foresees a need for graphic artists as increasing emphasis is placed on visual appeal in business, whether in product design, advertising, marketing or television.

Like other Southwestern states, New Mexico is poised to grow. However, traditionally growth in this state has not matched the phenomenal pace of its neighbors. Where Arizona and Nevada surged in population and job creation, in the last two decades, New Mexico has experienced many ups and downs. The construction industry, usually a leader for growth states, has declined since 1985 in New Mexico. Still, as the state marches toward the 21st century, it expects an increase of nearly 21 percent in this sector or more than 6000 new jobs created.

If the employment numbers sound promising, remember New Mexico is a small state economically with only 1.5 million people and 568,000 civilian non-agricultural jobs. With a per capita income of just $13,140, it ranks 45th among the 50 states. Unemployment runs slightly higher than the national average, but cost of living is parallel.

The fastest growing industries to the year 2000 are all in the services sector which is expected to increase by 94.7 percent. Personnel supply services should experience 88.5 percent growth, and health and allied services is expected to increase more than 78 percent each.

While the New Mexico Department of Labor predicts a job growth rate at somewhat larger than the national average, most opportunities occur in lower paying markets and remain concentrated in the Albuquerque, Santa Fe and Las

Cruces area. Albuquerque, which accounts for 235,000 of the 547,500 jobs in 1988, will continue to be the major job market. Baxter Healthcare and Metropolitan Life Insurance Company expanded recently in Albuquerque as have Martin Marietta, Motorola and Intel.

These gains help to offset the loss in military spending. The Star Wars ground-based laser project at White Sands Missile Range and the magnetic fusion project at Los Alamos National Lab both were curtailed. However, the stealth fighter was transferred to New Mexico from Nevada.

Outside the cities, rural New Mexico continues to be heavily dependent on farming and mining, a pattern repeated throughout the Southwest.

New York

It's a long-standing American tradition to go to New York to look for a job, one that's been celebrated in movies and plays for a century or more. Rarely are the job seekers in these fictions disappointed—but then nothing lasts forever.

The recession has hit both New York State and New York City so hard that the unemployment rate has risen to levels not seen since the oil-crisis malaise of 1976. In February 1992 the unemployment rate was 8.9 percent for the entire state, up from 6.2 percent in the same month of 1991. For New York City (the five boroughs only) the rate soared to 10.9 percent, up almost 50 percent from the 7.3 percent in February 1990.

The number of jobs in New York State diminished by 267,000 in 1991. Every large city in the state lost jobs: Albany-Schenectady-Troy (9,000), Buffalo (4,000), Rochester (5,000), Syracuse (8,000), Binghamton (3,700), Poughkeepsie (4,400). New York City alone lost 169,000 jobs while the entire metropolitan statistical area—which includes Long Island and parts of Westchester and northeastern New Jersey—lost about 300,000 jobs out of a total of 8 million jobs.

Every sector of the state's economy lost jobs as well. In the crucial services area where all but eight states had some job growth, New York lost about 50,000 jobs and ranked dead last in the "Job Growth Update" survey issued by Arizona State University. Manufacturing, too, lost 50,000 jobs, and retail and wholesale trade, a traditionally strong part of the Empire State's economy with 1.7 million jobs in 1990, decreased by 75,000 jobs. Even finance, insurance, and real estate—to many the core of the New York economy—lost 13,000 jobs, a decline of 3.4 percent from 762,000 to 749,000.

After so much bad news it's not surprising that Governor Mario Cuomo decided not to run for president this year. While no one could blame one politician for all this, the economic turmoil in New York is surely the result of faulty planning—or better no planning at all—in Albany. And while the Republicans and Democrats continue to blame each other for the mess, the truth is that New York has been undergoing structural changes in its economy that started with the erosion of its manufacturing base more than a decade ago as a result of high taxes and competition from neighboring states. But New York's economic power is so enormous—it is second only to California's—that these changes were thought to have only minimal negative effects. Moreover, the artificial boom times of the 1980s helped to mask the underlying weaknesses. Nowhere was this more true than in New York City.

SPOTLIGHT ON
NEW YORK CITY

New York City, the heart and soul of New York State's economy, is the megalopolis many people believe is the greatest city in the world. Peerless in its attraction to the arts, New York City has over 500 museums and galleries, 21 symphony orchestras, 23 dance companies, more theaters and more actors than anywhere else, and the list goes on and on. It is also the home of the United Nations and of 780 landmark buildings, so no wonder over 17 million people a year visit here making New York a national leader in tourism.

In business New York is a world class center for banking, advertising, retailing, the securities industry, publishing, television, and fashion. Avon Products, Bristol-Myers Squibb, Colgate-Palmolive, McGraw-Hill, The New York Times Co., Pfizer, Revlon, Time Warner, and RJR Nabisco are just a few of the *Fortune* 500 companies headquartered here.

A glance back over that list will reveal that almost all of these industries suffered serious setbacks during the recession and only began to recover in late 1991 and early 1992. Most experts believe that the jobs in banking and retail sales will never reach the same levels again, nor will many traditional office jobs for clerical workers, but in the other major industries most of the white-collar jobs will rebound to their previous levels. Growth will be modest to be sure but opportunities will exist.

Of course in the professional and technical category of occupations there never was any meaningful decline, and demand for their services continues. The same is true for health care workers. On the other hand almost *none* of the blue-collar occupations in construction, machining, printing, or textiles is in demand and the projections for the future call for a steady decline.

On the positive side the New York City white-collar job market is so enormous in so many different fields that openings occur continuously. Aside from the anecdotal evidence of this in the help-wanted sections of all the major newspapers, one can draw the same conclusion for the numbers of people employed in various occupations. New York City, for example, has more bank tellers (26,000), waiters and waitresses (45,000), retail sales clerks (93,000), and sec-retaries (150,000) than most *states*, so even though such occupations won't grow in number, there will be thousands of openings due to turnover, promotions, retirements, etc.

Below is a list of New York City jobs that in 1992 the state Department of Labor projected would have openings each year until 1996. It is clearly a reflection of the changes taking place there, both economically and socially. Note well that almost all of the openings—9 out of 10—will come from separations: i.e. deaths, retirements, firings, and people leaving their jobs voluntarily.

New York City: Average Annual Openings, Selected Occupations 1992–1996

Occupation	Number Employed (1992)	Projected Employment (1996)	Average Annual Openings
Accountants, Auditors	37,310	38,090	710
Actuaries	770	830	20
Architects	4,520	4,700	100
Child Care Workers—Private	3,840	4,100	310
Computer Programmers	23,460	25,330	870
Computer Systems Analysts	16,120	17,980	460
Cooks, Restaurant	11,180	12,070	560
Fast Food, Short Order	9,430	9,670	870
Dentists	4,300	4,530	150
Doctors	24,420	23,990	550
Economists	2,380	2,540	100

New York City: Average Annual Openings, Selected Occupations 1992–1996 *(cont.)*

Occupation	Number Employed (1992)	Projected Employment (1996)	Average Annual Openings
Education			
Administrators	8,780	9,100	220
Engineers	22,310	22,270	480
Chemical	440	430	10
Civil	4,920	4,920	100
Computer	2,280	2,300	50
Mechanical	3,170	3,220	90
Nuclear	580	620	20
Engineering			
Technicians	20,510	20,990	610
Food Preparation			
Workers	26,760	27,850	1,770
Food Service and			
Lodging Managers	14,230	15,410	430
Health Care			
Occupations			
Home Health Aides	34,080	38,920	1,450
Nurses, Registered	60,340	63,680	1,440
Pharmacists	4,360	4,660	170
Physical Therapists	2,020	2,200	80
Respiratory			
Therapists	1,370	1,460	50
Speech Pathologists	1,330	1,430	50
Technicians	31,150	32,250	630
Lawyers	49,130	56,770	2,490
Librarians	6,060	6,130	130
Paralegals	7,030	9,250	490
Personnel Specialists	17,200	17,720	370

New York City: Average Annual Openings, Selected Occupations 1992–1996 *(cont.)*

Occupation	Number Employed (1992)	Projected Employment (1996)	Average Annual Openings
Physical Scientists	3,720	3,720	120
Psychologists	5,580	5,710	50
Real Estate—Agents	10,030	10,570	240
Real Estate—Brokers	7,560	7,940	180
Secretarial Workers	142,280	147,820	4,450
Securities—Sales	46,020	52,045	1,760
Social Workers	24,110	24,900	320
Teachers, Elementary	44,010	44,700	1,160
Teachers, Secondary	43,400	44,770	1,070
Travel Agents	5,970	6,430	330
Writers, Editors	9,940	10,320	310

Source: *New York State Department of Labor*

SPOTLIGHT ON ALBANY

Although most of the job news in New York's capital city has been bad, new Albany offices for two of the nation's largest insurance agencies have provided some good news. State Farm added almost 900 jobs to Albany's insurance industry when it moved some of its offices to the capital region in 1991. A similar move is expected by Metropolitan Life in 1992.

"The availability of both labor and land means people are moving some of their back office operations to Albany," said Jim Ross, a market analyst for the Department of Labor. "Many of these jobs don't have to be in New York City, so it doesn't matter if they're across the street or a three-hour drive away from Manhattan."

The insurance industry grew by more than 11 percent in 1991 to just over 9000 jobs, making it one of the fastest growing areas in an otherwise declining job market. Total non-agricultural employment stood at 414,700 in January of 1992, down 1.87 percent from the year before. Unemployment increased from 6.2 percent to 7.5 percent over the same period. Layoffs, cutbacks, and office closings on all levels of government contributed to those declining numbers. Another round of layoffs are expected in state government in April of 1992.

Aside from the insurance industry, the only bright spots in Albany are for workers in the machinery, electrical and electronic equipment industry, which grew by 600 jobs, or 4.9 percent, and those in the health services industry, which added 1000 jobs, a 2.0 percent increase.

SPOTLIGHT ON BUFFALO

With nearby Niagara Falls providing the cheapest power in the world, and a large skilled labor force, Buffalo has many resources. Alas, the city has been home to some of the fastest dying industries in the country over the last twenty years. Both the auto industry and the steel industry had large concentrations of workers at one time in Buffalo. But today, the only industries that are thriving in this snowy city are health services, one of the fastest growing industries nationwide, and retail trade. Even the fast-growing chemical industry is merely holding steady in Buffalo, according to John Slanker, a senior economist for the Department of Labor in Buffalo.

Total nonagricultural employment grew by 11,000 jobs, or about 2.1 percent in 1991, with the service-producing industries responsible for more than half the increase. Retail trade grew by 6.96 percent, or 7,300 jobs, while education services increased 8.51 percent, adding more than 800 jobs to a field that numbered under 10,000 until this year. Among the goods producing industries, construction and mining skyrocketed over the summer from 19,600 jobs to a high of more than 23,000, before settling down to 19,000. Still, the overall growth rate for the year was nearly 8 percent.

For the future, Buffalo is pinning its hopes on a free trade agreement between the U.S. and Canada, which will allow Buffalo to become a satellite city of Toronto, its neighbor 100 miles north. "Toronto is becoming a world capital market," said Slanker. "The Buffalo area can benefit greatly if some of the flow of commerce in Toronto comes down here." Slanker said he expects Buffalo to intertwine its economy with Toronto's over the next decade.

North Carolina

North Carolina is the tenth most populous state in the nation. In the past decade it has added nearly 700,000 jobs to its work force, making its growth the seventh largest during the 1980s.

North Carolina has the lowest unemployment rate of the most populous states and the highest rate of participation in the labor force. More than 65 percent of all residents over age 16 are working. The state's unemployment rate has been steadily dropping from a peak of 6.7 percent in May 1991 to a seasonally adjusted low of 5.7 in December. This compares with the national unemployment rate in December of 7.1 percent.

"The recession in North Carolina was over in May 1991," says James F. Smith, professor of finance at the University of North Carolina at Chapel Hill, "and 1992 should show a moderate but steady growth." This is all the more remarkable, Smith points out, because North Carolina has the highest participation of workers in manufacturing of any state. North Carolina has 28 workers out of 100 in manufacturing, compared to the national average of 17 out of 100.

The strong military presence in North Carolina is a factor in the economy of the state and cutbacks in military spending could have an effect, says Dr. John Connaughton, professor of Economics and Director of the Center of Business and Economic Research at the University of North Carolina at Charlotte. With the Rapid Mobilization Force located at Fort Bragg and the Marines at Camp Lejeune, North Carolina sent more troops to the Mideast than any other state. Their departure for the Gulf caused a virtual shutdown on the economy in the eastern part of the state.

While North Carolina showed a net loss of 2900 jobs in 1991, economists are predicting a net increase of 61,000 jobs by the end of 1992. Michael L. Walden, professor of agricultural and resource economics at North Carolina State University, predicts a moderate growth of 2 to 3 percent in the state's GSP (Gross State Product) which would mean 60,000 to 80,000 new jobs in North Carolina this year. Most job growth is expected in technically-oriented fields such as computers, R&D, pharmaceuticals and medicine, and manufacturing. Building permits are up. And Walden expects interest rates to keep falling and record low mortgage rates to get the housing industry going again.

One of the reasons North Carolina has done better than most, says Don Carrington, Deputy Director of Labor Market Information in Raleigh, is because of the diversity of its industry and expansion into foreign markets. North Carolina is a large exporter of pharmaceuticals and tobacco.

North Carolina is a major textile manufacturer with such companies as Burlington Industries, Cone Mills and Hoechst Celanese located in the state. IBM is a major factor in the computer field with over 5,000 employees in North Carolina. The city of High Point calls itself "The Furniture Capital of the United States" and R.J. Reynolds and Sara Lee are among the largest employers in the Triad. Two of the largest banks in the country are headquartered in Charlotte, and Aetna Life & Casualty and Jefferson Pilot are insurance companies with large facilities in the state.

WHERE THE JOBS ARE: The growth of employment in North Carolina has come primarily from the Piedmont Crescent, a 170-mile strip that takes in Raleigh-Durham, the Triad cities of Greensboro, High Point and Winston-Salem, and the Charlotte-Gastonia-Rock Hill, NC/SC metropolitan statistical area (MSA). According to Labor Market Information, the Piedmont Crescent has 65 to 70 percent of the jobs.

This area has three universities, two medical schools and the Research Triangle Park which employs over 34,000 scientists, technicians and support people. Research Triangle Park is one of the largest university-related research facilities with over 50 corporate, academic and government tenants specializing in microelectronics, telecommunications, chemicals, biotechnology, pharmaceuticals and environmental health sciences. It is located on 6,800 acres with the points of the triangle formed by Duke University in Durham, North Carolina State University in Raleigh and the University of North Carolina at Chapel Hill.

Fastest growing jobs in North Carolina are computer programmers, computer systems analysts/electronic data processing, medical assistants, and home health aides. Occupations with the greatest number of annual openings are retail salespersons, food preparation and service, general managers and top executives, and registered nurses.

North Dakota

Like other states in its region, North Dakota is struggling to make the transition from a rural, agriculture-based economy to an urban service- and manufacturing-based one. The service industry is the fastest growing segment of the state's economy, but much of North Dakota's prosperity still depends largely on the price of wheat (only Kansas grows more wheat).

More than ten percent of North Dakota's labor force of 311,000 is involved in farming, which is concentrated in the western portion of the state. But of course here as elsewhere farmers and their employees continue to lose jobs due to consolidation of farms by large companies, a trend that is expected to last at least throughout the decade. In response, some small farm owners have tried to switch to nontraditional crops, such as exotic vegetables, sorghum, and potbellied pigs, said Warren Boyd of Job Services North Dakota. He also noted that some farmers have even started fish farms in an attempt to hold on to their land.

The eastern portion of the state has a more diversified economy, with many more jobs in the service and manufacturing industries. This part of the state will be largely responsible for the moderate (0.7 percent annually) job expansion expected until the year 2000. Job Services North Dakota projects a 16 percent growth in the number of retail salespeople, an 18 percent increase in nurses, and a 52 percent increase in home health aides. Openings should also abound for waiters and waitresses, general managers and top executives, and janitors. Over the same time period, the number of farmers is expected to decline by 8.5 percent, while farm workers should decrease nearly 13 percent.

Manufacturing is still a strong segment of the economy and will add over 3,000 jobs, a 19 percent increase, by the year 2000. Mining is an important part of North Dakota's economy since the state has the greatest lignite coal reserves in the country; employment here is expected to increase by over 600 jobs (14 percent). Construction, too, is projected to grow, adding 1,300 jobs (a 13 percent increase) by the year 2000.

Although North Dakota is currently in a transitional period the prospects for job growth are very solid and limited only by small population growth. But the people here have always been hardworking and enterprising and there's no reason to believe those qualities will fade away now. In fact several signs point toward a new outlook on the future. For example, Grand Forks, the state's third-largest city, has responded to the changing job market with an economic development program that provides grants, low interest loans, and other forms of financial assistance to new or expanding small businesses. Since its inception in 1987, the program, which is paid for with a 1 percent sales tax, has created 650 jobs in a city of 50,000 residents.

Ohio

Not too long ago Ohio was one of the central players in that now seemingly forgotten tragedy of the gutting of America's manufacturing-based economy. It was the state most people thought of when they heard the term "Rust Belt," with its dire connotations of empty factories and double-digit unemployment. But since the drastic recession of the early 1980s, Ohio has returned to relative prosperity by finding economic redemption in the service sector and by getting a little help from the Japanese.

According to the Ohio Bureau of Employment Services the state will add approximately 42,000 new jobs each year until the end of the decade. In addition Ohio's slow population growth reflects an aging population that will soon cause an increase in job opportunities through retirements. Even manufacturing jobs are projected to increase (despite some losses in the latest recession), but by far the great increases will be in health and business services as well as retail trade.

Among the state's 20 fastest-growing occupations, 10 are related to health care. The greatest demand in Ohio is for registered nurses, with 2,300 new positions and 2,100 vacancies a year. There will also be almost 2,000 openings each year for licensed practical nurses. Medical assistants and home health aides will also be in great demand.

Ohio labor-market analysts also project strong job growth for computer-related workers, with the state's businesses creating more than 1,500 new jobs each year for systems analysts and programmers. Engineering, especially electrical and electronic engineering (800 new jobs or vacancies annually), will be a growth area as will accounting, where almost 800 new jobs a year should become available.

The businesses with the largest levels of annual hiring will be eating and drinking places, which often provide entry-level jobs at low wages. They are projected to create more than 4,000 jobs a year. Next among the leading employers are private hospitals, with more than 3,000 new jobs annually. Nursing and personal-care facilities will add another 2,300 jobs each year. Another major growth area—again, at relatively low wage levels—are services that provide temporary workers for businesses. In Ohio, these services are projected to add about 2,400 jobs annually. Although retail trade was sluggish in 1991—employment was essentially flat—the categories of retail salesperson and cashier are projected to provide more than 2,500 new jobs each year, albeit generally low-paying, entry-level positions. Annual turnover—as persons in those positions move into other job categories or leave the work force—is projected at approximately 11,700 positions.

But the service sector is not the only area targeted for growth. Ohio should, for example, be a good market for construction skills, adding more than 1,000 jobs a year for the rest of the decade, bucking a national downward trend. Other blue-collar jobs, including truck drivers, will also increase in number. Most importantly, however, the automobile manufacturing sector (which employs over 100,000 people) has shown a new resiliency. While domestic manufacturers have been hard hit by the recession, the state's two Honda plants—both located near Columbus, the state capital and the state's fastest-growing market—have been prospering. As a result, auto-related employment was up 8.2% in December 1991 from a year earlier. Troubles within the domestic auto industry contributed to slower growth in the Toledo area, which was the metropolitan area hardest hit by the recession, and the Dayton-Springfield metropolitan area.

As in most states, Ohio's job growth will be concentrated in its metropolitan areas, with 87 of every 100 new jobs appearing in one of eight metropolitan regions. The strongest growth will occur in Columbus, which is projected to gain one of every four new jobs statewide. Cleveland and Cincinnati will gain 19 of every 100 new jobs; nine will be in Dayton-Springfield; six will be in Toledo; five will be in Akron; two will be in Canton; and slightly less than two in every 100 new jobs will be in Youngstown-Warren, which will finally reverse years of declining employment. From 1976–1988, the heavily industrial area adjacent to Pennsylvania lost 9,600 jobs in all; goods-producing employment fell by a staggering 28,900 jobs.

The Youngstown area, however, did not mirror patterns throughout Ohio, which added more than 50,000 jobs a year from 1976 through 1988. Statewide, nearly 760,000 new jobs in the service sector offset the loss of 171,500 goods-producing jobs, most of them (167,000) in durable-goods industries. The remaining industries presumably had adapted to competing in a world market and thus were better prepared to withstand the effects of the 1991–1992 recession.

SPOTLIGHT ON
CLEVELAND

Over the last two decades, Cleveland has shed significant portions of a past that can only be described as grimy, polluted, heavily industrial, and rather drab. "What a difference 13 years makes," said Knight A. Kiplinger, editor-in-chief of *Kiplinger's Personal Finance Magazine* late in 1991 on his first visit to Cleveland in more than a decade. Cleveland has rebuilt its downtown area and lakefront, worked hard to attract new companies, enhanced its image nationally and internationally, and emerged with a stable, competitive industrial base.

The region has become highly diversified even though manufacturers continue to be among the largest employers in the region. Employment is expected to grow by an average of 0.8 percent a year through the end of the decade in the state's largest metropolitan area, just slightly slower than the state as a whole. The growth adds up to almost 8,000 jobs a year, and Ohio Bureau of Employment Service analysts project that all of the growth will be in the service-producing sector.

The Cleveland area's largest employer is the federal government, which has almost 20,000 employees in the region. The Defense Department Finance and Accounting Service accounts for 1,700 of those employees, and local development groups are seeking to gain a national center for the service. The regional centers would employ between 5,000 and 10,000. The Cleveland area also has NASA's Lewis Research Center, which employs more than 4,700 workers.

The region's largest private employers are Ford Motor Co., which has an engine plant and other operations employing 12,500 workers, and the Cleveland Clinic, an internationally recognized hospital and medical research institution that employs 9,400. In fact, hospitals and health services account for four of the region's top 12 employers. In addition to the Cleveland Clinic, they are MetroHealth System, 5,660 jobs; University Hospitals, 5,100 jobs; and Meridia Health System, 4,800.

As in all other regions, health care is a major growth industry in Cleveland for the 1990s. In all, the Cleveland region has more than 50,000 people employed in health services, and employment is projected to grow by more than 2 percent a year for the rest of the decade. The Cleveland area will require 500 registered nurses to fill new positions each year, and vacancies will raise total demand for RNs to almost 1,000 a year. The area is projected to need 500 physicians and surgeons a year to fill vacancies and new positions, 370 licensed practical nurses and more than 300 medical technicians.

Among managers, the biggest explosion in demand will be for health-services managers, up more than 3 percent a year with a total annual requirement of 85 workers. The largest number of managerial openings will be for general managers, a broadly stated category that will have more than 1,100 openings a year. The area also will need more than 200 food service and lodging managers a year, and it will require a similar number of managers for public-relations and marketing operations.

Education also will be a growth industry with more than 700 openings a year, most to fill vacancies created by employees leaving the work force. Computer expertise also will be in demand, with approximately 270 openings annually in the region, mostly for programmers and data-processing analysts. Demand for engineers will be relatively buoyant, with a projected 640 total openings a year. Positions for electrical engineers will grow by better than 2 percent annually.

One of the fastest growing sectors will be retail trade; the Cleveland area is projected to require more than 3,000 retail salespersons and cashiers a year, mostly to fill vacancies. Similarly, food and beverage service will experience strong growth, 1.2 percent gains per year.

Cleveland achieved its diversity after some very tough times in the 1970s and 1980s. Manufacturing employment in the Cleveland region lost 63,400 jobs between 1976 and 1988. Further losses are projected through the 1990s, but at a significantly slower rate, declining by 5,500 jobs in durable-goods production and 2,100 in nondurable goods.

Also, the region's industrial base in closely linked to the domestic automobile market, which was buffeted by the 1991–92 recession and fierce competition from Japanese automakers, some of whose products are assembled in Ohio, Kentucky and Tennessee. Over the 1990s, transportation-equipment manufacturing will decline by another 1,000 jobs in the Cleveland area, with all of the losses occurring in the motor-vehicle category.

Several of the area's largest employers are involved in the automobile industry to some extent. In addition to Ford's 12,500 jobs, General Motors Corp. operations employ more than 4,500 persons in the Cleveland area. TRW Inc., which has its headquarters in greater Cleveland, employs 3,500. The area also has two large steel operations, LTV with 8,200 workers and USS/Kobe Steel Co. at Lorain, with 2,900 employees. BP International, the London-based petroleum company that has its U.S. headquarters in Cleveland, employs approximately 3,550.

Cleveland's construction industry was ravaged in the 1982–1983 recession, when 8,500 workers—roughly one in four—lost their jobs. But construction has rebounded in the past few years, with employment now approaching 28,000. The industry is expected to add about 150 new positions a year.

The city has several development projects underway, including the $375-million Gateway sports complex, which will have a 42,000-seat ballpark for the Indians and a 21,000-seat arena where the Cleveland Cavaliers of the National Basketball Association will play its home games. The complex, near downtown, is scheduled to open in 1994. The North Coast Harbor development will have a $65-million Rock 'n Roll Museum, and a $48-million Great

Lakes Museum of Science, Technology and the Environment is scheduled for completion in 1996.

SPOTLIGHT ON CINCINNATI

Known as the Queen City, Cincinnati has a diversified economy that actually managed to increase employment despite the recent recession. In 1991, the seven counties in Ohio, Indiana and Kentucky that make up the Cincinnati metropolitan area added 2,700 jobs, with substantial gains in the service industries offsetting a 4,800-job loss in manufacturing industries. Combine this figure with the 21,000 jobs added in 1990 and it's easy to understand why the Cincinnati area has consistently had an unemployment rate below 5 percent for its 760,400 nonagricultural work force. And it's no wonder that the outlook for the future is universally seen as extremely positive.

Like other parts of Ohio and the nation, Cincinnati is projected to have strong advances in health services, business services, and retail trade. Even construction employment, which fell by 600 jobs in 1991, is projected to gain steadily through the decade. On average, construction will add about 300 jobs a year to 2000, when it will total approximately 35,000 workers. The region's manufacturing base, assisted by several healthy corporations, is projected to maintain stable employment levels through the decade, with a work force of about 144,000 workers—which was almost exactly the low point for manufacturing employment in 1991.

The region's largest employer is General Electric Co., which has a large jet-engine manufacturing operation in greater Cincinnati and employs 19,000 workers. The next largest employer is the federal government, which has major regional centers for the U.S. Postal Service and the Internal

Revenue Service. The second-largest private employer is Procter & Gamble Co., the consumer-products giant whose corporate headquarters is in Cincinnati. The company, whose brand-management strategies have set the standard for consumer marketing over several decades, employs 13,400 in the region.

Also based in Cincinnati are Kroger Co., the large Midwestern supermarket chain with 10,000 employees in the region, Armco, the diversified steel maker, which employs 6,000, and Cincinnati Milacron, a manufacturer of machine tools and robotic equipment with 5,000 Cincinnati-area employees. In the early 1990s, several well-known companies moved their headquarters to the Cincinnati area including Heinz Pet Products, James River Corp., and Mercantile Stores.

One reason for Cincinnati's historic prosperity has been its location on the Ohio River and at the intersection of rail lines and interstate highways. In recent years some of Cincinnati's growth can be attributed to the expansion of Greater Cincinnati International Airport in northern Kentucky. The airport is a hub for Delta Air Lines, and expansion projects include a $65-million new runway and a $315-million Delta expansion that will include 25 new passenger gates.

The largest contributor to Cincinnati's employment picture over the next several years is projected to be retailing, which will add more than 1,500 positions a year. For retail salespersons and cashiers, new positions and vacancies will total more than 2,300 job openings a year. While retailing was essentially unchanged statewide in 1991, the Cincinnati area added 1,500 jobs, to 148,600 positions, a 1.6 percent gain from 1990.

Health industries also will be adding significant numbers of jobs in the remainder of the 1990s, with an annual growth rate of 2.7 percent. The area will need 400 registered nurses for new positions—out of a total requirement of 757 RNs each year. In addition, the region will have annual openings for several hundred licensed practical nurses, nursing aides-orderlies, and medical technicians. Among the largest medical employers in the region, which has 9,400 beds in more than 30 hospitals, are the University of Cincinnati Medical Center, and Bethesda Hospital, each employing over 4000 workers.

While it does not have any large-scale computer manufacturing operations, the Cincinnati area will benefit from the large installed base of computer technology. Computer programmers and systems analysts will have more than 200 job openings annually, with more than three of four representing new positions. The area is projected to have 30 openings annually for computer repairers, and 23 of those slots will be new jobs.

Among professional and technical positions, accountants and auditors will be in demand, adding about 142 new jobs a year, and the region also will require 171 engineers to fill new positions. Total engineering openings are projected at 485 slots a year, with the strongest demand—nearly one in five—for electrical and electronics engineers. In addition, the region will have almost 500 openings each year for teachers.

SPOTLIGHT ON COLUMBUS

For the decades when Ohio was a significant component in America's manufacturing machinery, most of its industries were heavily concentrated in the state's northern tier. In the state's heartland, Columbus was the state's capital and the home of Ohio State University, which in turn was best known for the football teams of the late Coach Woody Hayes. For those who looked at the state from outside, Columbus was the boondocks, a pleasant but rather uninteresting city in Ohio's agricultural midsection.

But no more. The years have been kind to Columbus,

and its shortage of major manufacturers—it has the lowest concentration of heavy industry of any of the state's metropolitan areas—turned out to be an advantage. While parts of the state struggled to hold employment or actually lost jobs through the late 1970s and into the 1980s, Columbus underwent strong growth across a wide range of industries and service sectors. Its growth has been so robust—averaging 3 percent a year from 1976 through 1988—that the Columbus area could very well overtake Cincinnati as the state's second-largest metropolitan area (after Cleveland) by the next census count.

Although Columbus had been cited in news reports as a victim of the 1991–92 recession, it in fact experienced only a slowdown from the fast expansion in the late 1980s, when employment growth was exceeding 5 percent annually. By one measure, the region fared well through the recession; its unemployment rate was below 4 percent at the end of 1991. On average, the Columbus region is projected to create more than 19,250 new jobs a year—a healthy 1.42 percent annual rate vs. the state's 0.9 percent annual rate.

In all, the region is projected to have 36,300 annual job openings in a 750,000-member work force, with new positions accounting for 25 percent of those openings. Of the 10,280 new jobs each year, most—but not all—will be in the fast-growing services sector. Manufacturing will hold its employment at about 102,000 workers, with losses in durable-goods industries offset by modest advances in nondurables such as chemicals, plastics, and printing, all of which are projected to grow through the decade.

Like other high-growth regions, the strongest employment increases will be posted by health services and business services. While retail trade will continue to grow at a very fast pace—retail outlets will add one of every three new jobs in the Columbus area through 2000 and will account for an average of 2,650 new positions annually—these generally low-paid positions are not as significant as the growth in the health and business service categories. If anything, retailing can be looked upon as a barometer of a region's employment climate, with retail sales growing with income and particularly with disposable income.

Together, health and business services will be Columbus's largest employer by the end of the decade, with 110,000 positions, or roughly one in every eight jobs. Health care will be a significant factor, growing by 2.9 percent a year. Hospital employment will expand by 2.4 percent annually, a slower pace than in the 1980s, but total hospital jobs will be approaching 25,000 by the end of the decade. An additional component in health-care employment will be jobs in state-owned hospitals, which will grow by almost 200 positions a year, a 3.2 percent annual rate, with increases spurred by the opening of a new cancer hospital at Ohio State.

Demand for health practitioners is projected to be strong. The region will require more than 260 new physicians and surgeons a year to fill a projected 60 new positions and in excess of 200 vacancies. As is the case almost everywhere, registered nurses will be a strong growth market, with more than 350 new posts among more than 600 openings annually. The region also is projected to need 175 licensed practical nurses for all openings, and 225 medical technicians.

Business services also are expected to post strong employment gains through the 1990s. Jobs in finance, insurance, and real estate are projected to increase an average of 1,000 jobs per year, while demand for computer-associated workers will rise by an average of 4 percent annually.

The broad category of general managers will have almost 1,000 openings annually, with new positions accounting for better than one-quarter of the job slots. The region will require almost 500 accountants each year and a similar number of engineers. Lawyers will be in demand, with almost 300 openings annually. Like other regions, Columbus will have openings for the new popular job category, paralegals. Demand will grow by about 5 percent a year, but those gains can be attributed to the relatively few openings—on average, fewer than 40 a year. By 2000, the Columbus area is projected to have 650 paralegals, compared with more than 4,000 lawyers. Demand for teachers will grow by about 1 percent a year, with the region requiring more than 650 teachers a year to fill vacancies and new positions.

Despite the strength in the service industries, the largest single group of workers—more than 160,000 employees—is engaged in production and other traditionally blue-collar jobs. This area will generally grow at a slow rate, 0.7 percent a year on average, through the decade. Manufacturing will hold its ground, while construction employment is projected to increase by an average of more than 1 percent a year from peak levels of 28,000 workers late in the 1980s. Hefty gains also are projected for truck drivers, with employment in the trucking and warehousing category growing by slightly more than 1 percent a year.

The weakest sector of the employment economy will be durable goods—despite the impact of Honda's automotive operations. Still, the strength of Honda's Marysville plant, located near the edge of the Columbus metropolitan area, will keep durable-goods job losses at relatively low levels. The Japanese automaker also plans to expand its East Liberty plant, which is located just outside the Columbus region.

Oklahoma

For generations, Oklahoma has lived off the ocean of oil and natural gas beneath its surface. The first well was sunk in 1897, and the Glenn field south of Tulsa was tapped in 1905. The oil derricks produced a succession of booms and busts that continues to the present day. When petroleum supplies became tight and the American economy sputtered, Oklahoma prospered. The last such oil boom occurred in the 1980s, and Oklahoma went on a building binge as the

U.S. slipped into recession. As the U.S. economy recovered and—perhaps more importantly—as crude-oil overproduction in the Middle East depressed prices at the gas pump, Oklahoma slipped into a deep recession, hitting bottom in 1986.

Since then, the state has been making steady progress, both in terms of absorbing the workers displaced by the oil bust and in rebuilding its economy in a slow, methodical way. As a result, the most recent national recession touched Oklahoma lightly. The state continued to add jobs in 1991, growing a very modest 0.21 percent, or 2,500 jobs, and lifting the state's nonagricultural job count to 1.2-million positions. In 1990, the state's nonagricultural jobs had grown by slightly more than 1 percent. Oklahoma State University's 1992 Oklahoma Economic Outlook forecast employment growth of 16,000 for the year, a 1.3-percent rate.

Unemployment at the end of 1991 was 6.4 percent of the 1.5-million member work force, a rate below the national average but up from 6 percent in December 1990. Still, 10 counties had unemployment rates above 10 percent, and three counties east of Oklahoma City had jobless rates ranging from 13 percent to 14.6 percent.

Oklahoma's overall employment increases represent a slow, steady addition to the job pool. Relatively few positions had annual growth rates exceeding 2 percent between 1986 and 1992, and those jobs with loftier growth rates had very few openings. For instance, annual demand for continuous mining machine operators expanded by 5 percent, but the total number of openings totaled six. Even such high-growth occupations as health care and retailing recorded modest growth during Oklahoma's climb out of the pit. Demand for retail salespersons grew by a modest 1.45 percent, and new positions for registered nurses expanded by a relatively subdued 2.12 percent. Oklahoma is estimated to have 777 annual openings for registered nurses, including about 300 new positions a year.

Nonetheless, the state does offer some opportunities. Demand for electrical engineers expanded by 3 percent annually between 1986 and 1992, with 140 annual openings. For electrical and electronic technicians, 2.6 percent annual growth added up to 66 new positions among 114 openings each year. Mechanical engineers had a 2.75 annual growth rate, with 105 openings. Despite a decline in positions for farm workers—down almost 800 jobs a year—demand is good for farm managers, with a 2.3 percent growth rate and 708 annual openings.

SPOTLIGHT ON
OKLAHOMA CITY

Outside the state capitol complex in Oklahoma City stands an oil derrick, a symbol of the city's one-time reliance on the petroleum industry. That economic dependence dates back barely a decade, to 1986. When crude prices plunged that year, so too did employment—both in the fields and in the city's office towers. In a year, Oklahoma City lost 28,441 jobs, or about one in every 11 positions. Oklahoma City also is paying another price for its failed pursuit of an economic mirage. In 1983, building permits for single-family homes soared to 8,412. By 1988, only 1,757 permits were issued, and preliminary 1990 census figures indicated a 9 percent vacancy rate in single-family homes. For office space, the vacancy rate is 25 percent, compared with a historic rate of about 6 percent, and one-third of the square footage in the city's core is unoccupied. In short, the construction industry plummeted into a deep recession, and prices for housing declined.

Today, Oklahoma City's private and public sectors are seeking to build a diversified economy with a healthy balance between service and production industries. Development officials are attempting in particular to attract aerospace, distribution, and back-office operations into the city.

In 1991, the region increased employment by 1.27 percent, adding 5,400 jobs to 430,800 positions. Unemployment declined at the end of the year to 5.3 percent, a marked improvement over the previous year's 6.4 percent jobless rate. While it has reduced its reliance on oil, Oklahoma City continues to be dependent upon another very large employer, government, whose payroll account for 95,000 workers. Various governmental units are the region's five largest employers, headed by the state itself with 32,200 employees. It is followed by Tinker Air Force Base, which has 22,700 civilian and military employees; the University of Oklahoma in nearby Norman; and the Federal Aviation Administration's Mike Monroney Aeronautics Center, which has 6,000 employees and trains all of the nation's air-traffic controllers.

The next largest employer is the Oklahoma Medical Center, a six-hospital complex that employs almost 6,000 workers. Other major medical employers in the region are St. Anthony Hospital and Baptist Medical Center, each with about 2,100 employees; South Community Medical Center, 1,656 workers; and Mercy Health Center, 1,400 employees. Within the services sector, health-related occupations offer the best prospects for job growth.

The region's next two largest employers are AT&T Network Systems, with 5,300 workers at a plant manufacturing communications equipment and computers, and General Motors, which has a 5,300-employee assembly plant in Oklahoma City. Bridgestone-Firestone manufactures tires in the region and employs almost 1,800. Dayton Tire is to move its corporate headquarters and 50 jobs to Oklahoma City from Akron, Ohio.

Oklahoma Employment Security Commission officials expect the state's next burst of growth to come from computer and software operations, and Oklahoma City already has a major player in Seagate Technology, a leading manufacturer of mass-storage disk drives—popularly known as hard disks—for personal computers. Seagate employs 2,300. Xerox also has a manufacturing operation for toner and developer in Oklahoma City, where it employs 300 and will be adding another 83 positions.

The region's job acquisitions have been solid without the addition of any large operations. Boeing Co. is scheduled to hire 200 workers for its aircraft and marine operations, and the federal government will add 145 employees for a unit to combat drug traffic from a base at the Monroney Aeronautic Center. Continental Carlisle Inc., a locally based plastics manufacturer, will add 100 employees in the early 1990s, as will Southwest Wood Processing Inc.

SPOTLIGHT ON
TULSA

Like Oklahoma City, Tulsa once was heavily dependent on the oil industry. It too was hammered when boom turned to bust in the 1980s, and its office-vacancy rate, almost 25 percent, is a vestige of the overbuilding that occurred in that period. Tulsa, in the state's northeast quadrant, has diversified like Oklahoma City, but it has sought to concentrate the diversification in manufacturing, a sector where it lost 1,700 jobs—all of them in durable-goods manufacturing—in 1991.

At the end of 1991, the Tulsa area's unemployment rate stood at 6.1 percent of its 343,400-member work force. The Metropolitan Tulsa Chamber of Commerce reported that the region had a net gain of 6,600 jobs in 1991, with the strongest advances in trade (3,900 jobs) and construction (1,500 jobs), which reversed a downward trend. Residential housing permits in the region were up by 5.8 percent over 1990 levels, and development officials indicated the pace of building was increasing in 1992. Services added 1,300 jobs, although growth in health services was minuscule. Government employment added 1,200 jobs, including 900 additions to the state's payroll.

Based on projections developed by the National Planning Association Data Service, the region's job market will grow by 2.4 percent in 1992, adding more than 7,700 jobs. Manufacturing will almost erase its 1991 losses with the creation of 1,350 new positions, services will grow by almost 3,000 jobs and government will add another 1,700 posts.

For years, Tulsa has been a major player in the aerospace industry and—although at least one endangered operation is based there—will remain strong in that area for some time. The region's largest employer, with 8,000 workers, is American Airlines, which has its principal maintenance facility near Tulsa International Airport. Also located there is American's SABRE flight-reservation system.

Just to the south of the American operation, Rockwell International and McDonnell-Douglas share a World War II-vintage former bomber plant where very modern aircraft are built. McDonnell, which employs more than 3,000, builds subassemblies for the MD–80 commercial aircraft. Rockwell, with a 2,000-worker payroll, has scaled back its employment for the endangered B–1 bomber, but it also builds fuselage and wing subassemblies for Boeing's 747 aircraft.

NORDAM, a 20-year-old aerospace and defense firm, has developed components that enable older commercial-jet engines to meet new noise regulations. The component kits, which cost up to $3 million per plane, have been sold to six airlines, including Lufthansa and Air New Zealand. NORDAM employs 1,070 in the Tulsa area. Other large employers are Sun Oil Co. and Ford Motor Co., which has a glass plant.

The region also is becoming a center for national rent-a-car reservations with the relocation of Dollar Rent A Car Systems Inc.'s headquarters and 280 jobs to Tulsa from Los Angeles. Two other divisions of Chrysler-owned, Tulsa-based Pentastar Transportation Group Inc.—Thrifty Rent-A-Car System Inc. and Snappy Car Rental—also are based in the region.

Scheduled to move into the region is Delaware-based

TeleCall Inc., a telemarketing firm that was to employ up to 1,000 workers by mid–1993. Kimberly-Clark announced plans for a $17-million expansion to a Kleenex plant that would boost employment.

Oregon

Over the last twenty years Oregon has earned a reputation for being earnestly against most of the less desirable elements of contemporary life including smoking, pollution, unrestrained economic development, and, most of all, transplanted Californians ("No Californicators" said a well-known highway billboard a little while back).

The predictable result has been comparatively slow population growth—only 8 percent in the 1980s—at least until very recently. In the latest report from the Census Bureau, covering the period April 1990 to July 1991, Oregon turned out to be the fourth fastest growing state in the union as the population surged by 80,000 or 2.8 percent. Only Nevada, Alaska, and Washington surpassed Oregon and in each case the reason behind the increase was the availability of jobs.

In 1991 Oregon added over 17,000 nonagricultural jobs ranking it eighth among all the states. It led the nation in the number of jobs (3,700) added in finance, insurance, and real estate and was sixth in the services category adding approximately 9,000 jobs in 1991. While these numbers are not enormous they are very impressive in a state that ranks 29th in total population (2.8 million).

According to all the economists polled by the Western Blue Chip Economic Forecast this growth trend will continue over the next two years in all sections of the economy except manufacturing, where employment could decline or at best grow by only 1 percent. (In 1991 there was a significant decline of over 7,000 jobs, 3.4 percent.)

The state Department of Labor's projections for the rest

of the decade see most job growth—over 90 percent—taking place in the services sector with health care, retail trade, and food preparation and serving leading the way. Helping to support the growth in services will be the continued increase in tourism, especially in the northeastern region around the Columbia River Gorge area (rated one of the top scenic drives in the nation), and along the Pacific coast. Spending on tourism increased by over 30 percent between 1989–91 and jobs by about 20 percent.

Oregon's natural splendor as well as its comparatively sane approach to economic growth have been attracting new businesses over the last decade and slowly transforming the state's economy. While agriculture and forestry will remain important sectors in the state's economy, they will not contribute to the job growth picture. Finance and high tech industry will—and so the state foresees steady increase in the need for engineers, lawyers (a 48 percent growth in positions is predicted, in fact), computer professionals, and financial specialists.

SPOTLIGHT ON PORTLAND

Just over 1.4 million people live in the Portland metropolitan area, almost half of the state's total population. In 1991 this metro added almost 7,000 jobs, about half the total for the state. By the year 2000 state economists project further increases of over 20 percent in total wage and salary employment, perhaps 130,000 jobs or more.

Most job growth will of course take place in the services with retail sales and health care leading the way. Kaiser Permanente medical center, the largest health care employer in the area (6,000 employees), projects 15–20 percent growth over the next five years and sees continuous openings for nurses, physical therapists, pharmacists, medical technicians of all kinds, and nurse's aides and orderlies. (Other leading health care employers in Portland are Legacy Health Systems and Sisters of Providence Health Care System.)

Retail sales will grow in the Portland area in part because of increasing population but the experts also expect a significant rise in the number of eating and drinking establishments. According to a recent report in the *Portland Oregonian* Portland ranks 12th among the 50 major markets in per capita spending in this area, although it is only the 27th largest metro in the nation.

One reason the experts have been so optimistic about Portland's economic strength is that in recent years the city has developed a very strong high tech base. Nicknamed the "Silicon Forest" it is now home to major electronic and software companies including such well-known names as Tektronix and Intel, both of which employ over 4,000 people. In general, however, it's good to keep in mind that these industries are not currently in a boom time so jobs may not be as plentiful as rising stock prices might lead one to believe.

Its new high tech image often blinds outsiders to the fact that Portland has long had a strong manufacturing component in several fields: wood and paper products (Weyerhauser, Georgia Pacific are here), clothing (Nike, Jantzen), food products (Ore-Ida, Lamb-Weston), heavy metals and aluminum (Oregon Steel Mills, Reynolds Metals), and aerospace (Boeing of Portland). But as noted above the manufacturing sector is not projected to grow in any meaningful way.

There are several ship-related industries as well because Portland is a vital port of entry ranking 21st in the nation in commercial tonnage handled (over 30 million in 1989). It is a leading port for the export of wheat to Pacific Rim nations and one of the largest for the importing of Japanese and Korean automobiles.

Obviously Portland has many elements that could provide the basis for a dramatically expanding economy and work force. But a managed growth approach is what people want here so expansion will be slow and deliberate. Portland could become a model city for the nation, or it could wither because it refused to encourage a rebirth of manufacturing.

Pennsylvania

Former steelworkers in Bethlehem, laborers laid off from Allentown apparel factories, and retired railroad workers across the state don't need government analysts or economic forecasters to tell them that Pennsylvania's economy has undergone tremendous upheaval in recent decades.

For thousands of such workers, one glance at the crippled factories in their hometowns tells the story: the manufacturing giants that once composed the backbone of the Keystone State's economy are now fighting for their lives.

According to analysts for the state Department of Labor and Industry, Pennsylvania lost 245,700 manufacturing jobs between 1975 and 1985. Nowhere have these losses been more glaring than in the once-mighty steel industry. Since those Department of Labor statistics were compiled, the state's two largest steel companies, Bethlehem Steel and USX Corp., have instituted massive layoffs, and USX has all but closed a huge plant in Bucks County that, in its heyday, employed nearly 10,000.

The face of Pennsylvania's economy is undeniably changing, and with it, employment prospects for the state's workers. But the jobs outlook here is not as grim as many might expect. The state that continues to lead the nation in the production of pretzels, potato chips, and mushrooms will add 362,900 new nonagricultural jobs by 1995, bringing the total number of people working in Pennsylvania to 5,102,000, an increase of 7.7 percent over 1984.

Throughout the state, the growth that will offset manufacturing's losses will come primarily in the services sector.

From Erie in the northwest to the Philadelphia metropolitan area at the state's opposite end, workers can expect to find jobs in health services, social services, and retail, according to labor department projections.

Among those who shouldn't have trouble landing jobs throughout Pennsylvania this year are paralegals, systems analysts, psychologists, travel agents, janitors, and flight attendants, according to "Outlook: 1990–2005," published last fall by the U.S. Department of Labor's Bureau of Labor Statistics. Of the thirty occupations projected to experience the greatest growth, half require college degrees or other advanced training, and half are in health services.

Losers across the state will be clerical workers, who by 1995 no longer will represent the largest occupational group, as they did in 1984. Their numbers are expected to drop from 17.2 percent of all jobs to 16.8 percent in 1995.

But the future is bright for those with expertise in computer programming and repair, and computer-assisted design. In their outlook through 1995, Bureau of Labor economists predict that Pennsylvania will find its economy buoyed in the next decade by advanced technology. As manufacturers try to regain a competitive edge by streamlining operations and, in some cases, trimming work forces, analysts foresee widespread opportunity for skilled workers who can use such techniques as computer-assisted design to help firms implement advanced technology.

Like most northeastern states Pennsylvania has some pockets of prosperity and many areas in a depressed state. Particularly healthy are smaller urban areas, including the Allentown/Bethlehem area, about 60 miles north of Philadelphia, said Steven Cochrane, senior economist with the Wefa Group of economic analysts based in suburban Philadelphia.

The two former steel towns, which are treated as a single entity by government researchers, will echo the state's growth in health services, retail, insurance, and real estate. In addition, the region will experience a 48 percent increase in repair services employment and another 48 percent increase in jobs for securities and commodities brokers.

The Erie metropolitan area, the state's third largest behind Philadelphia and Pittsburgh, will mirror those trends, although growth will be slower. Erie is distinguished from other areas in the state by a projected 45 percent growth in heavy construction employment.

Harrisburg is projected to post one of the best job-growth rates in the state through 1995. In addition to the expected areas of health care and other services, the state capital's future holds strong gains in amusement services, but a decline in the numbers employed by the state government. State analysts predict job growth in air travel, credit and real estate companies in and around Harrisburg.

Lancaster County, the formerly rural and still predominantly Amish enclave west of Philadelphia, will be the site of the state's greatest employment growth, the Department of Labor projects. Job gains in Lancaster will reflect those throughout the state, with the strongest industries being health services, real estate, insurance and other services.

Lancaster and Allentown are comparatively prosperous, Cochrane said, because real estate there is less expensive than in Philadelphia or Pittsburgh, yet the areas afford easy access to major roadways and lie within an industry corridor that extends down the east coast from New York to Washington, D.C.

SPOTLIGHT ON PHILADELPHIA

Lying almost in the middle of that activity corridor is the Philadelphia metropolitan area. And like practically every other American city, big or small, Philadelphia is sending out a call for health care workers, especially nurses.

While other workers may be scrambling for jobs in a

highly competitive market, nurses in and around America's fourth largest city can practically write their own ticket— right down to salaries that often are considerably higher than those of their colleagues elsewhere.

"Nurses are paid quite well in Philadelphia. It's a phenomenon of this market that there is actually a bit of a bidding war for nurses here," said Cochrane.

Robust growth in the number of health care jobs is a common prediction among economic analysts nationwide. But according to Cochrane, Philadelphia more magnifies than mirrors that trend, thanks to a heavy concentration of hospitals and five medical schools in the eight-county Philadelphia metropolitan area. (As defined by the U.S. Bureau of Labor, that eight-county area includes three New Jersey counties.)

And health care opportunities aren't limited to nursing, said Edward J. Murray, of the Pennsylvania Department of Labor's research and statistics unit. Opportunities for dental hygienists, EKG technicians, emergency room technicians, physicians' assistants, physical therapists, medical records technicians, and home-health practitioners also abound.

Overall, the number of health industry jobs, which are included in the services sector by government analysts, more than doubled in Philadelphia over the past decade, according to Bureau of Labor figures.

Led by growth in health care, Philadelphia in the 1980s gained 94,000 service jobs, according to the Bureau of Labor Statistics. Service-sector jobs are expected to continue growing through the '90s, although less rapidly than during the previous decade, the bureau predicts.

Service sector gains in the '80s were not enough to offset the nearly 177,000 manufacturing jobs lost in Philadelphia between 1969 and 1990. Surrounding suburbs lost another 38,000, and economists expect the manufacturing decline to continue.

A concentration of research labs and pharmaceutical companies, including Eli Lilly & Co., Smithkline Beecham,

Wyeth-Ayerst Laboratories International, Marsam Pharmaceuticals, and a division of the Upjohn Co., means probable jobs for chemists, bio-chemists, and lab technicians, Cochrane points out.

Web Christman, an economist for the Philadelphia Industrial Development Corp., urged serious job-hunters to probe deeply into the city's economic underbelly.

"For instance, transportation equipment is on no one's list of winners. But that happens to be a niche specialty in Philly. This is one of the leading centers for manufacturing auto parts. And if you think about it, that tends to be recession-proof," he said.

SPOTLIGHT ON PITTSBURGH

Pittsburgh once was known as the Smoky City. It is no longer smoky. Pittsburgh is still known as the Steel City. It is no longer the city of steel, either.

Through the 1980s, Pittsburgh has undergone a wrenching transformation from an industrial region to a service-based economy. The transformation has been so complete that the Pittsburgh and adjacent Beaver Valley metropolitan areas now have a smaller-than-average share of their jobs in the manufacturing sector. Only 13 percent of the Pittsburgh area's jobs are now in the manufacturing sector, compared with 20.5 percent in Pennsylvania as a whole and 18.1% in the nation. Beaver Valley had 18.4 percent of its jobs in the manufacturing sector in 1990, but that percentage is dropping precipitously.

The loss of blue-collar production jobs has resulted in some very large population losses—roughly twice as large as had been projected for the four-county Pittsburgh metropolitan area. Allegheny County, which includes Pittsburgh, lost 113,000 residents to 1,336,449 in 1990—a larger decline than for Philadelphia, which lost 102,000 residents through the 1980s. Pittsburgh itself declined from 423,959 residents to 369,879 in 1990. In the 1960s, the city's population exceeded 600,000.

Nonetheless, Pittsburgh is something of an anomaly. Such large changes in the population and employment base would add up to a depression in other areas. While undergoing this large outmigration, however, Pittsburgh was winning accolades as one of America's most livable cities—in the early 1980s, Rand-McNally's Placed Rated Almanac declared it to be the country's most livable city and it was third (behind Seattle and San Francisco) in 1989. As it lost jobs, Pittsburgh underwent a second downtown renaissance—the first was in the late 1950s—with the addition of PPG Industries' headquarters building and other major construction projects. In addition to PPG, Pittsburgh is the home of 11 other *Fortune* 500 companies, including Westinghouse Electric and H.J. Heinz.

Despite the heavy jobs losses, Pittsburgh entered the 1990s with an unemployment rate below the national average. At the end of 1991, the region had a 6.1% unemployment rate in a work force of 1.27 million, a full percentage point below the national unemployment rate. The immediate Pittsburgh region sustained negligible job losses of 0.1 percent in 1991, losing 3,700 manufacturing jobs while service industries added 3,400 jobs.

Among the 1991 manufacturing losses were 1,100 jobs in primary metals, the category that includes steelmaking. In the late 1970s, before the local steel industry collapsed, steel employment in the Pittsburgh and Beaver Valley regions totaled 90,000 jobs. In 1990, only 28,900 of those jobs remained. The loss for the Beaver Valley was especially stark; it lost 85 percent of its primary-metals employment, which fell to 4,000 in 1990.

For the job seeker, Pittsburgh also is something of an anomaly. Clearly, it has no demand for blue-collar manufacturing employment. But its declining population and growing service industries will provide opportunities, particularly in business services and health services. Through the middle of the decade, the region is projected to have an average of 42,500 job openings annually. The Beaver Valley, located along the Ohio River and abutting Ohio, will have significantly fewer job opportunities, adding an average of only 2,000 jobs to its economy annually.

The opportunities in Pittsburgh, as throughout most of the country, will break into two distinct groups: Those that require little education and offer low pay, and those that have high educational demands with relatively high pay. For instance, the jobs with the largest number of openings each year will be for janitors and cleaners (2,300 annual openings), retail salespersons (2,165 openings) and security guards (1,878 openings). They are low-paid positions, often have minimal benefits and frequently are part-time positions.

The next largest requirement in the region will be for registered nurses, with 585 new positions each year among 1,100 annual openings. Similarly, the region will require 344 physicians a year. Pittsburgh has for years been a major medical center and employs more than 80,000 medical-services workers, including 30,000 in professional capacities. Among Pittsburgh's industries, health care is the second-largest employer behind retailing, whose employment is approximately 175,000. Hospitals, most of them within Pittsburgh, account for 11 of the region's 50 largest employers.

Allegheny General Hospital is the region's 13th largest employer, followed by Presbyterian-University Hospital— located in the city's bustling Oakland section, a center for both medical services and colleges—in 17th position. The region also is projected to need 250 licensed practical nurses a year and 440 nursing aides-orderlies.

The region's largest employer is the federal government, followed by Westinghouse, which has both research and manufacturing facilities in the area. Next is the University

of Pittsburgh. Other principal higher-education employers
are the Community College of Allegheny County (34th largest employer), Duquesne University (35th) and Carnegie-
Mellon University (45th). Demand for college instructors
and professors will be strong, with projected openings of
550 a year.

The fourth largest employer is USAir Inc., which has its
principal hub at Greater Pittsburgh International Airport. A
proposed midfield terminal for the airport and other projects
are expected to stabilize construction employment at more
than 40,000 jobs. The region's largest remaining steel-
related employer is USX Corp., the former U.S. Steel,
which is the area's ninth-largest employer. Allegheny Lud-
lum Corp. is 14th, and the Alcoa is 32nd.

With so many headquarters operations, including those
of Mellon Bank of PNC Corp., Pittsburgh will be a strong
market for business services. The region will have an average of 3,000 openings a year for managers and administrators, and it will require more than 450 accountants and
auditors each year to fill new positions and vacancies.

Computer services will be in strong demand in the Pittsburgh area. The region is projected to require more than
350 programmers and computer-systems analysts a year to
fill new positions and vacancies caused by losses from the
job market, such as retirements.

Rhode Island

Job seekers in the Ocean State can expect rough seas until
the third quarter of 1992, as Rhode Island struggles to recover from the combined effects of a state, regional and
national recession.

Leonard Lardaro, an associate professor of Economics at
the University of Rhode Island, predicts that the state's
joblessness rate will peak at between 10.5 percent to 11

percent before a modest recovery begins in the third quarter of 1992. "Unless you have something specific lined up or very special skills, I wouldn't burn any bridges," was Lardaro's advice to out-of-state job seekers. "There's still just a lot of uncertainty."

According to recent information released by the Rhode Island Department of Employment and Training, the largest number of jobs openings over the next three years (until the beginning of 1995, which is the forecast endpoint) will be found in the service, clerical, professional, technical and related fields. However, the bulk of these positions will be replacements for existing openings and will not be the result of economic expansion.

According to state projections, there will be between 400 and 500 openings each year until 1995 for professional nurses, nurse aides, cashiers, waiters/waitresses, guards and doorkeepers.

About 700 sales clerk positions will be open each year, while more than 600 openings each year will await prospective secretaries and general office clerks. Some 200 to 300 annual openings are projected for accountants and auditors, fast food workers, technical sales representatives, child care workers, bartenders, truck driving occupations, accounting clerks and licensed practical nurses.

Annual vacancies of 150 to 200 jobs are expected for assemblers, secondary teachers, receptionists, restaurant and coffee shop managers, lawyers, automotive mechanics, production packagers, gardeners and groundskeepers, typists, stock clerks and restaurant cooks.

Unchecked worker's compensation, utility and other costs have made it difficult for Rhode Island businesses and industries and have forced them to look for ways to cut costs—and payroll. Construction and manufacturing have been especially hard hit.

Almac Supermarkets Inc., one of the state's largest employers, instituted a freeze on full-time positions in 1991 and reduced its part-time work force by 400 people. Human resources director Don Volino said he expects the company will hire some part-time employees this year—as well as some retail managers—but will continue to avoid new full-time hires to cut costs. The company employs 1,083 full-time workers and 2,600 part-timers.

The state also has suffered significant losses in real estate, insurance and banking; employment in these sectors has been falling since 1988 and is not expected to return to 1988 peak levels until 1994.

In 1991, the Rhode Island Shared Deposit Indemnity Corp. (RISDIC) collapsed, prompting the collapse of the state's savings and loan institutions. Fleet/Norstar, the Rhode Island-based banking giant, has consolidated operations in Maine and New Hampshire; fortunately, cost-cutting moves were not as dramatic in the corporation's home state. However, Lardaro said that the state remains unable to attract large insurance companies—and the job opportunities they offer—largely because of the high cost of doing business in Rhode Island.

The news is not optimistic for those seeking government jobs, either. Federal government employment is expected to grow 1.3 percent this year but is projected to fall in 1993 and 1994. State and local government employment is expected to drop by 5 percent this year and new, modest growth is not expected until 1994.

The only good news recently was the decision by American Power Conversion to expand their operations. The West Kingston based company—a leading manufacturer of uninterruptable power supplies for computers and other high-tech equipment—recently announced its intention to hire up to 1,000 workers within the next year or so, as plans proceed to take greater advantage of Providence's port city status.

Lawyers, medical personnel and other service sector workers are expected to do well, provided they can wait until 1993 or 1994 for an economic upturn; when job growth resumes, it could mean an additional 8,600 jobs above 1992 employment levels.

Health care, as well as toy and jewelry manufacturing, continue to do well compared to other job sectors; health care is the state's largest private industry with a total of 41,000 workers.

Rhode Island Hospital in Providence employs 5,100 workers, which makes it the state's second largest employer. Employment director Lucinda Wilmot reported that the recession has put a dent in the turnover rate but said openings remain in phlebotomy, medical accounting, third-party billing entry, medical records and coding and quality assurance. The number of applications for each job is up, as workers from hard-hit sectors—including construction—look for a way to make a living.

South Carolina

While South Carolina has not seen the spectacular growth of several other Sunbelt states with a huge migration of retirees or tremendous business development, its population grew by almost 12 percent during the 1980s, slightly greater than the nation as a whole which grew by 9.8 percent. The state has also remained on a steady, progressive economic course. Employment opportunities vary with the landscape. In the western part of the state, the job market is stable because of the high tech corridor in the corner clipped by Interstate 85. In the central region around Columbia, the employment opportunities are more scarce because of a hiring freeze in state government and a tight budget at the University of South Carolina. On the coast, the employment rate is more volatile, reflecting the ebb and flow of tourism in Myrtle Beach and Hilton Head. Charleston, on the other hand, has had strong job growth for the past two years.

Like many other states, South Carolina's work force is becoming more and more service-oriented. In 1991 despite a decline in jobs in conservation, manufacturing, trade, and finance the total number of jobs in the state remained about the same as the year before, 1.56 million, because services grew by 13,000 jobs, the fifth largest increase in the nation. In 1990 South Carolina was the leading state in job growth in the services sector.

Still, manufacturing plays an important role here. South Carolina is one of the top five manufacturing states in the country, with about 22 percent of its work force employed in this sector. While that number has decreased dramatically in the last two decades, it is expected to remain stable until at least the end of the decade. The state is a large producer of auto component parts, chemicals, plastics, designer fabrics, synthetics and specialty fibers, and lumber and pulp products. Other signs for manufacturing growth are good: Hoffman-LaRoche recently moved to the Florence MSA, Pirelli Tires opened a facility in Lexington County, and so many German companies have moved into one northern area that a local highway is known as the "autobahn."

Manufacturing directly influences the major increase projected for jobs in trucking and warehousing. Between 1986 and 2000 jobs in the industry are expected to increase by 73.3 percent, thanks to the emergence of several distribution centers welded together by an excellent and extensive state highway system.

Overall, nonfarm employment has been projected to grow by 34 percent or 473,080 jobs between 1986 and 2000, according to the state's Employment Security Commission. The overwhelming number of new jobs—seven out of every 10—are expected to be in the service industries. Business services will take the biggest jump, 119 percent during this period, with most new jobs in data processing and the fast-growing temporary employment market. An increase of more than 60 percent is expected in restaurants and bars, especially in tourism areas along the coast and in retirement communities. The aging population, coupled with advances in medical technology, will foster a 50 percent increase in employment in the health services, especially in such areas as outpatient care and nursing homes. Education services are expected to grow, especially in vocational and trade schools in several areas of the state with high illiteracy and high school dropout rates.

With a 1991 unemployment rate of 6.6 percent, South Carolina has weathered the recession better than many other states. And, according to some experts like Prof. Frank Hefner of the Economics department at the University of South Carolina, the worst of the recession is over, and the state is poised for a strong recovery. While the first quarter of 1992 is expected to be flat, Hefner predicts a fourth quarter growth of about 40,000 new jobs, with another 30,000 in 1993. Other experts believe that it will be some time before that state gets back to growing at the rate of 50,000 to 60,000 jobs annually as it did in the 1980s.

One black cloud on the horizon is military cutbacks. The Air National Guard base at Myrtle Beach has been closed and the Charleston Navy Yard has been downsized, effecting secondary companies as well. North Charleston is also expected to feel the pinch of military cutbacks.

Although South Carolina is still a relatively poor state (it ranks 43rd in per capita personal income among the 50 states) it is clearly making headway in developing a diversified economy. As the state's population continues to grow so too will job opportunities but at a nice, slow southern pace.

South Dakota

Most Americans are likely to have an image of South Dakota as a vast windswept plain with waves of wheat and soy beans, and perhaps Mt. Rushmore glistening off in the distance. While such outward appearances may still hold true they no longer reflect the reality of the state's way of life. For over the last decade South Dakota has been transforming its economy to mirror the rapid decline in the need for agricultural workers by actively wooing large service-oriented corporations to locate their key operations here. The result was a 15 percent increase in nonfarm jobs during the 1980s with the major jump coming since 1986 when 51,000 jobs were added in only five years.

In a more heavily populated state this wouldn't mean very much but for South Dakota, with a total population of 700,000, with only 310,000 nonfarm workers, the result has been an unemployment rate far below the national average (3.1 percent in December 1991). In fact in Sioux Falls, the state's largest city, the rate has been so low (an incredible 2.5 percent) that the business community was forced to take dramatic steps to fill its employment needs. Under the auspices of the Sioux Falls Development Foundation the city ran ads in *The Wall Street Journal* giving details about job opportunities and providing an 800–number for further information.

"When the ads ran, the phone lines were jammed and the service we hired to handle the calls had to double their staff," said Dan Scott, vice president of the Development Foundation. "The response to the program from around the country was overwhelming." An estimated 2,500 calls were received.

Scott said a major factor in creating the need for more workers in Sioux Falls was the relocation to the area by several large financial services firms including Citibank, Bank of New York, and Sears Payment Systems.

"The area has become known as the credit card processing center of the United States," he said. The credit card firms moved to South Dakota to take advantage of the area's comparatively cheap operating costs and the state's central location, he noted.

Other factors have contributed to the growth trend in the services industries. Legalized gambling in the Black Hills region in the southwest part of the state has generated numerous jobs in lodging accommodations and also in the food services. Additionally, an increased number of elderly residents, combined with improved technology in the medical fields, has led to substantial growth in job opportunities in the health care services.

"The medical sector of our economy has enjoyed explosive growth. In the last few years, it's been phenomenal," said a business leader in Sioux Falls. Between 1986 and 1991 in fact 5,000 jobs were added throughout the state and the projections for the rest of the decade are just as encouraging. By the year 2000 job growth for all health care occupations in South Dakota will be very solid especially for nurses (another 1,500 or so will be needed) and nursing aides and orderlies (also around 1,500).

Other strong growth occupations are waiters and waitresses (2,500 more needed through the year 2000), child care workers (925), general office clerks (925), hand assemblers and fabricators (880), mostly for the computer and office equipment industry, retail salespersons (830), and janitors and cleaners (815).

Tennessee

Tennessee's employment picture mirrors that of many Midwestern states; the metropolitan areas will be gaining jobs in the next few years—the fastest growing will be the Nashville area of central Tennessee—while more rural areas will be stagnant, at best. The good news is that the booming automotive industry growing up around Nashville is spreading into rural areas, and one operation is planned for the lightly populated area near the Georgia border.

In general, the state has a diversified economy that suffered some effects from the 1991–92 recession but—like other Midwest states—was still recovering from the wreck of its aged industrial base in the late 1970s and early 1980s. Researchers at Middle Tennessee State University's School of Business reported that the state's employment bottomed out in March, 1991, and then launched a weak and somewhat erratic recovery.

The state's economy is projected to have almost 120,000 job openings each year through 2000, with a robust proportion of new positions—nearly one in three. The largest growth, more than 9,500 jobs annually, will be among professional and technical employees—Tennessee is projected to need 470 computer programmers and analysts, 380 new accountants, 300 new engineers, and 260 additional lawyers each year. Demand will be particularly strong for registered nurses, with more than 1,100 new positions a year, and a similar demand will exist for teachers.

At the same time, production and repair workers will also be in demand, with more than 8,500 new positions a year. In all regions of the state, the Middle Tennessee researchers noted, manufacturing employment exceeds the national average. The growth is projected to occur despite the continued weakness in the garment and textile industries, which will lose still more jobs through the 1990s. Agriculture also will maintain its long-term slide, but service occupations are projected to add more than 7,500 jobs a year.

SPOTLIGHT ON NASHVILLE

After a downturn in the late 1980s, the Nashville area in north-central Tennessee appears to be poised for the largest employment growth in the state during the early 1990s. Nashville's rebound appears to have begun just as the United States economy slipped into recession. Like other regions of Tennessee, employment bottomed out in March, 1991 before resuming a steady upward climb. Tennessee Department of Employment Security projections place job growth at 1.89 percent a year in the immediate Nashville area through 2000 and 2 percent annually in the counties surrounding Nashville, the self-described "Music City USA." The only area with a comparable projected growth rate is the Knoxville area, but its employment was heavily pounded by the recession, as was the adjacent Chattanooga area. During the recession period, Nashville and the state's far northeastern corner—including Johnson City, Bristol and Kingport—posted the strongest employment gains. The state's overall job growth rate is projected to be 1.56 percent a year.

Nashville-area development officials estimate that the economy is adding about 10,000 new jobs annually in the early 1990s. That growth rate—in an economy that had a 511,000-member work force in late 1991—was well below the go-go period in 1985 and 1986, when Nashville was adding 30,000 jobs a year. But it also is an improvement from the latter years of the decade, when a construction and real-estate slump held job creation below 10,000 a year. Skilled workers and executives are in demand; one survey of Nashville-area employers found that 40 percent had a difficult time finding qualified applicants for their openings.

Music and tourism indeed are still big businesses in the metropolis that is the home of the Grand Ole Opry, but the auto industry is the engine currently driving the central Tennessee employment picture. One reason that central Tennessee is bucking the trend of less production employment nationally is an abundance of land in rural counties around Nashville and a ready work force. Another reason is an excellent roads system, at the intersection of three major interstate highways—I–65 from north to south, I–24 from northwest to southeast, and I–40 from east to west.

The largest component of the Nashville area's automotive boom is the Nissan Motor Manufacturing USA plant in Smyrna, located about 20 miles southeast of the city. The Japanese automaker, which employs about 3,800 workers, is expected to add 2,000 production jobs in the next several years. It should be noted, though, that the U.S. operations of the Japanese automakers tend to be very selective in their hiring, looking for a strong work ethic and personal flexibility in handling assignments as much as manual skills.

The other major automotive operation offers few prospects for employment in the next few years. The Saturn plant in Spring Hill, about 30 miles south of Nashville, has been slow to get off the mark, paralleling sales of the General Motors-inspired line of automobiles. The plant is turning out a quality product that has been favorably reviewed, but the recession and the Saturn's long-delayed launching in the early 1990s had the plant operating at half-capacity in early 1992, say economic researchers who follow the industry. When the plant reaches full capacity—if indeed that ever occurs—Saturn could produce additional jobs in the region.

The region scored a coup when the merged Bridgestone-Firestone Inc. tire company placed its headquarters in Nashville, moving there from Akron, Ohio, the nation's longtime tire capital. Bridgestone previously had its corporate base and production operations in central Tennessee, and it plans to build a new plant in the state. Nashville also has a Ford Motor Co. glass plant, and landed a Ford Motor Credit operation in late 1990.

The large automotive operations in central Tennessee were preceded by smaller automotive manufacturers. By one estimate, the area has more than 100 automotive suppliers, making everything from arm rests to electronic actuators for auto heaters. In addition, the Nashville Chamber of Commerce's aggressive search for new companies netted Tridon Ltd., a Canadian auto-parts manufacturer, in late 1990.

Air transportation also received a substantial boost in the late 1980s when American Airlines located a hub in Nashville. American maintains a crew base in Nashville and is estimated to have resulted in more than 1,000 new jobs for the area.

The region also has a substantial printing industry, with

well over 4,000 jobs, and employment growth is projected to outpace the Nashville area's average increases. Southern Baptist and United Methodist printing operations are located there, and Gannett has a plant where *USA Today* and outside jobs are printed.

Nashville also is a significant player in the nation's continuing health-care employment boom. The region's largest private employer, with more than 10,700 employees, is Vanderbilt University and Medical Center, which has a well-respected medical school in the city. Hospital Corp. of America, the nation's largest owner of hospitals with 130, is also based in Nashville. The city and its surrounding Davidson County are projected to need 400 registered nurses a year—half of them representing new positions—every year, and more than 280 licensed practical nurses to fill new and existing positions.

Nashville area development officials said they believe the slippage in construction and financial services has stopped. Building permits for Davidson County were up in November 1991 after a long decline, and office vacancy rates are at their lowest level since 1984. The financial-services industry has been battered by the consolidation of banks and bank holding companies in the Southeast.

Long a center of insurance operations, Nashville has obtained the U.S. headquarters of Willis-Corroon, a London-based insurer. Other operations placing their headquarters in Nashville have been Berol USA Inc., the pencil maker, and the National Federation of Independent Businesses.

Tourism has been a component of Nashville's economy for decades, and both the music industry and the tourism business continue to generate jobs. Opryland USA Inc. is the region's second-largest private employer, with almost 8,000 jobs, and the sprawling Opryland Hotel has announced plans to build another 1,000 rooms.

SPOTLIGHT ON MEMPHIS

Tennessee's second largest metropolitan area has lost jobs to the national recession, but its location, its Federal Express connection, its health-care industries and its federal-government facilities have offered some protection from a severe slide. Like other parts of the state, western Tennessee's employment bottomed out in March, 1991, and Memphis Area Chamber of Commerce officials said the region added over 8,800 new jobs in 1991. The area's total work force is approaching 500,000.

The Memphis area's largest single employer is Federal Express, with more than 18,000 employees. The company's phenomenal expansion has made transportation a growth industry for Memphis, which is located on the Mississippi River as well as at the intersection of major highways and rail lines. In all, the transportation sector grew from 33,000 to 47,000 jobs between 1985 and 1990, a 7 percent annual growth rate.

A job freeze at Federal Express, imposed as the Memphis-based company sought to consolidate its forays into the European and Asian markets, led to a small 0.6 percent decline in transportation employment in 1991. In addition to Fed Ex, Memphis is a hub for Northwest Airlines, which reduced its flights through the city in the early 1990s. The region has 23 air-freight companies as well as 200 motor-freight concerns and 100 freight terminals.

Despite the 1991 jobs freeze, Fed Ex's influence is significant, and development officials say they cannot fully gauge the effect. For instance, several computer-repair and electronics-parts companies have located in Memphis to take advantage of quick shipping turnarounds. Among the companies with repair or parts operations in Memphis are McDonald's, Centel, Xerox and IBM. The computer segment is projected to have moderately strong growth through 2000, adding about 130 new jobs each year.

The region's largest employer is health-care services, with approximately 40,000 jobs. The entire services segment grew by 2 percent in 1991, and health positions were a major part of the growth. The largest medical employers are Baptist Memorial Hospital, with more than 7,000 positions, and Methodist Hospital, which employs 5,000. Memphis's medical-services sector is projected to have strong growth, with roughly 1,100 total job openings each year. Demand for registered nurses and licensed practical nurses will be strongest, with new positions accounting for more than one in every three job openings.

Along with the medical services, Memphis has developed a good market for medical manufacturers and equipment. Schering-Plough HealthCare Products employs 1,700 in the region, and Smith & Nephew Richards Inc., a manufacturer of orthopedic and surgical equipment, has 1,250 employees. In its effort to build the region's manufacturing employment, Chamber of Commerce development officials have targeted the medical-manufacturing industry as well as specialty chemicals, printing-publishing and food processing. Specialty chemicals, particularly those based on edible oils, already have sizable operations in the region and employ 8,000.

The manufacturing sector accounts for approximately 60,000 jobs in all, and durable-goods makers added jobs in 1991. Bucking a national and regional trend, the Memphis area added textile employment in 1991, up almost 5 percent to 2,200 jobs, but the region continued to lose furniture-manufacturing jobs—principally to rural areas of Mississippi, the region's neighbor to the south. The paper industry, whose regional participants include International Paper (1,350 jobs) and Kimberly Clark Corp. (1,060 jobs), was flat in 1991. The area's largest manufacturer, with 2,600 jobs, in Cleo Inc., a maker of gift wrap and bows.

With almost 32,000 workers in two defense installations,

the federal government is a major employer in the Memphis area. The Memphis Naval Air Station employs more than 16,800, and the Defense Supply Depot accounts for another 15,000 jobs.

Texas

For decades, Texas prospered by poking holes in the ground and poking holes in the sky. In several regions of this large and diverse state, oil was the currency of prosperity, and it created unprecedented wealth for a few of its residents. Oil companies competed to build the tallest building in town as the Houston skyline soared toward the heavens in the early 1970s. (Banks and financial companies ultimately would build the city's tallest skyscrapers.) Dallas became a symbol of rapacious and ostentatious wealth when it gave its name to a long-running television series whose message was that greed, if not good, at least was highly profitable and modestly entertaining.

Texas also prospered from a legacy of powerful and adroit politicians, beginning with Sam Rayburn and extending beyond Lyndon B. Johnson, the native son from Stonewall who succeeded to the presidency when John F. Kennedy was assassinated on a visit to Dallas in 1963. An era of manned space exploration, launched by Kennedy and pursued by Johnson, was controlled from Houston, and the control room there became a familiar site to millions of Americans as they watched their countrymen first walk on the moon in 1969. The Houston Space Center now bears Johnson's name.

Beginning with the Rayburn era, Texas also became a major defense contractor, and the combination of oil and government dollars ignited a building boom of such proportions that it can only be described as Texan. Houston sprawled over more than 500 square miles, and the metropolitan areas of Fort Worth and Dallas grew so wildly that they appeared to be poised to link up along Interstate 30.

The boom began to unravel in the early 1980s, when the expectation of $100-a-barrel oil evaporated and Houston's real-estate market crashed. The bust went statewide in 1986, when crude fell below $20 a barrel and the oil patch plummeted into depression. Much of Texas historically has been described in economic terms as counter cyclical: When the rest of the country was thrust into recession by high energy costs, Texas prospered. Similarly, while the nation had a sustained economic expansion through much of the 1980s, Texas fell into a deep recession as the oil patch dried up.

Since the mid–1980s, Texas has been diversifying and rebuilding its large and highly complex economy. Where oil, cattle, banking and real estate once drove the economy, health care, high technology, computers, aerospace and biotechnology now are major factors in Texas. Today, the state has pockets of strong growth, particularly in the southern half. The northern half, especially around Dallas and Fort Worth, still has deep-seated problems that will take much of the 1990s to resolve and should be of concern for any job seeker.

Texas did not avoid the 1991–92 recession, but it did manage to add jobs, with statewide employment growing by 0.95 percent in 1991 after a 2.05 percent advance in 1990. The 1991 growth amounted to 67,500 jobs, raising Texas' job count to 7,193,000. Even modest growth amounts to big numbers; Texas' total number of new jobs was the largest in the nation by a factor of two, more than doubling the growth in Arkansas, which added 32,500 jobs.

Economists who contribute to the respected Western Blue Chip Economic Forecast pegged 1992 employment growth at 1.7 percent and at 2 percent in 1993. "Our dependence on the oil and gas sector has declined," said panel member M. Ray Perryman of Perryman Consultants Inc. in Waco. "We've been a net loser in jobs in mineral extraction and manufacturing facilities directly tied to oil and gas drilling activity. On the other hand, we've seen a lot of increases in the production of high-tech equipment (such as electronics and telecommunication apparatus), air transportation, health care and aircraft manufacturing. In doing so, we have established a notable presence in the growth industries of the future. We have a lot more jobs, and fewer of them are tied to natural resources.''

Indeed, Texas has a lot of jobs, the third largest total after California and New York, both of which lost employment in 1991. As a consequence, Texas will certainly have job openings in all of its major industries. But, with declines in such major areas as manufacturing, job seekers should expect considerable competition for most positions. The boom days, when a petroleum engineer or a construction worker could come into town and find work by sundown, are over—probably forever.

Beneath the raw figures, problems remain. The 1991 job growth was concentrated in two areas, services and government. The services category added 38,200 positions, but 32,100 of them were in health care—an area experiencing strong demand almost everywhere in the country. The one bright spot was engineering and management services, which added 2,200 positions to a total of 154,400 jobs statewide.

The growth in government employment has to be of concern for two reasons. For one, it most likely is not sustainable in a period of fiscal restraint. Second, the larger payrolls most likely will be paid for with higher taxes, which will affect buying power in the state. Most of the 1991 increase was concentrated in state employment, which added 14,300 jobs and raised the payroll by 5 percent to 298,400. One economist characterized state-government spending through that period as ''out of control.'' In all, government employment increased by 2.2 percent, or 28,700 jobs, to 1,330,700 in 1991 after a whopping 5.64 percent increase in 1990.

Also increasing was retail-trade employment, although

food—either in grocery-store or restaurant jobs—accounted for all of the growth. Retailing grew by 0.8 percent, 13,800 jobs, to 1,746,900 positions. All other areas of retail employment except food declined, reflecting both weakness in the national retail sector and in the state economy. Employment at general-merchandise stores across the state was down by 3,500 jobs; eating and drinking places posted the strongest advance, gaining 20,000 jobs over the year.

Construction advanced by 4,200 jobs in 1991, a healthy 1.24 percent gain after a 4.5 percent increase in 1990. Construction employment, totalling 342,600 at the end of 1991, continued its long climb out of the real-estate crash. Its strength also is expected to be concentrated in the southern half of the state.

Manufacturing's slide accelerated in Texas during 1991, with a loss of 15,800 jobs, or 1.6 percent, to 970,600 positions after a modest 0.16 percent decline in the previous year. Previously, manufacturing had been rebounding, growing by 3.3 percent in 1988 and 1.7 percent in 1989. As in most states, durable goods took the biggest hit, losing 22,800 positions. The biggest loser was aircraft manufacturing and parts, which shrunk by 8,800 jobs. Industrial-equipment manufacturing declined by 4,200 jobs, including another 1,500 jobs lost in the oil-field machinery category.

Nondurables advanced by 7,000 jobs, including a gain of 4,100 jobs in chemical industries, which are concentrated in the southern half of the state. Also on the positive side for that region, petroleum refining added 1,800 jobs, to 28,300 positions. Oil and gas drilling are still major factors in the state, employing 167,300 at the end of 1991. That total was down 7,200 jobs, more than 4 percent, in a year. Another major employer statewide, banks and other financial institutions, continued to decline in 1991, when employment fell by 4,200 jobs to 123,500 positions, mirroring the national trend.

Among Texas' major metropolitan areas, Houston, Austin and San Antonio added jobs in 1991. Houston was the largest gainer in both total jobs and percentage gain, up 0.78 percent. Austin's employment grew by 0.73 percent, and San Antonio advanced by 0.53 percent. Dallas and Fort Worth both had sizable declines in employment. But the state's strongest growth occurred in smaller metropolitan areas. The state's fastest-growing metropolitan area was Victoria, located southeast of San Antonio, which added 1,400 jobs, a 4.9 percent advance to 29,900 positions.

Perhaps the most impressive gain was in the Beaumont-Port Arthur area east of Houston, near the Gulf of Mexico and the Louisiana border. It grew by 3.82 percent, or 5,600 jobs, to 152,200 positions. This area benefitted from expansion by petrochemical companies and a resulting increase in construction employment. Other sizable growth areas were Brownsville-Harlingen, at the state's southern tip, which grew by 2,700 jobs, and the Killeen-Temple area, between Dallas and Austin, which added 2,000 positions. McAllen, near the Mexican border, and Brazoria, south of Houston, each added 1,600 jobs.

El Paso, in far West Texas and adjacent to New Mexico and Mexico's Chihuahua state, is expected to be the state's fastest-growing large metropolitan area in 1992. In 1991, it grew by 0.76 percent, an increase of 1,600 jobs to 212,500. The Odessa and Midland areas of West Texas also experienced strong growth in 1991, with employment expanding by 3.15 percent in Odessa and by 2.45 percent in Midland.

So there are undeniable signs of economic strength throughout this vast state, signs that indicate solid if not spectacular job growth over the next few years. Here are some details about possibilities in the major metropolitan areas.

SPOTLIGHT ON HOUSTON

Of Texas' major metropolitan areas, Houston has mounted the most successful recovery from a largely doleful decade in the 1980s. In 1991, its regional employment grew by 12,700 jobs to 1,643,000 positions. Among the nation's 36 largest metropolitan areas, that was the third-largest number of new jobs, after Omaha and Indianapolis. The rate of increase, 0.78 percent, was the fourth best in the country, after Denver, Seattle and Milwaukee. At the end of 1991, Houston's unemployment rate stood at 6.0 percent, up from 5.4 percent a year earlier.

Paul Coomes, associate professor of Economics at the University of Louisville, has developed an economic performance index for American metropolitan areas that provides a combined measure of job and income growth. According to that index, Houston was the fourth best-performing large metropolitan area in the United States in 1991, following Las Vegas, Fresno, Calif., and Seattle. Houston scored 113.07 with the years from 1987 to 1989 serving as a base of 100.

Houston achieved its 1991 job gains by holding the line on manufacturing employment and adding large numbers of service jobs and government positions. Trade employment advanced modestly, while all other classifications lost jobs. Oil production lost some more jobs, declining by 1,700 positions to fewer than 70,000 workers, but petroleum processing and refining added 500 jobs over the year. Business-services employment fell by 1,700 jobs, and retailing registered no growth. Banks and other financial institutions continued to pare their work forces, reducing employment by 1,600 jobs in 1991.

Goods-producing jobs remain a large and significant factor in Houston's economy. In 1991, 21.5 percent of

Houston's nonagricultural work force was involved in manufacturing, oil drilling, refining or construction. Employment in durable-goods manufacturing fell by 1,000 jobs to 96,000 workers, and nondurables added 1,000 jobs largely on the strength of refining and petrochemicals. Another growing area was paper manufacturing, which expanded by 5.9 percent in 1991 to 3,600 jobs.

Construction, although regarded as an area of growth into the mid–1990s, fell by another 2,400 jobs to 107,400 positions. The real-estate collapse that began in the early 1980s persists; the cost of housing in the Houston region remains relatively low although the median price of a single-family home rebounded in the late 1980s, and office space is plentiful.

Among Houston's largest companies, energy continues to be king: the top three by revenues are Tenneco Inc., Entron Corp. and Coastal Corp. The fourth-largest is Sysco Corp., a fast-growing food marketer and distributor. The region's largest manufacturing companies are Cooper Industries, which makes electrical and other equipment, and Compaq Computer Corp., the long-successful competitor to IBM in the personal-computer market. In the early 1990s, though, Compaq's profit margins were pinched by makers of inexpensive PCs.

Outside of manufacturing, a major gain occurred in amusement and recreation services, which grew by 3,000 jobs to almost 20,000 positions—an advance of 17.8 percent. The increase reflects the growing significance of tourism in both the Houston economy and in the Texas economy generally.

The strongest gains, though, were in health services, which added 4,600 jobs and raised total employment to 103,700. Over the past several decades, Houston has become internationally known for its medical center, and health-related companies are 11 of the region's 50 largest employers. The Texas Medical Center—comprising 14 hospitals, two medical schools, two nursing schools and other institutions—employs 51,000. In addition, the Sisters of Charity Hospital and Memorial Health Care Systems are major employers. At the beginning of 1992, the region had openings for therapists of all types, X-ray technicians and registered nurses.

After services, government added the largest number of jobs to the Houston economy, growing by 8,100—3.8 percent—to 218,600 jobs. Federal employment expanded by 9.7 percent to 27,200 jobs. A principal federal employer is NASA's Johnson Space Center, located 25 miles southeast of Houston's center in Clear Lake City. The center's human resources office said in early 1992 that entry-level engineers and secretaries were the most-frequent hires.

SPOTLIGHT ON
AUSTIN

The state capital, with its economy and employment stabilized by nonstop growth in government hiring, paused in the 1980s before resuming strong growth that will continue through the 1990s. Despite the recession in 1991, Austin-area employment expanded by 0.73 percent, adding 2,800 jobs to 386,300 positions. Unemployment edged up to 4.7 percent at the end of 1991 from 4.6 percent a year earlier, but its rate was well below both the national average and the jobless levels in other major Texas cities.

When Texas' economy took the oil-patch blow in the mid–1980s, Austin felt the effects. Employment dropped sharply in 1987, rebounded slightly in 1988 and bounced back over 1986's employment peak of 360,400 in 1989.

The Greater Austin Chamber of Commerce forecasts that employment will grow by 3.2 percent in 1992 and 3.6 percent in 1993 with the addition of 12,500 jobs in 1992 and 14,600 in the latter year. The chamber, which also forecast an unemployment-rate rise to 4.9 percent in 1992 before dropping back to 4.7 percent the following year, indicated that all job sectors will grow in each year. But the engine for the region's growth will be its burgeoning high-technology industry, which has both nationally-based players and its own home-grown participants.

The chamber reported that, according to its calculation of annual average employment, manufacturing grew by 2,000 jobs to 51,000 positions in 1991. The Texas Employment Commission's December-to-December comparison indicated a decline of 400 jobs in 1991. But the basic trend is undeniable; in a decade, Austin added 20,000 manufacturing jobs, an increase of 65 percent. In the 1980s, more than 150 manufacturing operations were established in Austin, and two-thirds of them fell into the high-technology category.

At the beginning of 1992, that sector contained 400 companies that employed 45,000 persons in all job categories. The chamber forecast that employment in the high-tech area will grow by 3.9 percent in 1992 and 4.2 percent in 1993. In 1991, Motorola Inc.—a major manufacturer of computer chips and other electronic equipment—announced that it was adding 2,440 workers in Austin. Other large manufacturers include IBM and Advanced Micro Systems. During the late 1980s, local start-ups began to have an impact on the high-tech world, particularly in the area of personal computers. Among these companies are Dell Computer, CompuAdd, Austin Computer Systems, Techworks, Radian, Ross Technology and XETEL. Among the areas expected to register strong growth in coming years are office automation, instruments and semiconductor-related businesses.

In the area of service employment, computer software is a growing factor in the region's job mix. The chamber estimated that 20 software firms locate in Austin each year. The area also has become a center for research and development, with public and private expenditures swelling to $1.3 million in the late 1980s. A major research facility has been announced by 3M Corp., which is moving several divisions from St. Paul to Austin. Other large employers in the area are Lockheed, Abbott Labs and Texas instruments.

Service employment, which accounted for 26 percent of Austin's jobs, was forecast to grow by more than 4 percent in both 1992 and 1993. Business-services growth will outpace gains in medical and professional services. American Airlines announced in 1991 that it would locate a reservations center with 500 jobs in Austin, and Apple Computer announced plans for a customer-service center with more than 400 employees.

The region's largest employer is government, which provides paychecks to 28 percent of all Austin-area workers. Despite the pending closing of Bergstrom Air Force Base in the fall of 1993, total government employment is forecast to grow by 2 percent a year.

The region appears to be poised for a construction boom, and the chamber forecast jobs growth of more than 8 percent in both 1992 and 1993. Office vacancy rates still exceed 15 percent, but multifamily residential housing is nearing capacity. Single-family home construction in 1991 grew by 44.6 percent over low 1990 levels. The construction activity is expected to reverse the decline in banking and financial employment, a sector that peaked at 25,600 jobs in 1986 and fell steadily to 23,100 positions in 1991. The chamber forecast modest growth, almost 1 percent in 1992 and 3 percent the following year.

SPOTLIGHT ON SAN ANTONIO

Like Austin, San Antonio suffered from overbuilding and the statewide malaise of the mid–1980s. Like Austin, its future lies in high technology, particularly in biotechnology. Unlike Austin, though, manufacturing is not a significant part of the employment picture in San Antonio. In 1991, the South Texas region added 300 manufacturing jobs, but production jobs constitute only 8.2 percent of the San Antonio economy.

The big gun in San Antonio employment—and potentially a cloud on its future growth—is the military. The site of the Alamo bristles with federal facilities, starting with Fort Sam Houston, which employed more than 18,000 in 1991. Right behind it are Kelly Air Force Base, with 17,423 workers, and Lackland Air Force Base, with 15,739. Not far down the list of San Antonio's leading employers is Randolph Air Force Base, 8,279 jobs, and it is followed by Brooks Air Force Base, where another 2,871 were employed in 1991. Another major federal facility is the Audie Murphy VA Hospital, with a total payroll of 2,321. The military's contribution to the local economy is estimated at $3 billion a year. Altogether, government employment accounts for a whopping 23.6 percent of the region's 527,900 wage-and-salary jobs, far above the national average of 17 percent.

San Antonio officials, burned by the cycle of feverish growth and recession in the 1980s, have charted a course of gradual growth, and the region's economy expanded by 2,800 jobs in 1991, a 0.53 percent increase. In addition to the small manufacturing gain, San Antonio added jobs in the transportation sector, in services and, of course, in government. Construction remained unchanged at a depressed level, trade jobs fell slightly and the large group of financial, insurance and real estate positions fell by 1,600 to 37,400 jobs. Outside of the military, the region's largest employer is United Services Automobile Association, an insurance and financial services company that employs 9,100. The San Antonio-based operation is undertaking a 1.5-million square foot, $100-million expansion.

San Antonio's most significant growth potential appears to be in biotechnology and health care. Operating in the area are the 2,500-employee Southwest Research Institute, the third largest applied research institute in the country, and the Southwest Foundation for Biomedical Research. The latter organization eventually will be housed in the 300-acre Texas Research Park, which has been developed with grants from Concord Oil Co., H. Ross Perot, local business people and the city. The Research Park's anchor tenant is the University of Texas Institute for Biotechnology, and the institute for Chemical Research and Drug Development is scheduled to locate there.

While biotechnology is still a small contributor to total employment, the medical community is a major employer, providing paychecks to more than 40,000 persons. The military also is a significant participant in the region's medical community. Fort Sam Houston contains the Brooke Army Medical Center, the Academy of Health Sciences and the Institute of Surgical Research, which has an acclaimed burn center. The region's largest medical employers are the University of Texas Health Science Center, with a payroll of 4,000; the Baptist Memorial Hospital System, with 3,800 on its staff; Southwest Texas Methodist Hospital, with 2,600 employees; and Santa Rosa Medical Center, which employs 2,286.

Humana Inc., which operates two 1,000-employee hospitals in the city, was scheduled to open a $17-million Humana Heart Institute in the spring of 1992. San Antonio is making provision for its future needs in this employment area. The city's Northside Health Careers High School was created to prepare students for medical professions.

The region also will be a player in two other growing fields: tourism and international trade. Fiesta Texas, a $100-million recreation center and musical theme park, is scheduled to employ 200 people full-time and provide 2,000 seasonal jobs. It will join Sea World of Texas, the largest marine theme park in the world, and an active convention trade. The city currently is building a downtown domed stadium.

Other construction projects include a $3-million Bausch & Lomb plant for making Ray Ban sunglasses that will

employ 1,000; a $5-million Colin Medical instruments fa-
cility to build vital-signs monitoring equipment that will
hire 400; and a $150-million Golden Aluminum plant that
will produce rolled aluminum for cans and employ 200.

San Antonio and the remainder of South Texas are
expected to benefit from increased trade with Mexico under the Free Trade Agreement. Already the wholesale-
distribution center for South Texas, San Antonio added
1,200 jobs in the transportation sector in 1991. The region
also is adding back-office services to its employment mix.
Sears Telecatalog Center employs 2,500 part-time workers
in San Antonio, and West Telemarketing Corp. employs
150 full-time workers and 500 part-timers. Southwest Airlines' reservation center employs 568 workers.

SPOTLIGHT ON
DALLAS—FORT WORTH

Despite an attractive and well-designed downtown—with
structures created by I. M. Pei and Frank Lloyd Wright—
Dallas is losing the battle to the suburbs, much as many
northeast and midwest cities suffered a large outward migration in the 1960s and 1970s. The flight is symbolic and
symptomatic of the changes Dallas has undergone in the
1980s. For many years a financial center, Dallas no longer
is the headquarters for any major financial institutions. Its
oil industry dried up in the mid–1980s and has shown no
signs of the resurgence that has occurred in the southern
half of the state.

The Dallas region lost 3,100 jobs in 1991, a decline of
0.22 percent to 1,384,200 total wage-and-salary employment. Drilling, which employed only 17,900 in 1990, lost
another 300 jobs in 1991. Construction, also in a relatively
depressed state, lost 3,300 jobs to 43,900. But the biggest
loser was manufacturing, which fell by almost 8,000 jobs,
a 3.6 percent decline to 211,000 positions in 1991.

The category that covers banks and other financial institutions lost 2,100 jobs, ebbing to 122,200 positions after the 1.7 percent fall. Government and services added more than 1 percent each to their employment, and the category that includes trucking and air transportation added 1,900 jobs to 85,000.

If Dallas was in a recession, Fort Worth was entering a deeper trough. The city 30 miles to the west of Dallas lost 8,100 jobs from an economy with 585,600 positions. The 1.36 percent fall was the worst performance by any Texas metropolitan area, and the future is clouded by layoffs in the aerospace industry there and the closing of Carswell Air Force Base. One bright spot in 1992 was General Motors' decision to retain the Arlington assembly plant, sacrificing a plant in Ypsilanti, Michigan.

Still, manufacturing fell by 14,000 jobs, or 12 percent, to 102,100. Construction also suffered a heavy hit, losing 1,900 slots and declining to 20,300 jobs. Only transportation, services and government employment registered 1991 gains.

Despite the downside, the Dallas–Fort Worth area is a very large market, and openings will occur for almost all types of workers. Like San Antonio, Dallas is developing biotechnology, and it has a base of high-technology and research-and-development companies. High-technology companies among Dallas' 10 largest employers are Texas Instruments, Electronic Data Systems and E Systems Inc. Other large employers are AMR Corp., General Dynamics Corp., LTV, and Cullum Cos.

Utah

In 1990–91, a period when the rest of the country was in decline, Utah's job growth rate was estimated at 3.1 percent, or 22,400 new jobs. Utah has now experienced four consecutive years of 3 percent or better growth—a rate which has not been seen since the 1976–79 period.

The state's high growth has not gone unnoticed. In the past year, Utah has been touted as a great place to work and live by nearly every major national publication including *Financial World, The London Times*, the *New York Times, Kiplinger Personal Finance, Money, Fortune, Business Week* and others.

As a result of national recognition and economic strength as compared to the rest of the nation, Utah experienced net in-migration for the first time since 1983. According to the state's 1992 Economic Report to the Governor, "Not only did we undergo in-migration, but the magnitude of 19,000 is the highest level in more than a decade and the third highest in 40 years." Almost as significant, the population boom was spread around. In-migration occurred in 25 of Utah's 29 counties.

Currently the Salt Lake City and Provo-Orem areas are hot spots for employment. Of the 16,000 new jobs created in Utah in 1991, 10,600 were in Salt Lake City, and 5,600 in Provo-Orem. Statewide, total employment is projected to increase from 808,000 jobs in 1990 to 1,324,000 jobs in 2020. These numbers include those self-employed and those working in agriculture.

Long-term, Utah expects to have a population of 2,715,000 by the year 2020. As it predicts an average annual growth rate of 1.5 percent beginning in 1990, Utah should be the eighth-fastest growing state in the 90s. While growth will be slower than in the previous decades, it is still projected at twice the national growth rate for the same projected period.

Short-term, however, Utah does not expect to entirely escape the national recession. Officials cite a distinctly smaller pool of expanding companies now exists for Utah to compete for and excessive debt and low consumer confidence on the part of consumers and businesses as factors that will affect investment in 1992. Nevertheless, expansion is big business here. One of only four states which allow for limited-liability companies, Utah is a right-to-work state that provides tax credits to companies in economically distressed areas. United Parcel Service, Franklin International Institute, J.C. Penney, Piper Impact, Morton International, Defense Logistics Agency, Sears Discover Card, Boston Company Financial Series and other companies all have announced expansions for 1992.

Utah's job opportunities are expanding because new employers are moving into the state and, at the same time, existing corporations are experiencing impressive growth. In 1991, new and expanding industries in Utah included McDonnell Douglas, Sears Payment Systems, Kennecott, Wal-Mart, UP&L Gadsby Plant, Black Diamond, Charter Oak Partners, Shopko, Softcopy, Novell, Jahabow, Sorex Medical, Aerotrans Corp., Gates Rubber Corp., Morton International, Zero Corps. Continental Airlines, Compeq Manufacturing, Kern River Gas Transmission, Flameco, GTE Health Systems, Borden, Rexene, Arrowhead Dental Laboratories, Delta Center, Gull Laboratories, Morton Airbag and others.

Most notable of the new and expanding industries were Novell of Utah County and Morton Airbag of Box Elder County. These represent two of the fastest growing industries in the state. Novell is a leader in network systems operating software linking desk tops to mini and mainframe computers, while Morton Airbag is the leading manufacturer in that fast-growing field. Morton expects to expand from 1,200 employees in 1991 to 4,500 by 1995, while Morton will add another 400 people over the next twelve months.

These examples illustrate two of the three top-growth industries which are helping Utah emerge as a leader in economic growth, computer-related services and equipment, and automotive airbags. The third industry experiencing substantial growth in Utah is telemarketing. Although telemarketing jobs are criticized as being low pay, low skill, research indicates this is not always the case. The economic report to the Governor emphasizes that some telemarketing opportunities, such as those with Fidelity, Inc.

in Salt Lake City, pay "substantially more than the average wage for all industries."

In just ten years, Utah has made a dramatic switch toward becoming a service-based economy. One reason Utah is attracting new employers such as telemarketing is the state's illiteracy rate, reported to be the lowest in the nation. Consequently, while a decade ago Utah's industrial profile was mostly made up of mining, construction and manufacturing, those sectors are no longer growing.

Amid all the cheering, a note of caution must be sounded. Annual personal income growth fell from a peak of 9.3 percent in the third quarter of 1990 to 7.4 percent in the second quarter of 91. And unemployment figures also crept upwards, from an 11-year low of 4 percent in April 1991 to 5.4 percent in November. Personal income, while rising, still comes in at only 76 percent of the U.S. figure.

As is the case in other Rocky Mountain states, Utah illustrates that dichotomy which exists between employment opportunities in the metropolitan and non-urban areas. Utah often refers to the "two Utahs," a fact of life in most Rocky Mountain states. Much of this is attributed to the nonmetro areas' struggle to move from a natural resource-based economy to a trade-based economy. While the majority of Utah's counties prospered, four rural counties lost population in 1990. In the future, the state is counting on increased tourism and an upswing in natural resource prices (especially copper) to help smooth that transition for the nonmetropolitan areas. Utah wants the entire state to benefit from these prosperous times.

So Utah seems to be solidly on the road to a growth economy that will be creating new jobs every year for the foreseeable future. But bear in mind that this is a sparsely populated state with a *total* work force of only 765,000. So although job growth in 1991 was strong (4.2 percent), only 16,000 jobs were added. Still growth of any kind is a positive sign for job seekers.

Vermont

Like most of the New England area, Vermont has been hit hard by the recession. According to Arizona State University's Economic Outlook Center, nonagricultural job growth here declined more than 3 percent from 258,000 in December of 1990 to 252,000 in December, 1991. Particularly hard-hit were jobs in the manufacturing industry, which are currently at their lowest level since 1977, according to Mike Griffin, Chief of Research and Analysis at the Vermont Office of Policy and Information. The decline has been distributed fairly evenly throughout Vermont, though the northeast section seems to have been hit harder than the rest of the state. Jobs in Burlington, the state's largest metropolitan area, declined at the same rate as the statewide average, while those in the capital region of Barre-Montepelier avoided any decline in job growth.

Nonetheless, Vermont is expected to post modest growth for the rest of the decade in all areas of the state and in all industries except for agriculture. Vermont's entire nonagricultural labor force numbered 245,750 in 1991. The state's Occupational Information Coordinating Committee projects an average annual growth rate of 2.23 percent through the year 2000. This could be wishful thinking on the state's part unless recovery from the recession begins very soon.

The lion's share of that growth will come in the area of retail sales, which was projected to increase a whopping 45.3 percent between 1987 and 2000. A large number of new jobs, however, will come in production, operation, and maintenance. Already the largest group of workers in the state, this occupational group is expected to grow by more than 20,000 positions over the same period.

Virginia

Simply put, the recession of the early 1990s has stopped fast-moving Virginia dead in its tracks.

During the 1980s its population grew by almost 16 percent to just over 6 million people. Its economy, jolted by massive increases in defense spending, rolled on to new heights and the future looked very promising as strong job growth occurred in every sector. In 1991, however, Virginia had a net job loss of over 18,000, with only services and government showing modest gains. Moreover, every metropolitan area except Bristol (which is very small) had net job loss figures for the year. While the effects of this recession will not be permanent, the ending of the cold war and the subsequent reduction in our military commitments certainly will.

For job seekers today the growth areas of the 1980s remain the best bet for the short term. Hospitals, retail trade, local government, research and development laboratories should be among the top job producers. Northern Virginia is suffering the worst economic downturn in the state—in large part because of the collapse in real estate prices. In 1991, the region lost 7,000 construction jobs and 4,000 retail-trade jobs. Yet the area's long-term job picture is bright. Services added jobs in 1991, with growth registered in health-related industries. The federal government will remain strong in terms of job possibilities (see the entry, "Where the Jobs Are in the Federal Government").

The largest number of jobs will continue to be centered in Virginia Beach (where tourism has exploded in recent years) and Richmond, the state capital. Nearly two-thirds of total employment growth in the next eight years is expected to occur in the services and retail trade. For example, McLean-based Mars, the food company, and Richmond-based Best Products, the retailer, are among the state's largest private employers with 24,000 and 14,000 jobs respectively.

For the savvy job hunter, Virginia does offer opportunity just off the well-tread path. Manufacturing registered slight increases in the last decade, even if it accounted by 1990 for a smaller percentage in employment as a whole. In southwest Virginia, Bristol actually gained employment in 1991. Buoyed by the stability of the local coal economy, the southwest recorded a slight 8 percent gain in goods-producing industries, such as machinery and electrical equipment. Retail trade remained stable.

Virginia's economy remains basically very strong and high. Per capita personal income, which increased dramatically in the 1980s, should help it through the recession. Still the period of exceptional job growth has passed so job seekers have to be selective about the areas of Virginia they can count on to find work.

SPOTLIGHT ON RICHMOND

Despite recent layoffs due to the nagging national recession, the Richmond-Petersburg area remains a vital part of the state's economy, accounting for 16 percent of nonagricultural employment. In the last decade the region recorded remarkable growth, adding more than 40,000 service-related jobs and 20,000 positions in retail trade. Moreover, manufacturing declined only slightly, losing just over 1,000 slots.

These patterns are projected to continue. The Richmond manufacturing base is considered very stable, with major employers such as Allied Chemicals and James River Paper. As many as 92,000 manufacturing and construction job openings are expected in this decade. Government employment should follow a similar trend. As the state capital,

Richmond has long been identified as a rock-solid center for government jobs, adding about 4,000 state positions in the last decade. Budget cutbacks have made government employment prospects less than rosy, but slight advances are expected after the recovery sets in.

Of course, services should continue to be the major job producer with 45,000 openings anticipated and encouraged by the steady demand for health services at area hospitals. Openings are expected for paralegals, medical technicians, computer operators, and clerical workers. With its modest downtown skyline and proximity to Washington, D.C., Richmond counts several corporate headquarters, including Reynolds Metal Company, Philip Morris USA, and Ethyl Corporation. In turn, the expansion, and a corresponding increase in population, should fuel retail employment. Like many cities, however, Richmond has lost major downtown retailers to suburban malls and shopping centers. Many of the some 23,000 retail job openings will likely be found in suburban-based discounters such as Wal-Mart and Kmart.

SPOTLIGHT ON NORFOLK—VIRGINIA BEACH— NEWPORT NEWS

During the 1980s this became an area of strong growth and relative influence. Population grew by a solid 20 percent and nearly 200,000 new jobs were added. Norfolk is the U.S. Navy's largest homeport and shipyard, so much of this success was related to increases in defense spending— as much as 3 percent of the total U.S. defense budget is allocated to this region. With defense cuts looming large, fears of the future overwhelm the relatively serene past.

During 1991 unemployment remained below 6 percent and fewer than 4,000 jobs out of 585,000 were lost. Driven hard by low-paying jobs in the tourism sector, this region has avoided the disastrous aspects of the recession but job losses are not uncommon especially in construction, finance, insurance, and real estate. According to regional planners such as John W. Whaley, the recovery will take place slowly throughout 1992. Health-care services should not be affected by defense cuts but the other sectors will be.

In brief, except for a few employment areas, a watchful waiting outlook is the best approach to take here, at least through the end of 1992.

Washington

Washington has been one of the more rapidly growing states in the nation for several decades. Drawn by the extraordinary natural beauty of the place as well as its strong, expanding economy, more than 1.5 million people have been added to the population in only the last 20 years. Most of this population growth has taken place in the Seattle-Tacoma metropolitan area (the last census revealed a 22 percent increase in one decade) so every economic development in this region has consequences statewide. And recently the watchwords for the labor market have been the ones that should give job seekers pause: ''changing'' and ''mixed.''

The statewide unemployment rate rose steadily during the last part of 1991 and early 1992, hovering close to 8 percent at times. Although the Seattle area had a small net gain in the number of jobs at the end of 1991 compared to 1990, the state as a whole had more than a 3 percent decline, losing 16,000 jobs. State officials remained predictably optimistic but there are signs of change everywhere. The region's traditional industries of forest products, aerospace, agriculture, and fisheries are currently in a state of flux.

Legislation protecting old growth forests has reduced the supply of timber, thus creating a 2.7 percent decrease, from

41,600 to 38,800 in jobs in the lumber industry from the third quarter of 1990 to the same period in 1991. Projections for employment from 1995 to 2005 indicate a leveling off in the number of jobs to around 45,300 statewide.

The national recession has seriously affected the aerospace industry. Cutbacks on orders from around the country caused Boeing to announce a lay-off of approximately 6,500 employees in early 1992. This lay-off was not foreseen during the third quarter of 1991 by forecasters who had been predicting employment growth in this industry from 111,800 in 1998, to 123,500 in 1995, and 131,400 by 2000. However, since 40 percent of Boeing's products are currently traded abroad, sales estimates and profits for the future are not tied exclusively to the U.S. market so these recent lay-offs were seen by most observers as temporary.

With approximately one-third of the state's area devoted to farming, and its proximity to the ocean, agriculture and fishing have long been important to the economy of Washington. Apples, cherries, wheat, and potatoes are the major cash crops. Although the total earnings of agriculture and fisheries employees were projected to increase by over 25 percent between 1988 and 2000, the number of jobs should decrease in the agricultural sector from 81,800 to 76,600; the fisheries anticipate a rise in employment of over 40 percent, from 45,300 to 64,900 jobs, during the corresponding time period. Increased research in fish farming opportunities in Washington is fueled by the rising demand for seafood in the U.S. and abroad.

Construction and retail trade saw a downturn in the last quarter of 1991. However, both industries are expected to recover by mid–1992, and modest but steady growth has been predicted from 1995 to 2000. The 136,200 construction jobs in 1988 are predicted to swell to 153,500 by 2000. Retail positions should rise from 423,200 in 1988 to 504,900 by the turn of the next century. State and local government employment grew by 4.2 percent (324,700 to 338,400) from 1990 to 1991. Various forecasters have predicted growth in government work, some estimates as high as 9 percent, translating to 369,000 jobs by 1996.

Services employ about 23 percent of all the workers in Washington, 630,800 out of 2.5 million. Despite suffering some setbacks in 1991, projections indicate a 25 percent rise in the number of service jobs in the next eight years. The increases in demand for services is across the board: auto repair, recreation, lodging, business, health, legal, and education.

Dennis Fusco, Chief Economist for the Employment Security Department of Washington, predicts that "the Washington economy will be able to skirt the recession's full impact and still grow despite the national economy's slipping in the last twelve months." He cites Boeing as a major component of Washington's economic stability because "as Washington's largest employer, Boeing has been able to maintain a stable employment base due to a four year backlog on commercial orders."

Commercial projects account for around 80 percent of Boeing's business. Also, the "growth of the state's economy during the late '80s and early '90s carried this state through until as late as December of 1991." Fusco projects that Washington's economic growth rate will be back up to its historical average by 1993, and the unemployment rate should run "close to or below the national average."

The long-term prospects for Washington's economy are even stronger. Its location on the Pacific rim makes it an ideal center for foreign, Alaskan, and West Coast trade. The ports of Seattle, Tacoma, Bellingham, and Olympia are linked with each other and the Pacific via Puget Sound. The Tri-Cities area and Vancouver (Wash.) are located along the Columbia River, which also connects to the Pacific. Several ports in Washington also open directly onto the ocean. Washington's export dollars per capita now run twice the national average and with U.S. trade, especially with Asia, poised for even greater expansion that figure should increase significantly.

SPOTLIGHT ON
SEATTLE-TACOMA

Over 1.1 million people are employed in the Seattle-Tacoma area, more than half of all the workers in the state. In 1991 it ranked third among major metros (behind Houston and Denver) in the number of new jobs added, over 11,000 altogether. Services, government, and retail sales increased while manufacturing, construction, and wholesale trade decreased.

In early 1992 the unemployment rate remained below 7 percent in Seattle, significantly below that of the state's, which hovered around 8 percent. Tacoma's was higher than Seattle's but basically they both reflected a flattened-out economy.

As mentioned earlier so much of Seattle-Tacoma's future will depend on the true health of Boeing with its 90,000-plus work force. Nonetheless, there is increasing diversity here; other major employers include several utilities (U.S. West Communications, 8,500 employees, Puget Power, 2,500, Seattle City Light, 2,000); financial institutions (Seafirst Bank, 5,900, Security Pacific, 4,500); airlines (United, 3,000, Northwest, 2,200, Alaska, 1,500); and retail trade (Safeway, 10,000, Sears, 8,400, Nordstrom, 6,000). High tech companies have been successful here but they don't create a great many jobs—witness that the world-famous Microsoft employs only 3,000 people.

This is very much a professional, white-collar area and growing more that way each year. In King County, for example, 80 percent of all the job openings over the last five years have been in white-collar sectors. According to Gary Bodeutsch, Director of Labor Market and Economic Analysis at the state's Employment Security Department, the professional occupations, especially lawyers and even architects, have been growing at far above the average national rate. So too have health care occupations, and computer systems analysts and programmers.

So although the outlook for this part of the country is mixed for job seekers, the highly educated and the well-trained will fare well at least over the next few years.

West Virginia

A West Virginia Division of Employment Security official, with both clarity and economy, described the state's job picture in early 1991: "West Virginia is, as usual, out of step." Indeed, West Virginia shared little of the good times associated with the 1982–1990 economic expansion and registered some gains only as the national economy began to slip toward recession. A state that practically defined the term "Appalachia," West Virginia may be "almost heaven" in song, but it is almost nothing for the job seeker in the early 1990s. Between now and 2000, West Virginia is projected to create less than 5,000 new positions a year, a very modest 6 percent of all job openings annually, and one in three of those new positions will be unskilled, low-paid retailing or food-service jobs.

West Virginia has pockets of stability and even some growth surrounded by mountainous, rural areas that have never enjoyed any real prosperity—even when coal was king. The problem with West Virginia's mineral wealth, a state employment official noted, was that the coal and other basic products were shipped out of state for processing. The jobs were elsewhere, and in time the mining jobs disappeared. Coal is still a major industry in West Virginia, but it no longer is a large employer. By the end of the 1980s, the state had about 28,000 coal miners, out of a total work force exceeding 700,000.

In its recent history, West Virginia always has had more people than jobs, and it lost 8 percent of its population in the 1980s, declining to 1.8 million residents in 1990. The growth of its work force late in the decade reversed a trend that had been continuing since the 1970s. In short, West Virginia has been plagued with a labor surplus for decades, and nothing will reverse that trend in the next few years. Still, the state offers some opportunities for job seekers who fit into specific niches.

The biggest surge in West Virginia employment most likely will come from the federal government, and largely as a result of Sen. Robert Byrd's efforts to assist his state. The powerful senator has secured the FBI fingerprint center for the Clarksburg area, and it is scheduled to provide some 2,500 jobs in the near future. Also, 700 jobs are scheduled to be added at the Bureau of Public Debt in Parkersburg, raising employment there to 1,900 by 1994.

SPOTLIGHT ON CHARLESTON

The state capital and West Virginia's largest city, Charleston is probably the brightest spot on the state map. Despite the recession, a considerable amount of job-producing construction is underway in the south-central part of the state. A regional economic development official said most of the construction is split between institutional and commercial jobs, although some industrial work is on the books. Rhone-Poulenc AG Company is building a $40-million chemical-manufacturing facility near Institute, site of a large Union Carbide installation.

Among the other Charleston-area construction projects are a $6-million business park, a regional postal distribution center, a major state prison and a regional jail. (No, the state is not experiencing a crime wave. West Virginia's selling points include a low crime rate, one of the lowest in the country, and an inexpensive cost of living.)

Economic-development officials said the state's modern telecommunications system is also helping the area to attract back-office operations. Group Hospital Medical Services, based in Washington, D.C., will be moving 735 jobs to remodeled quarters in Charleston. Most of those jobs will require some computer proficiency but will pay up to $8 an hour.

Although not encountering a technological boom, Charleston will be getting a small research and development group that will be hiring 35 to 40 engineers, the development official said.

On the manufacturing front, no change is good news, and Charleston development officials expect some modest gains after dark days in the 1980s, when unemployment zoomed to 18 percent. A Canadian manufacturer is scheduled to build a plastics recycling plant in the area.

The construction growth extends as well to the state's eastern panhandle area around Martinsburg. With the growth in federal employment both in the District of Columbia and surrounding states, the commuting ring is now extending into West Virginia's easternmost area. Other major construction projects are power plants between Morgantown and Clarksburg, in the state's northern segment, and a $25-million psychiatric hospital in Weston, located south of Clarksburg. Construction was West Virginia's growth industry as the 1990s began, adding 8.8 percent more jobs from fiscal 1989 to the end of fiscal 1990.

SPOTLIGHT ON WHEELING

As much as any other part of the state, the Wheeling area is going against the flow. While steel is a declining industry in many parts of the country, it is experiencing a rebound after some very tough times in the area known as West

Virginia's northern panhandle. Nonetheless, steel hardly represents a growth industry; over the last two decades, the United Steelworkers of America has lost more than one-quarter of its membership.

Weirton Steel, the nation's largest employee-owned company, is the state's largest employer, ahead of three public-sector employers, West Virginia University, the state highways department and the U.S. Postal Service. In partnership with Nissan Steel of Japan, Wheeling-Pittsburgh Steel is adding a new fabricating line as part of a $550-million Japanese investment in the region.

Economic-development officials believe the most likely area for job development lies in back-office business services. Chesapeake and Potomac Telephone, for instance, is running some collections and data-processing functions out of Wheeling. The operation has been adding approximately 100 entry-level jobs a year. Wheeling's largest employers are two hospitals, a part of the fast-growing medical-services sector. Statewide, health services are projected to account for one of every eight new jobs each year, with West Virginia requiring a total of 880 registered nurses and 530 licensed practical nurses each year to fill vacancies and new positions.

SPOTLIGHT ON PARKERSBURG

Located on the Ohio River about 100 miles downstream from Wheeling, Parkersburg has remained stable, in part because it has no mining and relatively little heavy manufacturing. Its largest operation is a Du Pont chemical plant, and Parkersburg also has a General Electric plastics plant. With the Bureau of Public Debt, where all U.S. Savings Bonds are printed and ultimately destroyed, they are the area's largest employers. Economic-development officials are seeking light-manufacturing operations for the region, and its airport industrial park now is filled to capacity.

Wisconsin

Only eight states added more than 15,000 jobs to their work force in 1991; Wisconsin, surprisingly, was one of them. With such success during a recession it's no surprise that prospects for the future are not in the least bit guarded.

Wisconsin bills itself as ''America's Dairyland,'' but its economy includes much more than farming. Although agriculture—both dairy and meat—dominates the economy of the eastern part of the state, the eastern region has a high concentration of manufacturing employment (machinery production in the southeast, including Milwaukee, and paper products manufacturing further north). Tourism, particularly in the beautiful northern part of the state near Lake Superior and on the Door County peninsula in Lake Michigan, also constitutes an important sector of Wisconsin's economy.

Wisconsin's population growth provides evidence of the health of the state's economy: While Ohio, Michigan, and Iowa have lost population in recent years, Wisconsin's population has not only increased but has done so at a rate that outstrips those of both Indiana and Illinois. During the 1980s almost 200,000 people were added to the census figures, a growth of 4 percent.

From 1985 to 1990, the number of business establishments in Wisconsin grew by more than 13,500. These new concerns ranged across service industries (a 17 percent increase in the number of companies), finance/insurance/real estate (17 percent), wholesale trade (16 percent), transportation/public utilities (12 percent), construction (11 percent), manufacturing (11 percent), and retail trade (7 percent). In 1990, businesses constructed nearly seven million square feet of new industrial space and invested more than one billion dollars in capital projects, which resulted in the creation of almost 5,000 new jobs. Areas represented by these expansions ranged from food products to litho printing to leather goods to industrial equipment, to name just a few. Medical services also represent a major employer in Wisconsin—hospitals statewide employ more than 78,000. The Wisconsin Department of Industry, Labor and Human Relations (DILHR) predicts a 12 percent growth in the number of Wisconsin jobs between 1985 and 1995. The leading fields are service and professional and technical occupations, which the DILHR calculates will grow by 16 percent. The DILHR also estimates growth in sales professions at 15 percent, followed by the managerial sector (14 percent) and clerical and production and maintenance areas (8 percent each).

Well-known American companies are located in Wisconsin, including Harley-Davidson (Milwaukee), Miller Brewing (Milwaukee), Lands' End (Dodgeville), American Family Insurance (Madison), Rayovac Corporation (Madison), and Oscar Mayer Foods (Madison). In 1992 Kimberly-Clark will open a $90 million plant in Neenah as well as expand their nearby Lakeview plant. These additions will increase the number of jobs Kimberly-Clark provides to more than 7,000, 25 percent of which have been created over the past five to six years. Similarly, Great Lakes Instruments, a manufacturer of devices for measuring and controlling water, will be expanding its work force by 25 percent when its new Milwaukee plant opens.

In addition to Milwaukee and Madison, the Racine/Kenosha area about 20 miles south of Milwaukee also has job opportunities. The J.I. Case Company, which manufacturers tractors, employs 3,000 people; S.C. Johnson & Sons (better known for Johnson Wax) provides jobs for 2,600; the Western Publishing Company has 1,500 emloyees; and Twin Disc Inc. (maker of clutches and transmissions for boats and heavy equipment) and St. Luke's Hospital each employ

1,000 people. Other cities that offer the chance for employment include Green Bay and Oshkosh.

Businesses choose to locate in Wisconsin for a wide variety of reasons. First, Wisconsin's location and transportation facilities furnish easy access to regional, national, and international commerce. Wisconsin boasts international airports, major rail lines, interstate highways, and access to Great Lakes shipping through ports on Lakes Michigan and Superior. Second, the highly rated University of Wisconsin system, the numerous private colleges and universities, and the extensive network of two-year and technical colleges produces a large pool of educated and skilled workers. Third, health care spending throughout the state increased at the lowest rate in the country between 1980 and 1990, in large part due to the widespread availability of HMOs. Wisconsin also had the lowest per capita hospital expenses in the Midwest at $629 per person, well below the national average of $746 per person.

SPOTLIGHT ON MILWAUKEE

The Milwaukee metropolitan area (including the four counties of Milwaukee, Ozaukee, Washington, and Waukesha) encompasses nearly 1.4 million people, the 31st largest metro in the United States.

Manufacturing has traditionally occupied the largest sector of employment. Because of the rapid growth of service-oriented jobs and a leaner manufacturing sector, however, the number of service employees surpassed the number of manufacturing workers for the first time in 1986. In 1987 (the latest figures available) the city had 181,500 service jobs (26.0 percent of the total nonfarm wage and salary employment) while manufacturing provided 168,600 jobs (24.2 percent). Other major sectors of employment included the government (11.7 percent), transportation and public utilities (4.9 percent), and construction (3.3 percent). Different types of manufacturing in Milwaukee include motor vehicle parts and accessories, industrial machinery, plastic products, leather tanning and finishing, and beer brewing. Historically, Milwaukee's unemployment rate has trailed that of the United States as a whole, and that pattern has continued even through the recession when it remained below 6 percent.

Milwaukee's largest employers fall into both the manufacturing and service sectors, with particular emphasis on health services. Briggs and Stratton, a manufacturer of engines for lawn mowers, provides the most jobs in the area, 7,000, followed by WFSI (a health-care organization), which employs 6,500 people, and Aurora Health Care, which employs 5,400. Other major Milwaukee-area employers are Wisconsin Bell and Allen-Bradley (an electronics manufacturer) at 4,500 people each, and General Electric Medical Systems Group, A.O. Smith (auto and truck frames), and Quad/Graphics at 4,000 people each. General Motors' two area auto parts plants provide a total of 3,600 jobs in the area.

Based on recent trends, the Metropolitan Milwaukee Association of Commerce predicts that future growth will occur primarily in the service sector, particularly in the areas of health, business, educational, and legal services. In addition, growth has occurred in finance, insurance, and real estate and in wholesale and retail trade. Standard and Poor's recently confirmed this optimistic view by giving the city an AA+ credit rating.

SPOTLIGHT ON MADISON

Seventy miles to the west of Milwaukee lies Madison, Wisconsin's second largest city and the state capital. Dane County, which includes Madison, is the state's fastest growing county. In 1990, the area recorded an increase of 7,500 jobs—a 3.6 percent rise over 1989. Most of these jobs were in manufacturing, government, retail trade, and services. Since 1980, the number of jobs in the county has increased in services (a 52 percent rise), finance (48 percent), wholesale and retail trade (39 percent), transportation and utilities (30 percent), manufacturing (29 percent), construction (26 percent), and government (5 percent).

Throughout 1991 the unemployment rate here was below 4 percent, and for obvious reasons. Madison's largest employers are the state government (40,200 jobs), the Madison Metropolitan School District (3,150), Wisconsin Physicians' Service Insurance (3,145), Meriter Hospital (3,100), the United States government (3,000), American Family Insurance (3,000), and Oscar Mayer Foods (2,800).

American Family is building their new national headquarters in Madison, which will create a projected 20,000 new jobs when completed. The Wisconsin Department of Labor and Human Relations predicts the following increases in the number of employment positions in Dane County between 1988 and 2000: service, 25.9 percent; executive, administrative, and managerial, 25.5 percent; agriculture services, 25.5 percent; marketing and sales positions, 24.6 percent; professional, paraprofessional, and technical, 22.3 percent; administrative support/clerical, 17.2 percent; precision production, craft, and repair, 15.8 percent; and operators, fabricators, and laborers, 13.7 percent. These estimates represent a total of 50,000 new jobs in the Madison area.

Wyoming

Wyoming is probably the place to go if you are looking for work in the great outdoors or if you want to live without hordes of people cramping your space. Only Alaska has fewer people per square mile than Wyoming's 4.7 (compared to neighboring Utah's 21.0, or Colorado's 31.8) and even that figure is declining as people continue to leave the state in a slow but steady stream. At the last census (1990) Wyoming ranked last in total population (453,588) after a decline of 3.4 percent since 1980.

Despite this fallback in population the total number of nonagricultural jobs increased by over 4,000 during 1991 and unemployment remained below 6 percent. About 75 percent of Wyoming's small work force of 237,000 is involved in the service sector, with about 40,000 employed in retail trade and almost 15,000 in eating and drinking places. Tourism is responsible for much of this especially in the northwest part of the state, home of Yellowstone National Park and its nearly three million visitors a year.

Government, relatively speaking, is a major employer in Wyoming with over 57,000 people, 36,000 of whom work for local agencies. Of these 21,000 are teachers, which is the only occupation that will witness a moderately strong increase in new job opportunities over the next several years.

A number of specific occupations are expected to see some growth in the next year. They are (with total number of openings expected each year until 1993): secretaries in all fields (750), general managers and top executives (502), salespersons (428), waiters and waitresses (391), registered nurses (268), and nursing aides and orderlies (238). These figures are from the state's Department of Employment and may be a bit optimistic as Wyoming's work force continues to shift.

Agriculture, cattle ranching, and mining remain key aspects of Wyoming's economy despite the declining number of workers in these areas. Indeed, the vast majority of Wyoming's land is used for grazing by cattle ranchers. And no other state in the country produces more coal. However, while technology has increased production in these fields, it has also put many Wyoming residents out of a job. Many displaced workers who have moved to the urban areas around Cheyenne and Casper have discovered that the only jobs available are low skill, minimum wage jobs, said Mike Paris, executive director of the Wyoming Occupation Coordinating Council. How this will all play out in the years ahead remains to be seen.

WHERE THE JOBS ARE

OCCUPATION

The Five Standard Professions

Accountants

There are about 1 million accountants in the United States and only 10 percent of them are self-employed. With so many working in the corporate sector it's not surprising that the recession has seriously rattled this once unflappable profession. The current situation is a far cry from the booming 1980s when an accounting degree was a ticket to the fast track in business. The hours were long, pay was high, and promotions were frequent. But when the bottom fell out, so did many of the keepers of the bottom line.

However, even in a recession, the books must be kept. Financial planning becomes more important than ever—so accountants are still finding jobs in selected areas. According to a survey by Robert Half International, a major recruiting firm, several types of accountants are in demand, especially in the credit and collection fields. "In slow economic times such as these, specialists who can increase the flow of of payments into a company—credit and collections, accounts receivable and cash management experts—are in greatest demand," says Max Messmer, chairman and CEO of Robert Half.

Another specialty in demand is the "forensic" or investigative accountants who look for financial wrongdoing or mismanagement, arising in many cases from mergers and the recession. "Investigative accountants are being called in to advise companies whether to declare bankruptcy or take the necessary steps to remain solvent," Messmer said.

To keep payrolls at a lower level, both corporations and public firms are relying on staff or junior accountants with one to five years' experience rather than more highly paid middle managers. "The stronger demand for more junior accountants is, in part, a response to financial pressure," said Messmer. "They are being given increased responsibility as companies strive to boost productivity."

And going one step further, many companies are hiring on a part-time basis only. "We find that both public accounting firms and corporations are trying to keep the head count low but they still need the manpower to do the work," says Frank Riniti, a partner with Source Finance, a national placement agency. He notes increased demand for accountants on a per diem basis: "We are placing people at positions for periods of three months up to a year. Some of these companies laid off so many people that they now don't have enough to get the work done." The demand for temporary work is "across the board" in all types of firms, says Riniti.

Full-time hiring is found in pharmaceutical companies and hospitals, according to Riniti. "The pharmaceutical industry as a whole is expanding, partly pushed by demand for new drugs. The health care field is also doing well, particularly hospitals. Accountants with specialized knowledge of hospital work, especially the insurance reimbursement end, are constantly in demand," he says.

Several studies have found other areas of growth. Robert Half reports increased demand in import/export, biotechnology and manufacturing, especially for auditors, cost accountants, and in some areas of the country, accounting generalists. In Source Finance's 1991 *Salary Survey,* experts predict growing demand for accountants with tax, audit and consulting experience on an international level to deal with the newly formed European Common Market and Pacific Rim countries.

Another strong area is small- and mid-sized financial services companies. "The big boys are laying off, but the smaller firms which invested more conservatively and stayed away from junk bonds are doing some hiring because they have weathered the recession better," said Michael Zaremski, placement manager for Robert Half in New York.

When jobs are available, industry-related experience, knowledge of computer spreadsheet programs, and certification as a CPA or CMA are all assets, if not requirements, for many positions. "The more qualified you are the better chance you have of getting hired," said Riniti. "Firms are hiring qualified people, even over-qualified people."

Architects

For the nation's 85,000 architects, these are not easy times. Conventional wisdom in early 1992 claimed that there was good news and bad news for architects looking for work: the good news was that the job market was not going to get much worse; the bad news was it is going to be this way for some time.

Employment problems in architecture (and its allied fields like construction and engineering) is a leading indicator of downturns in the economy, and it lags behind other occupations in picking back up when the economy rebounds. Or as James Vermeulens, president of Vermeulens, Inc., a Toronto-based consulting firm of construction economists, notes, in recessionary times architects tend to "go in faster and come out slower."

Complicating matters, architecture tends to remain locally based. Even in an age of increasing national and global business, most architecture firms are small (some 80 percent employ 10 or fewer and over 60 percent have only one architect on staff) and closely linked to their local economies and contacts within their communities. In the 1980s this meant that as different regions of the country offered the opportunity to work, architects could relocate to follow the economy: from Texas to New England, from New England to California, wherever new building was being done. But now, an informal national survey conducted by Richard Fitzgerald, Executive Director of the Boston Society of Architects, at the end of 1991 delivered a clear message: "no work anywhere." Indeed, forty of the forty-eight respondents recommended that architects "stay put."

Nonetheless, Vermeulens said when the economy rebounds not all regions will be equal in terms of creating architectural work. He points to regions that have suffered longer down times as the most likely candidates to begin to grow again and he includes oil-producing states like Texas and mid-central cities such as Cleveland and Cincinnati in that group. Further, architects provide services to many kinds of clients: retail, commercial, residential, institutional, educational, and the government. Some of these sectors, particularly commercial and residential, have been hit harder than others and some, such as institutional and government, are expected to remain steady.

For someone already established, it means stay where you are; for someone just starting out it means being willing to look for work in many places and many guises. Stephen Dill, Vice President of Consulting for Architects/Boston, agrees there are no easy answers but counsels that architects "as professionals or individuals in the 1990s be flexible and willing to creatively consider each opportunity." Wherever that may be.

Dentists

For most adult Americans, a visit to the dentist is associated either with middle-aged decay or with the remembrance of childhood terrors. Despite the fact that we know how important their work is, how vital to good health, dentists are rarely afforded the same respect as doctors or even lawyers.

No wonder all polls say the status of dentists is not very high.

One thing that does remain high for America's approximately 150,000 professionally active dentists is the size of their incomes. The average net income of dentists in general practice who were incorporated was approximately $140,000 according to a recent survey. Many dentists hold more than one job as well.

High income and steady, relatively stress-free work helped to increase the number of dentists by more than 30 percent during the late '70s and early 1980s. Since the population grew by only 10 percent during that period, there has been a marked increase in competition among dentists. One sign of this is the use of the cut-rate dental clinic in shopping malls and department stores around the country.

Despite the upsurge in the number of dentists, and the fact that kids don't get cavities at the same rate (about 40 percent have none) because of fluoridation, predictions for opportunities in the next decade are positive. The Bureau of Labor Statistics, for example, estimates that new positions will grow by 15 percent. The reasons are simple: Since 1975 the number of Americans covered by dental insurance has more than tripled to over 90 million, so those covered will be more likely to visit a dentist. Also, Americans—and American teeth—are aging, requiring more dental care. In addition the number of students enrolled in dental school has declined by a full third to about 4,000 so competition should decline.

Doctors

With all the current talk about controlling the costs of health care it's not surprising that some people are convinced that there are too many doctors in the United States. In fact predictions of a doctor glut date back to the mid–1960s when there were fewer than 300,000 practicing physicians, about 160 per 100,000 people. By 1988 there were over 510,000 and a rate greater than 210 per 100,000, but nevertheless no one today talks too seriously about an oversupply, at least not on the national level. The Department of Labor predicts that the number of doctors will grow rapidly over the next ten years and so do the medical schools, who turn out about 15,000 graduates a year.

What is different today is the heavy concentration of established physicians in the prime metropolitan areas meaning that many new doctors have to consider geographic location as well as medical specialty when planning their futures. The state with the highest concentration of physicians in 1988, the latest figures available, was Maryland with a rate of 325 per 100,000 population (doubtless the presence of the National Institutes of Health distorts this figure), followed by Massachusetts (322), New York (307), and California (242). The states with the smallest concentration of MDs were all those with a high percentage of people living in rural areas, Idaho (120), Wyoming (134), Alaska (138), South Dakota (138), Arkansas (144), Iowa (145), Oklahoma (145), Indiana (151), and South Carolina (156).

Most doctors prefer to work in urban areas, with the lure of good salaries and the desire for social amenities allowing them to avoid the rural way of life. Some of this is being brought on by the rise of HMOs and other managed care systems, some by increasing specialization among the younger doctors who see no opportunities in sparsely settled regions. As a result by 1988 there were 111 counties in the U.S. with a total population of 325,000 that had no physicians at all. Over half a million rural residents lived in counties with no obstetric care and 49 million with no psychiatrist. The American Academy of Family Physicians estimates that 2,000 counties are underserved by doctors.

Since slightly more than 25 percent of all Americans live in rural areas the federal government recently decided it was necessary to provide incentives for doctors to practice in what it refers to as Health Manpower Shortage Areas (HMSAs). Administered by the National Health Service Corps this program provides for loan repayments (up to $20,000 a year for four years) as well as scholarships for any doctor willing to undertake primary care duties in these areas. Since most medical students have $50,000 to $60,000 in loans it's easy to understand the attraction.

The federal government is also pushing medical students to return to family practice (an estimated 35,000 are needed). The government's intention, probably mistaken, is that the general practitioner will charge less than the specialist, and not require as many tests, thus saving the taxpayer a lot of money. Since most Americans are far more concerned about getting the right treatment than saving money, as some critics point out, they will probably find a way to go to the specialist of their choice.

It's too early to tell whether or not the government's approach will cause more doctors to go into family practice. For now the specialities with the best potential for growth appear to be radiology, geriatrics, neurology, and emergency medicine.

For further evidence of the very solid future in store for just about everyone in medicine see *Health Care*.

Lawyers

It is not within the scope of this book to discuss whether or not there are too many lawyers in America, although we sure do have a lot of them. In fact 70 percent of all the lawyers in the world live in the United States. Over 730,000 people here have law degrees (up from only 486,000 in 1980, and 280,000 in 1970) and about 600,000 of them practice law today. Moreover, our law schools are graduating over 30,000 new ones a year.

Now the question that *is* germane to this book can be more readily addressed. If I go to law school will I be able to get a job? The chances are excellent that you will find a very good job if you do very well academically at a top-notch law school, very good if you do very well at a good law school, and good if you do well anywhere else. In 1990, according to the National Association of Law Placement, 84 percent of those graduating with a JD degree found work "substantially legal in character." About 28 percent of all graduates entered public service (government, public interest organizations, judicial clerkships, etc.), an area that continues to grow as the competition for high-paying jobs in the largest law firms grows more intense each year.

Most new lawyers (63 percent in 1990) still enter private practice and since the national bill for legal services is expected to rise in 1992 by 10 percent to $110 billion there should be enough to go around. In fact, according to the *National Law Journal*'s annual survey of the nation's largest law firms, 137 of the top 250 had a net increase in the number of attorneys in 1991. The two largest firms in the United States, Baker and McKenzie, and Jones, Day, Reavis and Pogue, grew by 61 and 57 new lawyers, respectively.

Firms that are expanding attribute their growth to new emphasis on specific practice areas. In other words if you want a good job in this field, as in so many others, learn a specialty. Today law firms that specialize in bankruptcy, corporate debt refinancing, and environmental law are faring much better than their counterparts whose expertise is in financial services and real estate. Firms polled by the *National Law Journal* report that bankruptcy is the number one area contributing to growth. Not surprisingly, many firms are restructuring to take advantage of these trends. One example is the top New York law firm, Skadden, Arps, Meagher and Flom, which has, according to the *Wall Street Journal*, expanded its bankruptcy and reorganization department from 20 lawyers two years ago to more than 80 currently.

Expansion is also taking place in the international law arena and American firms are stepping up their global presence. The collapse of communism, the reunification of Germany, and the scheduled opening of the European Common Market this year have raised the prospects of doing an increased amount of business with both Eastern and Western Europe. According to the NLJ survey, the nation's 250 largest firms have more than 2,000 lawyers in 244 branch offices in 48 cities around the world.

Brussels, Belgium, the capital of the European Community, is a city targeted by 27 of the top 250 firms for branch offices. There is a total of 217 lawyers from these firms in Brussels, up from 153 a year ago.

Reunified Germany is also encouraging American firms to open offices there by adopting a policy which allows foreign firms to practice before the German bar. Nine new offices were started in Frankfurt by firms in the top 250 in 1991.

Back in the U.S., corporate law departments are gaining new ground in the legal world not only in numbers but also in the power they have in dealing with outside firms. Many corporations have expanded the number of their in-house counsel due to the high cost of outside legal fees and complex litigation. More and more work is being handled by corporate law departments. Corporate lawyers often specialize within their companies in energy, antitrust, employment discrimination, product liability, and pension funds. The largest corporate staff is at American Telephone & Telegraph (909), followed by Exxon (454), General Electric (410), Prudential Insurance (204), and Ford (192).

It would be terribly misleading, however, not to mention some of the less-than-positive aspects about the current employment situation. Times are especially tough at large law firms for lawyers who have reached the limit of their tenure as an associate and are not offered a partnership, meaning they have to leave that firm. Although the numbers are not tallied by anyone there's sufficient anecdotal evidence to suggest that many are being caught in this pinch often quite unexpectedly. Some of this is the result of pressure from clients to reduce legal fees (see the entry below on "Legal Assistants"), and some from the increasing number of young lawyers who will work for less.

There are thus many talented lawyers out of work. While seeking full-time law jobs, some lawyers keep body and soul together by working through temporary placement agencies. The major advantage of using a temporary agency, besides the paycheck, is the chance to work at a top firm for several months and to build a stronger resume in a specialized area. The major temporary agencies include:

DC Legal Support Inc., Washington D.C.

Special Counsel Inc., New York

Lawsmiths, Los Angeles

Lawyer's Lawyer, Washington, D.C.

All of the above information concerns the short-term outlook for lawyers' employment. Over the next ten years or so, however, the Bureau of Labor sees a need for at least another 150,000 lawyers, perhaps as many as 240,000, so there should be sufficient legal work to go around even if we continue to create 30,000 new lawyers a year. Of course their number may begin to decline soon as the cost of law school begins to outweigh its financial promise.

Location should be a major consideration for all lawyers—new or experienced—seeking a job. In 1988, the latest year figures available, the American Bar Foundation calculated that there was one lawyer for every 473 people in the general population.

In that year the states with the highest concentration of lawyers were New York (1 for every 295 ordinary citizens); Massachusetts (1 for 318); Colorado (1 for 367); Connecticut (1 for 375); Alaska (1 for 387); New Jersey (1 for 393); Illinois (1 for 400); and California (1 for 402).

The states with the smallest concentration (many of which should offer excellent opportunities given their economic and population growths) were North Carolina (1 for 886 ordinary citizens); Arkansas (1 for 872); West Virginia (1 for 838); South Carolina (1 for 831); Mississippi (1 for 790); Alabama (1 for 777); and Indiana (1 for 765).

Of course the ultimate city for lawyers is Washington D.C., where they don't actually have to meet any ordinary citizens since there is a lawyer for every 40 persons.

Legal Assistants (Paralegals)   According to the Bureau of Labor Statistics this is one of the fastest growing professional occupations in America. By the year 2005 the number of legal assistants is projected to grow by over 75,000, an average of 5,000 a year. Job opportunities are available throughout the country, but according to the National Association of Legal Assistants, Inc. (NALA) in Tulsa, Oklahoma, most of them will be in major cities where the largest law firms are centered. NALA's most recent surveys indicate that future job prospects will be strongest in private firms with more than 90 attorneys, although a significant increase will also take place in all levels of government jobs. The federal government, for example, will utilize paralegals in almost every department, with the greatest number going to Justice, Treasury, Interior, Health and Human Services, and the General Services Administration.

The chief reason for this explosive growth is basically financial necessity. As more and more lawyers compete for business, especially in the corporate law field, the need to reduce the client's costs has become essential. Since legal assistants have an average billing rate to clients of $53 an hour while even first-year associates bill as much as $100 or more an hour, it is obvious why law firms are eager to show their clients how they are saving them money by using paralegals for everyday legal tasks.

There are several paths one can follow to become a legal assistant. Although a significant number of currently employed legal assistants have only an associate's degree there seems to be a trend toward more educational background as competition for these jobs leaps up. Many large firms, for example, simply look to hire college graduates and then train them in-house. More and more colleges are offering undergraduate programs for paralegals as well as postgraduate certification programs that can last anywhere from a few months to two years. (The American Bar Association has just begun to grant approvals to some of these programs and such certification is bound to help graduates seeking jobs.) In addition NALA has instituted a certification program that requires passing an exam that lasts two days; although this is a voluntary process there are signs that Certified Legal Assistants (CLA) are being hired more readily and at higher salaries. In 1990 the average annual compensation for CLAs nationwide was $29,900 compared to $27,700 for those without certification.

Science and Technology

Engineers

The outlook for today's 1.5 million engineers is not so much mixed as it is murky and confused. Because of the recent collapse of the Soviet Union and the imminent collapse of America's bloated defense budgets, thousands of engineering jobs will be lost in the near future, but how many will be replaced in other sectors of the economy—and how quickly—remains in the hands of the politician's budget-makers. The recent passage of the gargantuan transportation bill will unleash tens of billions of federal dollars into local economies and should create many jobs for civil engineers, design engineers and the like, but just how other funds may be diverted from the research and development of destructive weapons to more productive pursuits is not entirely clear, although some of society's needs are so pressing that speculation is not difficult.

According to many experts the most promising fields for engineers in the 1990s will be those related to the protection of the environment. Literally tens of thousands of engineering jobs are being created for the management of solid waste, the cleansing of toxic waste sites, as well as the monitoring and controlling of industrial pollution. (Of course older engineers will remember that in the 1960s nuclear power was the place to be while in the 1970s petroleum engineers were in the greatest demand, both fields with limited demand today.) According to the Association of Environmental Engineering Professors the universities are currently producing only about 2,000 of the 5,000 new engineers needed each year in this field. Employment opportunities exist throughout the country in both private industry (including the large corporations involved in oil exploration, and chemical production, as well as several major environmental engineering firms such as CH2M Hill in Denver) and at the federal, state and local levels of government as the enforcement of stricter pollution laws becomes essential for our future.

Chemical engineers will also benefit greatly from the "green movement." Many industries will be looking to chemical engineers to provide environmental experts, corrosion experts, etc., to supplement their staffs in the future. In particular Monsanto in Alabama and Mitre in Virginia are hiring chemical engineers: The Department of Energy is also seeking chemical engineers at the production reactor sites.

For mechanical engineers the job market also looks encouraging although the Bureau of Labor Statistics believes that most opportunities will result from the need to replace retiring engineers, rather than the creation of new jobs. Not surprisingly then most of the hundreds of ads for mechanical engineers we found in early 1992 were for those with five or more years of experience.

While the outlook is not exuberant, there are more employment opportunities for experienced electrical and electronics engineers than for most other engineering disciplines. The power industry—utilities, independent power producers and their suppliers—has been stable for some time but some parts of the country are still hiring. Those with openings in early 1992 included Central Hudson Gas & Electric (N.Y.), Green Mountain Power Corporation (Vermont), New York Power Authority (N.Y.), Western Farmers Electric Cooperative (Okla.), Tucson Electric Power Company (Ariz.), San Diego Gas & Electric (Calif.), and the Navajo Tribal Utility Authority (Ariz.). The Electric Power Research Institute (EPRI) in Palo Alto (Calif.) is looking for electrical engineers in their Electric Systems

Division. Other large companies seeking electrical engineers are SAIC in San Diego, and Martin Marietta in Orlando (Fla.). Some encouraging parts of the country for electrical engineers are Chicago, Washington, DC, and northern New Jersey.

Two other strong fields for electrical engineers include medical electronics and telecommunications. Some medical electronics firms that were hiring in early 1992 included Puritan-Bennett, Optical Sensors for Medicine, Abbott Laboratories, C.R. Bard, and Pfizer. Some hope in the telecommunications field includes Bell Labs, Bellcore, Inc., AT&T, and GTE.

Aerospace engineering and the companies devoted to it are as down as one would expect given diminishing defense and space-related budgets. It will be a while before these industries recover and become strong sources of employment, but it will happen.

The nuclear engineering field, which utilizes a wide variety of engineering disciplines, as well as those with nuclear training and experience, has been in a lull but is starting to bounce back. The power reactor business has, over the last 10–20 years, been the principal employer of nuclear engineers. Since, however, no new units have been ordered since the Three-Mile Island accident and several under construction have been cancelled, licensees (the owners and operators of the reactors) have not increased their need for nuclear engineers except in the areas of operations and maintenance. They have, however, maintained that need for a high quality engineering staff since safety and downtime are of vital importance.

The Nuclear Regulatory Commission (NRC), the overseeing regulator of the industry, has been seeking and hiring engineers in anticipation of the retirement of existing personnel who joined them in large numbers in the 1950s and 1960s when the business was starting in earnest and then again in the 1970s when a multitude of engineers became available at the end of the Apollo Project.

Within the next 10–15 years, the NRC expects a rebirth

of activity in the regulatory arena due to the need to review plans for new units of a standardized design as well as applications for renewal of existing 40-year licenses which are due to start lapsing around the turn of the century. Both these activities will require a large resource allotment by NRC and utilities as well as contractors to both.

The Department of Energy is also seeking to hire nuclear engineers for both the cleanup of the waste generated by government reactors used to produce weapons-grade material and for safe renewed operation of reactors (e.g., Savannah River in South Carolina) to be used for such in the future.

The preceding description of opportunities for engineers may strike some as a bit optimistic. We believe, however, that our own research has demonstrated that there are jobs available and we suggest the following approach to anyone seeking a job in this field.

An excellent and current source of such information is the technical journal or magazine usually published on a monthly basis. Examples include *Mechanical Engineering, Electrical World, Machine Design, Chemical Engineering News, Aviation Week and Space Technology Power, Nuclear News,* and *Graduating Engineer Magazine.* Each of these and others in more specific fields are available in any large or technical library and each has a standard section entitled something like ''Employment Opportunities.'' The articles and editorials in these trade publications should not be ignored—they occasionally include a discussion of a specific discipline or company that is currently in a strong growth period and may, therefore, be a source of immediate employment. This awareness of the company's current undertakings can be beneficial and discussion-provoking at the interview.

For a variety of engineering positions, several head hunters are doing some active advertising.

Another important source of current engineering employment opportunities is the On-Line Career Fair, which provides job seekers with a listing of available engineering positions with a variety of companies. A PC and a modem are all that's required; there are no fees and anonymity is possible if desired. Operated by Response Technologies Corporation (RTC) in Londonderry, New Hampshire, this system allows you to learn the background (including employee benefits) of those companies with the openings, and to leave a resume on-line so that the system can forward it to the employers of your choice. There are often several hundred jobs listed. Note that actual application to a specific company is not handled by the On-Line Career Fair, but names/addresses/phone numbers are made available for direct contact. This system is updated each week to assure currency. Hook-up to the system is accomplished by dialing (603) 432–2742. The password to be typed in when prompted is NEWJOB. To resolve problems or ask questions, prompt and courteous help is provided at (603) 437–7257 or (603) 437–7337.

No particular region of the country will have significantly greater demand for engineers beyond that dictated by population growth and economic development, but some organizations are more apt to be hiring engineers than others.

For example, a major source of engineering opportunities exists today in consulting firms. These companies vary in size from a handful to thousands of engineering employees. The smaller to medium-sized firms (less than 200–300 employees) are more stable and require substantial overtime when times are good but do not generally lay off when the work falls off. Frequent travel may be involved and weekly to monthly time away from home is often part of the job. Larger consulting firms are similar with regard to travel and time away from home but they are not known for stability or commitment to their employees. The peaks and valleys of contracts on hand dictate the number of engineers employed.

These consulting firms market their services to large, more stable engineering organizations in just about every field and discipline. They provide several crucial services including long- and-short term supplementary manpower for staff augmentation; they also contract for a specific project and handle it "cradle-to-grave" with minimal client oversight or they will simply provide specific expertise when required by an organization that does not keep such a specialist on their engineering staff. Marketing ability is often a job requirement as strong as engineering expertise. The larger consulting companies include Stone & Webster, Gibbs & Hill, Sargent & Lundy, Burns & Roe, Gilbert/ Commonwealth, Inc., etc. The trade journals are informative as to when these companies are hiring. In early 1992, for example, Sargent & Lundy was looking for a wide variety of mechanical and electrical engineers of varying experience although most openings call for 5–10 years or more of related work experience.

Several smaller consulting firms were interviewing for high quality engineers. Positions were available in several engineering disciplines, especially mechanical and electrical engineering at companies such as Dominion Engineering, Tenera, Harvey Personnel and Atometrics. Other small to medium-sized consulting firms that expect to be hiring during 1992 include Altran, Cygna, EPM, NES, Haliburton NUS and Impell. Several of these companies keep resumes on hand for "associates" or engineers who will be called if the company gets, or is looking to get, a contract where specific expertise is needed. Tenera keeps a file of "associates" 300 strong. A call to the personnel office of such a company will determine if they keep such a list. If so, they ask for no more than a resume to be kept on file. Such a system contributes to the stable nature of working full-time for the consulting firm.

There are also many openings today for various position levels, including department heads and deans, in the university environment. Salaries are generally less than equivalent experience would yield in industry but there *are* jobs here. Examples of those with positions recently available cover the entire country—Worcester Poly Tech, Univ. of Illinois at Chicago, Univ. of Colorado, Univ. of Iowa, Texas Tech Univ., Univ. of Dayton, Carnegie Mellon Univ., Univ. of Pennsylvania, Louisiana State Univ., Univ. of Houston, SUNY Institute of Technology at Utica/Rome, Arizona State Univ., Univ. of Oklahoma, Rensselaer Polytechnic Institute, Univ. of Delaware, Univ. of Massachusetts at Amherst, Univ. of Rhode Island, Univ. of North Carolina at Charlotte, Univ. of Alabama at Huntsville, Purdue Univ., Columbia Univ., Tulane Univ., Northeastern Univ., etc.

Finally, there are many engineering job opportunities these days outside the United States. The Leslie Corporation in Houston, Texas, is seeking mechanical engineers for jobs in Saudi Arabia. A program called USAID Electrification for the Atlantic Coast is now seeking experienced electrical engineers for remote area work in Nicaragua. Many industries in Japan have a high interest in American engineers especially in the fields of chemicals, electronics, automobiles, communications, information, shipbuilding, food, and pharmaceuticals. For further information on such opportunities, as well as in-depth insight into living and working there, a book has been published by ASME Press, entitled *Working In Japan: An Insider's Guide for Engineers*, available from the ASME Order Department at 1–800–843–2763 (FAX 201/882–1717) for $19.95 for ASME members and $24.95 for non-members. Excerpts appeared in the January 1992 issue of *Mechanical Engineering*. Mechanical engineering teaching positions are now being sought at the National University of Singapore. PhDs are in greatest demand and applications and information may be obtained from the North American Office in New York City at (212) 751–0331. (See also the entry, *Where the Jobs Are Overseas*.

Scientists

The job outlook for scientists will depend partly on two powerful and contradictory trends. On the one hand, the United States remains a highly technological culture dependent in many ways on its scientists' expertise; on the other hand, U.S. investment in research and development has begun to decline for the first time since the 1970s. This decline coincides with substantial increases by other countries, most notably Japan. Whether international competition in R&D will hasten American industrial decline or prompt a renewed effort to excel remains to be seen.

Predictably, certain specific fields will be affected more than others. Some 500,000 Americans are professional nonmedical scientists; experts in cutting-edge disciplines are more likely to join their ranks than those in more established areas. According to Betty Vetter, Executive Director of the Commission of Professionals in Science and Technology, the most promising fields are electronics, lasers, and biotechnology. "There's particularly intense excitement in the biological sciences," Vetter notes, "especially with the new work in genetic engineering." In addition, she notes that growing concerns about the natural environment will prompt scientific research and applications to solve problems of pollution and resource depletion.

Chemists

Some 80,000 chemists currently work in the United States. Most of these hold jobs in manufacturing firms—more than half in the chemical manufacturing industry, the rest throughout other industries. In addition, more than

19,000 people hold faculty positions in chemistry throughout academia. Job opportunities should be strong for the field overall for these reasons:

- The number of degrees granted in chemistry will not meet future demand;
- Research and development will continually expand;
- Demands for environmental protection will require increased attention from industry;
- The chemical industry is much healthier than in the early 1980s; and
- Demand for innovative pharmaceuticals, biotechnology, and other technological breakthroughs will increase.

Through the year 2005, the Bureau of Labor Statistics estimates new annual job creation for chemists at about 1,000 a year at best.

Geologists and Geophysicists   In the past, most of this country's 42,000 geologists have generally worked for the petroleum industry. Low oil and gas prices during the past decade have consequently suppressed the need for scientists in this field. The U.S. Bureau of Labor Statistics anticipates that employment for geologists will grow only as fast as the average for all occupations through the year 2000. However, any substantial increase in oil and gas prices will create strong incentives for petroleum corporations to hire scientists once again. In addition, other job opportunities may occur in areas of groundwater monitoring, toxic waste management and cleanup, and geophysical research into other environmental issues.

Physicists and Astronomers   Slightly fewer than half of this nation's 32,000 physicists are academic faculty members; the rest work for independent research and development laboratories, for the federal government, and for aerospace firms, electrical equipment manufacturers, engineering service firms, and the automobile industry. The job outlook for scientists in all these areas appears to be strong, although not consistently so. Many physicists—both academic and nonacademic—received their degrees during the 1960s and thus will approach retirement late in the present decade. On the other hand, the end of the Cold War and consequent cuts in the U.S. defense budget probably means cutbacks in weapons-related R&D, with obvious implications for physicists in related fields.

Biologists and Biotechnicians Of the approximately 100,000 biological scientists in the U.S. at the previous decade's end, roughly one-half held faculty positions in colleges and universities. Some 40 percent of the nonfaculty scientists work for federal, state, or local governments; most of the rest work for commercial or nonprofit research and development labs, hospitals, or the drug industry. For all these job categories, the job outlook is unusually bright. Biotechnology remains one of the most innovative fields anywhere in the sciences. Recombinant DNA and other techniques promise breakthroughs in agriculture, the pharmaceutical industry, medicine, and the environment. Most job growth will occur in the private sector.

Meteorologists This country employed only about 6,200 meteorologists by the late 1980s, with perhaps 1,000 more holding academic appointments. The overall outlook for scientists in this field is good, however, for two main reasons. First, the National Weather Service, which employs most U.S. meteorologists, plans to increase its hiring over the next ten years. Second, the private sector will create many new jobs in response to needs for private weather forecasting services for farmers, commodity investors, transportation and construction firms, and radio and TV stations.

Agricultural Scientists   Some 25,000 scientists worked in agricultural areas as of the late 1980s, with another 13,000 holding academic faculty positions in agricultural science. Over 40 percent of nonfaculty agricultural scientists work for federal, state, or local governments. Nonacademic agricultural scientists in the private sector generally work for commercial research and development laboratories, service companies, wholesale distributors, and seed or food products companies. The job outlook for agricultural scientists is good for several reasons: enrollments in related curriculums have dropped considerably in recent years; a disproportionate number of current workers will be leaving the work force and advances in biotechnology will heighten the need for employees within the private sector.

Key White-Collar Jobs

Human Resources Staff

Human resources, once known simply as Personnel, encompasses all areas of a company's dealings and relationships with its employees, from the hiring of new staff members to planning programs to assist people when they leave the company. Human resources also covers: training, compensation and benefits (including health care), labor relations, corporate safety and security, and, in many companies, in-house communications. More than 400,000 individuals are employed in corporate human resources, a field that has gained dramatically in status and importance over the last decade. Most experts predict above-average job opportunities over the next few years despite all the corporate downsizing.

Although companies and industries most seriously affected by the recession of 1991–92 (i.e., automotive, some retailers, some manufacturing) resisted hiring in the human resources field, most industries have continued to recognize the importance of maintaining a strong human resource bank within their corporate structure and are constantly searching for qualified individuals in the field. These include the software industry, pharmaceutical industry, bio-tech industry, and most areas of high-technology (except computer hardware). According to Robert LoPresto of the human resources consulting firm, Rusher, Loscavio & LoPresto in Palo Alto, California, "Since human resources is so dependent on 'intellectual property' or brain power it is natural that the best regions to seek employment are those close to major university centers such as the San Francisco-Berkeley area and Southern California in the West and the Boston area in the East.''

Although the field of human resources is constantly changing, there are key areas open to qualified people. For example: employment or staffing, compensation, employee benefits, training and development, and employee relations are areas showing strong positive growth. Because of the slowdown in the growth and activity of labor unions, the field of labor relations, though still a most important area, is not growing as fast as others. Says LoPresto, ''One of the most rapidly growing areas is the field of cultural diversity. This area, formerly identified with concerns of affirmative action, now addresses the growing influx of foreigners in the workplace as well as the interests and needs of minority workers.''

Another rapidly growing human resource area is training and development. Notes Helen Bensimon, American Society of Training, ''The need and importance to keep workers abreast with changing technologies has required companies to maintain and enforce their entire corporate training and development programs. Since people are the key link there is a tremendous need to locate qualified individuals and, in many cases, establish in-house programs to train the trainers. The entire field of data processing, for example, requires constant training and evaluation. Training in the field of health care technology is another area that has shown a tremendous growth in recent years.''

The Society for Human Resource Management (formerly the American Society for Personnel Administration) in Alexandria, Va. is a leading source of career guidance information.

Management Consultants

Management consulting, like any service industry, has been hard hit during the recent economic downturn. Outside expenditures on discretionary services are always the easiest costs to cut when belt-tightening is mandated. However, the management consulting industry has recognized these imminent problems and taken action to counter them. According to ACME, the association of management consulting firms, while revenue growth in the industry was low last year (probably under 10%) profitability was up markedly and may have reached record levels in some firms.

The small consultant firms are more likely to be found in major business centers, and the firms specializing in government work are found in the Washington, DC area. The large accounting firms with consulting arms have offices all over the country as do the largest of the others. There is a concentration of firms in the Boston area. In all cases, however, the availability of jobs in a given location will reflect the firm's market in that area and therefore will reflect the economy of the region.

There are some good signals for job seekers in the management consulting industry. According to Edward D. Hendricks, president of the Council of Consulting Organizations, Inc., cutbacks at large firms have gone about as far as they can, and many are now rehiring strategically to fill practice areas in which growth is anticipated or being realized. Firms are taking a hard look at the way they charge for their services, and their hiring is reflecting this new view. There are more hires of entry-level BAs rather than MBAs to pass on lower billing rates.

Jim Kennedy, publisher of *Consultants News* and the *Directory of Management Consultants,* and a long time authority on the industry sees a retreat from the consulting supermarket trend fostered by Saatchi & Saatchi several years ago although firms like Tower Perrin have continued to grow with their structure of a grouping of boutiques. Likewise, while Andersen Consulting is still the largest single firm, McKinsey & Company is reestablishing its claim to second place fighting off the onslaughts of the other accountant founded consultants. The Human Resources firms such as The Hay Group and Mercer-Meidinger show continued strength.

There has also been an increase in the hiring of established professionals with a specific expertise that can be translated into an immediate market advantage. In this way entrepreneurial niches can be built within the larger framework of the big firm. Likewise, senior consulting professionals whose specialty area has been eliminated by their firms are going out on their own and developing niche practices in specialty areas. These specialties range from the broad disciplines like marketing and strategic planning to the highly esoteric. A key specialty for many firms, both large and small, is the growing but ill-defined field of Information Management, the utilization of communications and information technology to provide competitive advantage.

Finally there is a trend toward hiring consultants with language skills (especially Spanish and Eastern European languages) reflecting the growth potential in these areas of the world. The restructured and stabilizing economies of Central and South America, and the wide-open newly emerging markets in Eastern Europe seem ripe for the services Management Consultants can offer.

Manufacturers Sales Representatives

Almost 2 million Americans work as sales representatives for the producers and distributors of thousands and thousands of products, everything from nails and screws, books and office supplies, to industrial robots and mainframe computers. Although most work for small companies an increasing number of mid-sized and even a few major corporations have discovered the benefits of hiring these representatives.

According to a spokesman for the Manufacturing Agents' National Association in Laguna Hills, California, ''With the economy in an uncertain condition this is one of the best times to consider becoming a manufacturers' representative. Since most reps work only on commission rather than straight salary, using sales representatives allows a manufacturer the opportunity to cut overhead by reducing in-house salespeople, who earn salaries even if business is bad.''

Since this seems to be exactly how business leaders are thinking, it's no wonder the Bureau of Labor Statistics projects this occupation as one of the fastest growing over the next few years with an increase of at least 50,000 jobs by the year 2000. Although the recession has had some negative effects since businesses and individuals are buying less, the long-term outlook is for continued employment growth.

This is not a job for everyone, however. Sales representatives must be independent types who can rely solely on their ability to sell to earn commissions. Their time is their own, so they must be strongly self-motivated. And they usually are. Recently, the Manufacturing Agents' National Association surveyed their members and found that the heads of the 1,200 largest manufacturers' representative firms had a median income in excess of $100,000.

A successful manufacturers' agent often needs technical skills as well as sales ability. Often they are the buffer between a customer's complaints or needs and the manufacturer. If the product requires sophisticated technical expertise the representative will be as well-trained in the technology as a company engineer.

Office Jobs

The largest major occupational group, this collection of office support and clerical jobs is expected to grow at a modest rate of 2 to 3 percent a year. Technological advances are expected to decrease the demand for stenographers, typists, word processors, and data entry keyers, while the demand for information clerks—reservations clerks, ticket agents, new accounts clerks—is expected to grow substantially. By the year 2000, jobs for receptionists will grow the fastest, at 47 percent, while the market for general office clerks should increase by the most jobs, 670,000. Typists and word processors will lose more than 100,000 jobs.

Overall, these jobs should grow about 12 percent, from just under 22 million in 1990 to about 24.84 million in 2000, according to the Department of Labor. In an expanded economy, this sector of the job market could grow 19 percent. The number of workers and rapid turnover within this category should mean lots of job openings throughout the decade. Statistics for all jobs within the industry, in order of growth, follow on the next page.

Job	1990 Actual Employment	Projected Growth (%) by 2005	Projected Growth(%) (Expanding Economy)
Receptionists	900,000	47%	55%
Dispatchers, private	138,000	31	38
Adjusters & collectors	1,058,000	24	31
General office clerks	2,737,000	24	31
Credit authorizers	240,000	24	30
Correspondence clerks	30,000	22	29
Personnel clerks	129,000	21	26
Real estate clerks	29,000	17	21
Secretaries	3,576,000	15	21
Advertising clerks	18,000	15	20
Computer operators	320,000	13	19
Office machine operators	169,000	13	18
Traffic clerks	762,000	13	18
Data entry keyers	475,000	12	18
File clerks	271,000	11	17
Customer service representatives	109,000	10	16
Mail clerks	280,000	9	15
Stock clerks	752,000	4	10
Weighers & measurers	37,000	4	8
Statement clerks	33,000	3	9
Order clerks	291,000	3	8
Production clerks	237,000	1	4
Financial records processors	2,860,000	−4	+1

Job	1990 Actual Employment	Projected Growth (%) by 2005	Projected Growth(%) (Expanding Economy)
Proofreaders	29,000	−5	−1
Stenographers	132,000	−5	0
Procurement clerks	56,000	−8	−4
Typists and word processors	972,000	−11	−6
Telephone operators	325,000	−32	−28
Statistical clerks	85,000	−36	−33

Operations Research Analysts

In the midst of all the praise we hear about the efficiency of Japanese and German business methods it is easy to forget that not too long ago these nations, among many others, held the U.S. system in the highest esteem. The rapid growth in the number of operations research analysts may mean that we are intent on winning back our preeminent position.

Generally speaking these people are problem solvers who utilize mathematical models to present managers with a series of possible outcomes that will help them make more informed decisions. They are employed in most industries and their numbers are expected to increase by over 70 percent, from 57,000 in 1990 to 100,000 by 2005. The requirements for employment are a fairly rigorous training in mathematics or quantitative methods with some knowledge of computer programming.

Public Relations Specialists

About 100,000 people currently work in this field and the outlook for the near future looks very promising. One reason for this optimism was highlighted during the recent recession, when major corporations turned increasingly to public relations to supplement their drastically reduced advertising budgets. "Corporations are spending more on public relations because they find they get more mileage in the media for their money than advertising," says Charlotte Klein, a public relations consultant and past president of the Public Relations Society of America.

Corporations especially, rather than public relations firms, are hiring "cautiously," according to Len Daniels, president of Placement Associates, a consulting and executive search firm in New York. "Many places are now understaffed because they cut back. I've seen an upswing and expect it to get better after the first quarter."

Daniels points to pharmaceuticals and health care as two public relations specialties with job openings. "Pharmaceuticals are growing very fast because of the rapid introduction of new products and the competitive markets," Daniels says. "Hospitals and nursing homes, especially outside of New York and the major metro areas, have empty beds and they are using public relations to try to fill them." Hospitals, especially in major cities, have been hurt by cutbacks in government spending so they are increasingly relying on public relations specialists for help to fill the gap with fundraising, special events and media placement.

In a related area, nonprofit organizations, especially those in the health field, such as the American Cancer Society, Planned Parenthood, and Red Cross, also have openings.

Another area experts point to is the entertainment industry, where often millions of dollars are spent promoting a movie and its stars before opening. In a related field, commercial and public television are feeling the competition from new cable channels and in response are putting more effort into public relations to get publicity.

Corporate public relations is growing for other reasons as well. All the recent layoffs, cutbacks, and downsizings have caused such tremendous morale problems among employees of large companies that many managers have tried to restore a positive attitude through increased use of newsletters, house organs and the like.

A relatively new but especially strong growth area within corporate public relations groups is the environmental field. Companies involved with waste management, nuclear power, and chemical production obviously need people to deal with this most important issue but increasingly almost all manufacturers have found a need for well-informed public relations staff.

Although only 10 percent of the public relations work force is employed in public relations agencies, these firms are a vital and growing part of the business. As in many other industries, the mid-sized public relations firms have weathered the recession better than the giants. "Small and mid-sized agencies are more tightly run and controlled than the big agencies. They don't have excess staff so as business picks up, as it has recently, these firms need to hire more people," said Daniels. Small agencies have staffs of three to 20, and mid-sized have staffs of 12 to 50.

Daniels cannot pinpoint one area of the country particularly strong with openings. "The openings are everywhere from major metro areas to corporate headquarters in suburban areas to plant sites," he says. But one key to getting a job is willingness to relocate. "If you want the best jobs be ready to relocate. If you're not willing to relocate there is little chance for career growth," he warns.

Purchasing Agents

Every major organization, whether a governmental agency or manufacturing corporation, maintains an active department responsible for the acquisition of materials or services required by the organization. Various jobs within the purchasing profession include: purchasing agents, buyers, inventory control and materials-management specialists, and contract administrators. There are approximately 400,000 individuals working in the field.

Unfortunately, the recession affected most areas of the purchasing profession in 1991 and early 1992. On the positive side, however, purchasing industry spokespeople are confident that when the recession eases the need for purchasing professionals will be as strong as ever as a myriad of companies, slowed by the economic downturn, re-gear to meet future demands. And even during the height of the recession, some industries such as pharmaceutical, food processing and manufacturing, and some areas of the communications industry showed an upswing and are hiring purchasing professionals. Also, according to Jean Henrichs, employment services coordinator for the National Association of Purchasing Management, "There are areas of the country in which purchasing jobs have opened up. Los Angeles, Chicago, and more recently, Houston have shown a positive trend. The primary areas of the field currently in demand include purchasing agents, contract administrators, inventory control specialists, and materials-management personnel."

Working in the public area is another matter. Although federal, state and local governments will spend in excess of $100 billion acquiring goods and services in 1992, the economic situation has had a major impact on the hiring of all personnel. Until additional funding filters into the public sector all personnel, including those in the purchasing field, will note a paucity of job opportunities. When the economy rebounds these jobs will again be available.

Key Blue-Collar Jobs

Mechanics, Installers, and Repairers

The various occupations in this category evidence one of the widest fluctuations of growth within a single sector of the labor market. Increases in the use of data processing equipment and biomedical equipment will bring with them a corresponding need for people to repair and install them. At the same time, labor-saving advances should cause a decline in employment for installers and repairers of telephones, televisions, and other types of communications equipment. Overall, America's 4.9 million jobs in mechanics, installing and repairing should grow 16 percent by the year 2000, according to the Department of Labor. In an expanding economy, the number of jobs could increase by 21 percent. Jobs for data processing equipment repairers will grow the fastest, an estimated 60 percent by 2000, while general utility maintenance repairers will increase by more than 251,000 jobs. On the flip side, jobs for communications equipment repairers are expected to decline by more than 48,000. Statistics for all jobs within the industry, in order of growth, follow.

Job	1990 Actual Employment	Projected Growth (%) by 2005	Projected Growth (%) (Expanding Economy)
Data processing equipment repairers	84,000	60%	67%
Electromedical equipment repairers	8,000	51	60
Aircraft mechanics	122,000	24	29
General utility maintenance repairers	1,128,000	22	28
Auto body repairers	219,000	22	28
Auto mechanics	757,000	22	28
Bus & truck mechanics	268,000	22	28
Heat, air conditioning & refrigeration mechanics and installers	219,000	21	28
Electric meter installers & repairers	14,000	18	24
Elevator installers and repairers	19,000	17	24
Tire repairers	81,000	17	23
Electronics repairers	75,000	17	22
Camera & photographic equipment repairers	7,000	17	21

Job	1990 Actual Employment	Projected Growth (%) by 2005	Projected Growth(%) (Expanding Economy)
Office machine & cash register servicers	73,000	13	19
Electronic home entertainment equipment repairers	41,000	13	18
Mobile heavy equipment mechanics	104,000	13	18
Millwrights	73,000	12	18
Bicycle repairers	15,000	11	16
Motorcycle, boat & small engine mechanics	50,000	10	15
Industrial machinery mechanics	474,000	10	14
Electrical powerline installers & repairers	99,000	9	14
Farm equipment mechanics	48,000	9	14
Precision instrument repairers	50,000	8	12
Musical instrument repairers and tuners	9,000	2	7
Riggers	14,000	0	4

Job	1990 Actual Employment	Projected Growth (%) by 2005	Projected Growth (%) (Expanding Economy)
Coin & vending machine services & repairers	26,000	− 1	+ 4
Home appliance & power tool repairers	71,000	− 1	+ 4
Telephone & cable TV line installers & repairers	133,000	− 30	− 26
Watchmakers	7,000	− 33	− 30
Communications equipment mechanics	125,000	− 38	− 35
Telephone station installers & repairers	47,000	− 55	− 53

Personal Service Jobs

Like the entire service industry, the personal service occupations should grow much faster than the national average. However, low status and pay for private household workers like cooks, housekeepers, and cleaners is likely to produce a decline of nearly 30 percent in the number of people in those jobs through the 1990s. But this contraction will be more than offset by the increasing number of people working as home health aides, personal and home care aides, and child care workers. Employment in the personal service occupations stood at just under 3 million in 1990, and is expected to jump 25 percent to 3.72 million by the year 2000, according to the Department of Labor. An expanding economy could bring about a 31 percent increase to just under 4 million.

Home health aides will post the biggest growth rate, 92 percent, as well as the biggest numerical increase in jobs, 263,000. Private household workers will be the biggest losers, dropping 227,000 jobs by 2000, a decrease of 29 percent. Statistics for all jobs within the category, in order of growth, follow.

Job	1990 Actual Employment	Projected Growth (%) by 2005	Projected Growth(%) (Expanding Economy)
Home health aides	287,000	92%	103%
Personal care aides	103,000	77	87
Flight attendants	101,000	59	67
Child care workers	725,000	49	55
Manicurists	25,000	38	45
Baggage porters	31,000	33	37
Amusement attendants	184,000	24	31
Hairdressers, stylists	597,000	24	30
Shampooers	14,000	21	29
Ushers, ticket-takers	48,000	13	19
Barbers	77,000	−1	+2
Household workers	782,000	−29	−25

Production Jobs

One of only three occupational groups to experience little, zero, or negative growth during the current decade (the others are helpers, handlers, and cleaners, and agriculture, forestry and fishing) the various production occupations encompass more than 100 different jobs. For this reason, it is convenient to break this broad category into two distinct groups: precision production occupations and operators, fabricators and laborers. The first category consists largely of skilled tradesmen and tradeswomen, while the second group is made up primarily of nonprecision machine operators.

Precision Production Jobs　There were more than 3 million precision workers in 1990 according to the Department of Labor. Their numbers are expected to increase only 2 percent by 2000, though an expanding economy could spur growth of 7 percent. Jobs for precision printing workers, like printing strippers and electronic pagination systems workers will increase the most (34 and 33 percent respectively) while the greatest numerical increase in jobs will be for precision metal machinists. Technological advances will mean that jobs for assemblers of electromechanical, electrical and electronic equipment will all decrease by more than 37 percent. Statistics for all precision production occupations, in order of growth, follow.

Job	1990 Actual Employment	Projected Growth (%) by 2005	Projected Growth(%) (Expanding Economy)
Printing strippers	32,000	34%	40%
Electronic pagination systems workers	12,000	33	39
Water treatment plant operators	78,000	29	39
Optical goods workers	19,000	29	34
Platemakers	14,000	23	29
Job printers	15,000	23	28
Camera operators	17,000	21	26
Jewelers, silversmiths	40,000	20	24
Custom tailors, sewers	116,000	18	23
Photo process workers	18,000	16	21
Cabinetmakers	107,000	13	19
Sheet metal workers	233,000	13	19
Bookbinders	7,000	13	18
Paste-up workers	30,000	13	18
Photoengravers	8,000	13	17
Furniture finishers	34,000	12	17
Wood machinists	46,000	12	17
Machinists	386,000	10	15
Upholsterers	64,000	10	13
Electric power plant operators & dispatchers	44,000	9	14
Aircraft assemblers	32,000	6	9

Job	1990 Actual Employment	Projected Growth (%) by 2005	Projected Growth(%) (Expanding Economy)
Dental lab technicians	57,000	4	10
Boilermakers	22,000	3	9
Tool and die makers	141,000	3	6
Stationary engineers	35,000	1	7
Inspectors & graders	668,000	−1	+2
Typesetters	14,000	−2	+1
Bakers, manufacturing	34,000	−4	−1
Shipfitters	13,000	−4	−1
Fabric patternmakers	16,000	−4	−2
Butchers & meatcutters	234,000	−6	−2
Gas & petroleum plant & system occupations	31,000	−11	−9
Metal fitters	15,000	−14	−9
Chemical plant operators	35,000	−14	−10
Machine builders	50,000	−17	−14
Shoe & leather workers	27,000	−19	−15
Electromechanical equipment assemblers	49,000	−37	−35
Electrical & electronic equipment assemblers	171,000	−48	−46

Job	1990 Actual Employment	Projected Growth (%) by 2005	Projected Growth(%) (Expanding Economy)
Laundry & drycleaning machine operators	173,000	23%	29%
Combination machine tool operators	93,000	23	27
Numerical control machine tool operators	70,000	23	27
Plastic molding machine operators and tenders	143,000	21	26
Photoengraving machine operators	98,000	21	25
Photo process machine operators and tenders	58,000	20	25
Printing press operators	224,000	19	24
Textile & garment pressing machine operators	84,000	14	19
Woodwork machine operators	64,000	12	18
Metal fabricators	34,000	11	18
Sawing machine operators	72,000	11	17

Job	1990 Actual Employment	Projected Growth (%) by 2005	Projected Growth(%) (Expanding Economy)
Bindery machine operators	71,000	11	16
Mixing machine operators	135,000	7	12
Welding machine operators	95,000	6	10
Non-garment sewing machine operators	131,000	5	8
Metal & plastic heaters	5,000	1	6
Slicing machine operators	88,000	1	5
Boiler operators	21,000	0	6
Heating equipment operators	7,000	0	4
Heat-treating machine operators, metal & plastic	21,000	0	j 4
Soldering machine operators	11,000	− 1	+2
Kiln & kettle operators	56,000	− 1	+3
Painting and coating machine operators	160,000	−1	+3
Furnace operators	22,000	− 2	+2
Paper goods machine set-up operators	59,000	− 3	+1

Job	1990 Actual Employment	Projected Growth (%) by 2005	Projected Growth(%) (Expanding Economy)
Textile extruding and forming machine operators	21,000	−3	+1
Filling machine operators	324,000	−8	−5
Movie projectionists	13,000	−9	−5
Electrolytic plating machine operators	43,000	−13	−10
Dairy processing equipment operators	18,000	−13	−11
Hand workers	2,675,000	−14	−11
Non-electrolytic plating machine operators	7,000	−15	−11
Cooking machine operators	31,000	−16	−14
Metal molding machine operators and tenders	38,000	−18	−15
Punching machine setters & operators	52,000	−18	−15
Chemical equipment controllers & operators	75,000	−19	−15
Gluing machine operators	35,000	−20	−16

Job	1990 Actual Employment	Projected Growth (%) by 2005	Projected Growth(%) (Expanding Economy)
Separating and still machine operators	26,000	− 20	− 17
Garment sewing machine operators	585,000	− 20	− 18
Lathe operators	80,000	− 24	− 22
Machine forming operators	174,000	− 25	− 21
Grinding machine operators	72,00	− 25	− 22
Drilling and boring machine operators	52,000	− 26	− 23
Foundry workers	10,000	− 26	− 23
Textile machine set-up operators & setters	42,000	− 27	− 25
Textile bleaching machine operators	28,000	− 28	− 26
Machine tool cutting operators & tenders	145,000	− 29	− 26
Textile winding machine operators	199,000	− 31	− 29
Electronic semiconductor processors	32,000	− 31	− 30

Job	1990 Actual Employment	Projected Growth (%) by 2005	Projected Growth(%) (Expanding Economy)
Tire building machine operators	14,000	−38	−34
Shoe sewing machine operators and tenders	18,000	−45	−43

Operators, Fabricators, and Laborers Half of this group of jobs is expected to grow over the current decade while the other half is expected to decline, according to the Department of Labor. The end result is an overall market of more than 17 million operators, fabricators and laborers that is expected to grow only 4 percent by 2005. Even in an expanding economy, this occupational group will grow no more than 7 percent. The expanding jobs are concentrated primarily in the printing and woodworking trades, but certain segments in all areas of this field show some growth. Jobs for laundry and drycleaning machine operators will grow fastest, at 23 percent, while the biggest numerical increase in jobs will be for 44,000 additional printing press operators. On the flip side, the current decade will be a tough one for sewing machine operators. Shoe sewing machine operators will see their ranks drop by 46 percent, while the market for garment sewing machine operators should contract by 116,000 jobs. Statistics for all precision production occupations, in order of growth, follow.

Transportation and Material Moving Jobs

Job growth in this sector will reflect a move from railroads and waterways to surface roadways. Jobs for truckdrivers should grow faster than the national average, while jobs for all rail transport workers (except subway and streetcar operators) and water transportation workers should decline over the current decade. Jobs for material moving equipment operators (e.g. crane operators and excavation machine operators), should increase at a slower than average pace. Overall, the number of jobs should grow about 19 percent, from just under 6 million in 1990 to about 7.13 million in 2005, according to the Department of Labor. In an expanded economy, this sector of the job market could grow by 25 percent. Both figures are about the same as the national average for all jobs.

Taxi drivers and chauffeurs will post the biggest growth rate, 22 percent, while the biggest increase in jobs should be in truckdriving, which will grow by more than 650,000 jobs by 2005. Able seamen, ordinary seamen, and marine oilers will be hurt most by the increase in truckdriving. The market for these occupations will shrink by 24 percent, a loss of more than 5000 jobs. Statistics for all jobs within this category, in order of growth, follow.

Job	1990 Actual Employment	Projected Growth (%) by 2005	Projected Growth(%) (Expanding Economy)
Taxi drivers	108,000	29%	35%
Operating engineers	157,000	28	36
Truck drivers	2,701,000	24	30
Hoist & winch operators	11,000	13	19
Excavation operators	74,000	12	19
Grader operators	93,000	11	18
Industrial truck & tractor operators	431,000	9	14
Crane operators	51,000	7	13
Ship captains & pilots	14,000	1	9
Ship and barge mates	7,000	−4	+4
Rail yard engineers	8,000	−5	−1
Locomotive engineers	16,000	−6	0
Railroad conductors	28,000	−14	−9
Railroad signal operators	35,000	−18	−13
Ship engineers	7,000	−19	−13
Seamen	22,000	−24	−18

Fastest growing occupations, 1990–2005
(Numbers in thousands)

Occupation	Employment 1990	2005	Numerical change	Percent change
Home health aides	287	550	263	91.7%
Paralegals	90	167	77	85.2
Systems analysts and computer scientists	463	829	366	78.9
Personal and home care aides	103	183	79	76.7
Physical therapists	88	155	67	76.0
Medical assistants	165	287	122	73.9
Operations research analysts	57	100	42	73.2
Human services workers	145	249	103	71.2
Radiologic technologists and technicians	149	252	103	69.5
Medical secretaries	232	390	158	68.3
Physical and corrective therapy assistants and aides	45	74	29	64.0
Psychologists	125	204	79	63.6
Travel agents	132	214	82	62.3
Correction officers	230	372	142	61.4
Data processing equipment repairers	84	134	50	60.0
Flight attendants	101	159	59	58.5
Computer programmers	565	882	317	56.1
Occupational therapists	36	56	20	55.2
Surgical technologists	38	59	21	55.2

Fastest growing occupations, 1990–2005 (cont.)

Occupation	Employment		Numerical change	Percent change
	1990	*2005*		
Medical records technicians	52	80	28	54.3
Management analysts	151	230	79	52.3
Respiratory therapists	60	91	31	52.1
Child care workers	725	1,078	353	48.8
Marketing, advertising, and public relations managers	427	630	203	47.4
Legal secretaries	281	413	133	47.4
Receptionists and information clerks	900	1,322	422	46.9
Registered nurses	1,727	2,494	767	44.4
Nursing aides, orderlies, and attendants	1,274	1,826	552	43.4
Licensed practical nurses	644	913	269	41.9
Cooks, restaurant	615	872	257	41.8

Note: These figures are based on a moderately growing economy.
Source: U.S. Bureau of Labor Statistics, Monthly Labor Review *(Nov. 1991).*

Occupations with the largest job declines, 1990–2005
(Numbers in thousands)

Occupation	Employment 1990	Employment 2005	Numerical change	Percent change
Farmers	1,074	805	−224	−20.9%
Bookeeping, accounting, and auditing clerks	2,276	2,143	−133	−5.8
Child care workers, private household	314	190	−124	−39.5
Sewing machine operators, garment	585	469	−116	−19.8
Electrical and electronic assemblers	232	128	−105	−45.1
Typists and word processors	972	869	−103	−10.6
Cleaners and servants, private household	411	310	−101	−24.5
Farm workers	837	745	−92	−11.0
Electrical and electronic equipment assemblers, precision	171	90	−81	−47.5
Textile draw-out and winding machine operators and tenders	199	138	−61	−30.6
Switchboard operators	246	189	−57	−23.2
Machine forming operators and tenders, metal and plastic	174	131	−43	−24.5

Occupations with the largest job declines, 1990–2005 *(cont.)*

Occupation	Employment		Numerical change	Percent change
	1990	*2005*		
Machine tool cutting operators and tenders, metal and plastic	145	104	−42	−28.6
Telephone and cable TV line installers and repairers	133	92	−40	−30.4
Central office and PBX installers and repairers	80	46	−34	−42.5
Central office operators	53	22	−31	−59.2
Statistical clerks	85	54	−31	−36.1
Packaging and filling machine operators and tenders	324	297	−27	−8.3
Station installers and repairers, telephone	47	21	−26	−55.0
Bank tellers	517	492	−25	−4.8
Lathe and turning machine tool setters and setup operators, metal and plastic	80	61	−20	−24.4
Grinders and polishers, hand	84	65	−19	−22.5
Electromechanical equipment assemblers, precision	49	31	−18	−36.5

Occupations with the largest job declines, 1990–2005 *(cont.)*

Occupation	Employment 1990	2005	Numerical change	Percent change
Grinding machine setters and setup operators, metal and plastic	72	54	− 18	− 25.1
Service station attendants	246	229	− 17	− 7.1
Directory assistance operators	26	11	− 16	− 59.4
Butchers and meat cutters	234	220	− 14	− 5.9
Chemical equipment controllers, operators, and tenders	75	61	− 14	− 19.1
Drilling and boring machine tool setters and setup operators, metal and plastic	52	39	− 13	− 25.6
Meter readers, utilities	50	37	− 12	− 24.8

Note: These figures are based on a moderately growing economy.
Source: U.S. Bureau of Labor Statistics, Monthly Labor Review *(Nov. 1991).*

Occupations with the Largest Numbers of New Jobs, 1990–2005
(Numbers in thousands)

Occupation	Employment 1990	Employment 2005	Numerical change	Percent change
Salespersons, retail	3,619	4,506	887	24.5%
Registered nurses	1,727	2,494	767	44.4
Cashiers	2,633	3,318	685	26.0
General office clerks	2,737	3,407	670	24.5
Truck drivers, light and heavy	2,362	2,979	617	26.1
General managers and top executives	3,086	3,684	598	19.4
Janitors and cleaners, including maids and housekeeping cleaners	3,007	3,562	555	18.5
Nursing aides, orderlies, and attendants	1,274	1,826	552	43.4
Food counter, fountain, and related workers	1,607	2,158	550	34.2
Waiters and waitresses	1,747	2,196	449	25.7
Teachers, secondary school	1,280	1,717	437	34.2
Receptionists and information clerks	900	1,322	422	46.9
Systems analysts and computer scientists	463	829	366	78.9

Occupations with the Largest Numbers of New Jobs, 1990–2005 (cont.)

Occupation	Employment		Numerical change	Percent change
	1990	2005		
Food preparation workers	1,156	1,521	365	31.6
Child care workers	725	1,078	353	48.8
Gardeners and groundskeepers, except farm	874	1,222	348	39.8
Accountants and auditors	985	1,325	340	34.5
Computer programmers	565	882	317	56.1
Teachers, elementary	1,362	1,675	313	23.0
Guards	883	1,181	298	33.7
Teacher aides and educational assistants	808	1,086	278	34.4
Licensed practical nurses	644	913	269	41.9
Clerical supervisors and managers	1,218	1,481	263	21.6
Home health aides	287	550	263	91.7
Cooks, restaurant	615	872	257	41.8
Maintenance repairs, general utility	1,128	1,379	251	22.2
Secretaries, except legal and medical	3,064	3,312	248	8.1
Cooks, short order and fast food	743	989	246	33.0

Occupations with the Largest Numbers of New Jobs, 1990–2005 *(cont.)*

Occupation	*Employment*		*Numerical change*	*Percent change*
	1990	*2005*		
Stock clerks, sales floor	1,242	1,451	209	16.8
Lawyers	587	793	206	35.1

Source: U.S. Bureau of Labor Statistics, Monthly Labor Review *(Nov. 1991).*

WHERE THE JOBS ARE

MAJOR INDUSTRIES

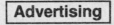

Advertising

Over the last five years employment in the advertising business has been rocked both by the sudden and dramatic merging of many large agencies and the rapid decline in consumer spending that has caused budget cutbacks in almost every sector of the economy. In 1991, for the first time in thirty years, American advertisers actually spent less money in aggregate to pitch their products than in the previous year. The 1.5 percent decline brought the amount spent for advertising to about $126 billion, still an enormous business enterprise by anyone's reckoning. While that decline forced the major advertising agencies to lay off staffers, overall cuts in the industry were not as severe as the headlines would lead you to believe. According to the Bureau of Labor Statistics, there were 230,100 people employed in advertising in 1991, a drop of 7,600 over the previous year.

Despite the cuts, there are some pockets of opportunity where jobs can be found. Health care, thanks to an aging population and a mania for medical services and drugs, is a fertile field for jobs. Business is so good that several ad agencies now deal exclusively with health care. A number of the mega-agencies own health-care subsidiaries such as Healthcom (Saatchi and Saatchi) and Medicus Interon International (D'Arcy Masius Benton Bowles).

"I've seen jobs go begging in the health care field. Medical ad agencies and corporations are looking for both creative and marketing people," says Lillian Studer, senior vice president at Jerry Fields Associates, a New York-based recruiting firm. "It's a very hot area now with high salaries." The best jobs, according to Ms. Studer, go to those with industry experience. But "creative" people with science backgrounds, with related sales experience, and even nurses, are also finding jobs.

Another area that has remained strong is sales promotion, which relies on in-store ads, displays, newspaper inserts, and sweepstakes to woo the consumer. Advertisers have switched money into point-of-sales advertising because they get faster results, according to Jon Lafayette, a reporter for *Ad Age,* who adds that agencies have begun special departments to handle sales promotion rather than deal with it on a piecemeal basis as had been done previously.

Several cities outside of New York are weathering the recession fairly well, according to Ms. Studer. She points to Chicago, Portland, Minneapolis, and San Francisco as cities each with several "very hot" ad agencies. In Portland, for example, Wieden & Kennedy have the Nike sporting goods and Subaru "What To Drive" accounts. Chicago ad agencies, with Leo Burnett leading the way, have garnered $500 million in new business in the last three years, according to *Ad Week.*

Despite the downturn, some industry observers and head hunters claim the picture has never been more rosy for talented copywriters and art directors. Richard Morgan, editor-at-large for *Ad Week,* explains, "To save money, many big shops abandoned their training programs so they are unable to cultivate and nurture their own talent. As a result there is a large demand for very talented, creative types." The demand is not limited to people with 20 years in the business. Even newcomers have a chance. "All you need to demonstrate is a couple of successful campaigns," says Morgan.

Judy Wald, head of her own New York placement agency, has seen an upturn in demand in the last six months. "Agencies fired too many people. They are now hiring across the board. The demand is especially for high level creative types and account managers," she says.

Agencies are always on the outlook for creative types as evidenced by an ad J. Walter Thompson North America ran recently in several trade publications and newspapers. The ad asks would-be art directors to submit ideas in response to several questions, ranging from coming up with a product every American teenager would buy to designing a symbol for love to replace the heart which has been deemed old-fashioned. As a result of a similar ad for copywriters and account managers several years ago, the agency hired 15 people.

Morgan of *Ad Week* has a final bit of advice for job seekers wondering where to make the next move: go to small shops. "Companies don't want to pay the freight and overhead for the big shops," Morgan says. "More business is being farmed out to small shops." The trend Morgan sees emerging, instead of one-stop shopping at a large ad agency, is that some advertisers are doing their own in-house research, turning to "boutiques" for the creative campaign, and doing print and broadcast placement through a media-buying company. As a result, Morgan predicts, "The account executive at the large agency may become extinct."

Banking

Looking for a job in banking these days takes more than a little courage and certainly a great deal of sophisticated research. The Bureau of Labor Statistics estimates that about 50,000 jobs were lost in both commercial banking and the beleaguered savings and loan industry in 1991 alone. This continues a trend that started in the late 1980s, when large banks realized they needed far greater assets to compete globally, and so began to seek out merger possibilities. As many large banks merged they were able to consolidate departments and save money by trimming workers.

About 1,100 banks have shut down since 1985 and just over 1000 more remain on the FDIC's so-called problem list. The number of savings and loan associations has been cut almost in half, from 4300 to 2500, through merger and failures. Another 250 could fail during 1992, according to the Department of Commerce.

Still, 1992 is expected to be a quiet year in banking and some bright spots in the job market are distinctly possible. Loan officers of all types, for example, will be needed because lower interest rates should send people back to borrowing. In addition, several of the mega-mergers (e.g. Chemical and Manufacturers Hanover) will be firmly in place this year and staff reductions should be replaced with new hirings as needs become more clearly defined.

Employment in banking will most likely continue to decline from its peak of 2.2 million or so (the industry study estimates a decline of 250,000 by 2000). But while fewer tellers and clerks will be needed, most analysts project strong growth in the marketing and services sector. With banks about to break into the securities business, people with sales experience or knowledge of this new field of endeavor could do very well.

Broadcasting

After decades of unparalleled growth, the broadcasting industry occupations should come down to earth in the 1990s. Growth will continue, but at a much more moderate pace. But jobseekers will always outnumber the relatively small number of jobs in this glamorous industry, since fewer than 100,000 people work in the entire field.

Cable television, the success story of the 1980s, will face much slower growth in the 1990s and beyond. Fears of government regulation and entry by telephone companies into cable broadcasting will keep rates (and profits) from growing too quickly. But the trend of cutting into the networks' audience should continue. Along with home video, cable reduced the prime time audience from 93 percent in 1975 to 64 percent in 1990.

In the 1990s more and more broadcasters will be competing for smaller and smaller slices of the viewing population. The networks and cable will both increasingly use ''narrowcasting'' to appeal to specific demographic, age, or ethnic groups. Increasing reliance by cable stations on their own original programming should lead to increased staff levels at cable stations.

The networks have also recognized that news shows are cheap to produce and have begun broadcasting more of them. That trend will continue into the 1990s. They will also be increasing their use of in-house production.

The strongest growth area, however, is likely to be at local television stations. Independent stations are increasing their news coverage in an attempt to compete with the networks, local network affiliates, and cable stations. Many advertisers are using local stations and local cable stations as low-cost alternatives to advertising on network TV.

Radio and Television News Announcers About 57,000 men and women worked as announcers for radio and television stations across the country in 1990, the vast majority of them in radio. Jobs in this field are expected to grow 20 percent by the year 2005, about the same as the national average. However, job openings should be few, because turnover is low and competition is high. Beginners generally have better luck at radio stations than television stations, which often hire only those with previous radio or television experience.

Radio and Television Reporters and Correspondents Like their studio counterparts, radio and TV reporters are expected to see job growth of about 20 percent by 2005. There were 13,000 reporters and cooresspondents working in television and radio in 1990. These jobs also attract an inordinately high number of applicants for a relatively small number of jobs. In general, the lower-paying the job, and the smaller the station's market, the easier it is to attain.

Camera Operators   About 13,000 men and women (but mostly men) worked as camera operators in 1990. That number should increase 37 percent by 2005, according to the Department of Labor. Despite rigorous working environments—the so-called hand-held cameras used by many camera operators can weigh up to 100 pounds—jobseekers almost always outnumber openings. Attractive salaries mean that competition is always high for these jobs.

Computers

Although this is now a $60 billion a year industry (based on the value of shipments), its greatest period of growth seems to have ended. Throughout most of the 1980s the computer industry became accustomed to double-digit revenue growth. According to *Business Week* magazine, however, it will be lucky to break 6 percent. The U.S. Department of Commerce estimates only 4 percent. The industry is, and this is kind, in transition, and it has been for a number of years.

Over 15,000 jobs were lost in the computer industry in 1991, most of them in the areas of administration, marketing, and sales support personnel. Dan Lacey, the editor of *Workplace Trends,* a newsletter that tracks corporate employment, claims that since January 1989 over 154,000 jobs have been cut by the computer industry, more even than the highly publicized cuts in the automotive sector.

It is doubtful that these jobs will come back in the same number since the revenue base of the industry is moving away from the expensive mainframe computers that generated so much revenue. More than 50 percent of the industry's revenues between now and 1996 will come from systems design and integration, software, and after-sales service. Other growth areas include workstations, which should increase 28 percent in 1992, computer networking, which is expected to grow 24 percent, and printers, which should grow 7 percent.

Computer Programmers and Systems Analysts   It is important to remember that the two most rapidly growing jobs for trained computer specialists are for the most part not connected to the computer industry. A good thing, too, since in general the industry is in a shaky period.

Systems analysts and programmers work in offices in almost every other industry. Systems analysts study business situations and design computer systems to meet the needs of each business. Programmers work under the direction of analysts and write the programs designed by the analysts. The most profitable futures for both analysts and programmers are in financial services (including banks, investment houses, and insurance companies), retailing operations, airlines, hotels and other travel industries, and industries that rely on a high level of customer service to generate business.

The outlook for the future continues to be exceedingly positive throughout the country although there is very keen competition for the best jobs, a situation that will grow even more intense as the number of college graduates in the field increases.

Increasing use of computers by businesses of all kinds means that demand for systems analysts should grow much faster than the national average by the year 2005. However, increasing specialization within this field means that competition for jobs will increase, threatening those who do not have specialized computer training or experience. Nevertheless, the number of systems analysts is expected to grow nearly 80 percent, to 829,000 by the year 2005, up from 463,000 in 1990. Unlike the computer industry itself, the turnover rate for systems analysts is slower than average.

Further automation of offices and factories, coupled with advances in health and medicine, will make the job of programmer even more important through the 1990s. Jobs for programmers should grow much faster than the national average by the year 2005, according to the Department of Labor. Competition for jobs is high. Jobs for both systems and applications programmers should be particularly plentiful in data processing service firms, software houses, and computer consulting businesses.

There were 565,000 computer programmers in 1990; their numbers are expected to swell 56 percent to 882,000 by the year 2005. Like systems analysts, programmers must keep abreast of changing technology and train and retrain constantly. Most of them can find work in every section of the country.

Construction

No other sector of the economy feels the immediate effect of a recession more quickly than construction. In the latest one people as always stopped buying new houses so housing-starts (a key indicator of the economy's health) declined, and rapidly too. Add to this the fact that during the 1980s the tax code encouraged wealthy citizens to invest in office space that no one needed so now many major cities have commercial vacancy rates near or above 20 percent. So it's not hard to understand why about 310,000 jobs were lost nationwide in 1991.

Although 14 states actually added construction jobs that year, the greatest number was 4,700 in Nebraska followed by 4,200 in Texas, and 3,400 in Utah, hardly enough to make up for the almost 47,000 lost in Florida or the 43,000 in California. Other states with major declines were New York (28,600), Massachusetts (21,000), and Georgia (19,200).

Despite this 5.2 percent reduction in jobs in 1991, the construction trades are still expected to grow by more than

20 percent by the year 2005, according to the Department of Labor. The industry as a whole, which currently employs about 4.5 million workers, will fare slightly better than the average for all other occupations.

Pipelayers will post the largest growth rate, 31 percent, but electricians will see the the largest numerical increase in jobs, 158,000. Statistics for all jobs within the industry, in order of growth, follow.

Job	1990 Actual Employment	Projected Growth (%) by 2005	Projected Growth(%) (Expanding Economy)
Pipelayers and fitters	55,000	31%	40%
Pavers	73,000	30	39
Electricians	548,000	29	36
Insulation workers	70,000	24	33
Hard tile setters	28,000	24	30
Painters	453,000	24	30
Drywall installers	143,000	23	30
Roofers	138,000	23	30
Glaziers	42,000	22	30
Plumbers	379,000	21	28
Carpet installers	73,000	21	26
Bricklayers	152,000	20	28
Metal workers	80,000	20	28
Carpenters	1,057,000	14	20
Concrete masons	113,000	13	21
Plasterers	28,000	13	20
Ceiling tile installers	20,000	11	19

Health Care

(See also the separate entries on Doctors and Dentists)

Anyone who is genuinely concerned about finding a job or who is truly worried that fewer jobs will be available in the near future should take a look at the health care sector for a big dose of optimism. Not only are seven of the 10 fastest growing occupations in the country in health care, but in literally every state and every metropolitan area these jobs are in great demand.

In this $666 billion health care industry one rarely even hears of "downsizing," the "lean and mean" approach, or even simple staff cutbacks. While most other major industries have been struggling in recent years, health care has grown by more than 10 percent every year since 1987. Total expenditures for health care now total $2,400 per person each year, and represent 12 percent of the US Gross National Product figures that are so significantly higher than other industrialized nations that the cost of health care has become a serious political problem.

Every politician today makes an issue out of health care costs but not one ever seriously proposes cutbacks in our commitment for the obvious reason that most voters want quality care regardless of the price tag. As the population continues to grow older (almost 13 percent are over 65, and the average age is now 33, up from 28 in 1970) and as medical technology continues to break new ground the chances are very good that this commitment will not diminish in the least. The manner in which we pay for health care services may change but this will not affect job growth in any way.

What will definitely change is a lowering of the percentage of dollars going to hospital-based care, and this will affect jobs. A new boom in home health care has driven up expenditures in this area by about 25 percent a year recently (in 1990 it totalled $7 billion and will easily reach $10 billion in two years). In the long run this trend will lower costs but will create more jobs since a larger number of patients can be cared for.

Administrators Although hospitals will remain the central organization in the so-called health care delivery system they will dwindle in number over the next decade, with perhaps as many as 450 shutting their doors. The people who manage them, however, will not be hard-pressed to find new jobs. Health care administrators of all kinds, from CEOs to billers and coders, will be in demand, say the experts, because their major functions—controlling costs, dealing with the government and with private insurance providers, assuring quality patient care—will be even more important in the future. In addition the creation of more nursing homes, clinics, HMOs, and large home-based care providers will require additional staff to handle the business operations of this enormous industry. Health care is seen as the proverbial growth area, one that will be a safe-haven for many professional occupations—computer professionals, etc.—as well as those directly involved with patient care.

Registered Nurses Registered nurses are ranked as the second fastest growing job in the U.S. with over 700,000 jobs expected to be added by the year 2005. The problem is that even experienced nurses find it hard to do such strenuous work for relatively low pay and not much prestige and as a result literally tens of thousands have given up practicing or take only part-time work. Some analysts believe that the shortage of nurses has reached crisis proportions and will be worse before it gets better.

But the pay is rising and enrollments are inching upward (200,000 in 1991) so as the job market tightens more men and women may turn to nursing and help to ease the shortage, especially when they realize that they can work almost anywhere they please. The states with the greatest demand are those that are still building their health care delivery systems, such as Kentucky, Tennessee, and Alabama, and the states with strong population growth including Arizona, California, Florida, and Texas (so great is the need in Texas that the famous M.D. Anderson Cancer Hospital in Houston offers a $500 bonus to any employee who helps find someone to fill several vacant positions). But even in areas hit hard by the recession—New England, Michigan, Pennsylvania—the demand for nurses has not abated.

Nor will it for the foreseeable future. According to the U.S. Bureau of Health Professions of the Health and Human Services Department there will be a need for as many as 20,000 new nurses a year for the next 30 years because of increases in the number of doctors, nursing homes, and home health services.

Physical Therapists The need for therapists of all kinds will also grow significantly over the next decade but recent breakthroughs in rehabilitative medicine have helped to create strong demand for physical therapists, whose numbers are expected to grow by over 4,000 a year. This may turn out to be a conservative estimate since this field is quickly developing specialties (pediatrics, neurology, etc.) that are having very positive results for patients on the mend. Over 100 colleges now offer degrees in this field and a B.S. degree has quickly become a minimum requirement. Competition to enter the best programs (the University of Vermont's, for example) is very sharp.

Respiratory therapists—working with patients who have breathing disorders—are also expected to be in strong demand and to increase in number by over 30,000 by the year 2005. A college degree is not required but you must have certification that coursework and training have been taken.

Technicians Also in very great demand are health technologists and technicians, the people who take the X-rays (now called radiologic technicians), sonograms, and EEGs, administer the blood tests, and work in the laboratories processing all those unneeded tests we keep hearing about. According to the Summit on Manpower, a consortium of 18 professional health care groups (including the American Hospital Association), over 20 percent of hospital technician jobs are vacant and enrollments in training programs are at only 50 percent of needed capacity.

The education needed to become a health technician ranges from one-year certificate programs to four-year baccalaureate degrees. Open to high school graduates (or the equivalent diploma holders), applicants should select from programs accredited by the American Medical Association, based on their career goals. In general, the more advanced the course of study, the more high level positions are available. Many students elect a shorter certificate program and then pursue higher levels of education while employed, taking advantage of tuition reimbursement offered by many hospitals. After completing a program, there are certification exams for each of the sub-specialties.

The Summit on Manpower is also targeting nontraditional sources for recruitment such as mothers returning to the work force and older Americans.

There is tremendous opportunity for high school graduates to complete a relatively short program and enter the technology field at a competitive salary. The status of these professions within the hospital is also on the rise.

For more information contact:

The Summit on Manpower
1825 K Street NW, Suite 210
Washington, DC 20006
(800) 432–3247

For a current list of accredited programs and wage information, write:

American Medical Association
Department of Allied Health Education and Accreditation
535 North Dearborn Street
Chicago, IL 60610

Podiatrists and Optometrists As the accompanying table makes clear, there will be an increased number of jobs for all the other major support categories in the industry. Among the so-called medical practitioners, podiatrists will continue to be a strong specialty as the number of people engaging in strenuous physical activities continues to grow; the Department of Labor estimates that podiatrists will number about 24,000 in 2005, up from 16,000 in 1990. Optometrists too will find new openings but at a smaller growth rate, as their numbers are projected to increase from 37,000 to about 46,000 in the same time span.

So across-the-board growth in health care occupations seems certain. Who exactly is going to pay for this ever-increasing financial burden may well be the central question of our next two or three presidential elections but it will not hinder the employment growth that in a very real way is keeping the national employment rate at a respectable level.

Psychologists Society's ever-increasing acceptance of the value of psychological counseling has helped to make this one of the fastest growing occupations in the country. The U.S. Bureau of Labor Statistics expects about 5,000 new positions to be available each year for the next decade or so. Most of the jobs will be for clinical pyschologists working in community mental health centers, in nursing homes, and in drug and alcohol abuse programs either in hospitals, clinics, or Employee Assistance Programs run by corporations. The AIDS epidemic and the public's increasing awareness of the extent of family violence will also bring a stronger demand for specialized psychological services. So too will the needs of the aged whose growing numbers are affecting all health care services.

According to the American Psychological Association (APA) increased opportunities for psychologists are also expected to occur in schools and in corporations as industrial psychology grows in importance in the human resources sector. In addition, with the rise in the willingness of third-party insurers to cover some of the costs of therapy more and more psychologists are expected to enter private practice (approximately 20,000 of today's 125,000 psychologists are self-employed). Finally, a surprising number of college and university teaching positions will be available over the coming years since over 20 percent of the current faculty are over the age of 55.

One note of caution for those not familiar with this profession: all supervisory positions and most meaningful responsibility require a doctoral degree; many entry level positions require a master's degree. On the positive side, the APA estimates that the unemployment rate for psychologists is less than 1 percent.

According to the APA, there were 17 clinically active psychologists for every 100,000 residents of the U.S. in 1989. In part because federal employee benefits pay a large part of the cost of therapy, the area in and around Washington D.C. had by far the greatest number of psychologists in proportion to the general population: 78 per 100,000. Among the states, Massachusetts led with 40 per 100,000, followed by New York (30), Maryland (27), and Vermont (27).

Some growth areas of the country that should have room for more psychologists are Seattle, Phoenix, Salt Lake City, Houston, Dallas, Columbus, and Cincinnati.

Employment Growth For Health Care Workers, 1990–2005

Occupation	Employment[1]		Avg. Annual Increase	Net Increase
	1990	2005		
Dental Assistants	176,000	236,000	4,000	60,000
Dental Hygienists	97,000	137,000	2,666	40,000
Dieticians and Nutritionists	45,000	56,000	730	11,000
Medical Assistants	165,000	287,000	8,133	122,000
Pharmacists	169,000	204,000	2,333	35,000
Pharmacy Assistants	83,000	101,000	1,200	18,000
Physicians Assistants	53,000	72,000	1,267	19,000
Podiatrists	16,000	23,000	466	7,000
Nurses Registered	1.7 mil.	2.5 mil.	46,670	700,000
Licensed Practical	644,000	913,000	17,933	269,000
Nurses Aides, Orderlies	1.3 mil.	1.9 mil.	40,000	600,000
Psychiatric Aides	100,000	134,000	2,267	34,000
Therapists Occupational	36,000	56,000	1,333	20,000
Physical	88,000	155,000	4,533	68,000
Recreational	32,000	45,000	866	3,000
Respiratory	60,000	91,000	2,066	31,000
Speech	68,000	91,000	1,533	23,000
All Others	26,000	40,000	933	14,000

Employment Growth For Health Care Workers, 1990–2005 *(cont.)*

	Employment[1]		Avg. Annual Increase	Net Increase
Occupation	1990	2005		
Therapy Assistants	55,000	89,000	2,266	34,000
Technicians				
Clinical Lab	258,000	321,000	4,200	63,000
EEG	7,000	11,000	266	4,000
EKG	16,000	15,000	None	−1,000
Emergency Medical	89,000	116,000	1,800	27,000
Medical Records	52,000	80,000	1,866	28,000
Nuclear Medicine	10,000	16,000	400	6,000
Opticians	64,000	88,000	1,600	24,000
Radiologic	149,000	252,000	6,866	103,000
Surgical	38,000	59,000	1,400	21,000
All Other Paraprofessionals and Health Technicians	409,000	588,000	11,933	179,000

1. Based on U.S. Bureau of Labor Statistical projections for a moderately growing economy and industry.

Source: U.S. Bureau of Labor Statistics, Monthly Labor Review, *November, 1991*

Insurance

The insurance industry is a vast and financially powerful sector of the U.S. economy. In 1991 alone premium receipts totalled over $283 billion for life insurance, and $226 billion for property and casualty insurance (including $95 billion for auto insurance). The industry is also one of the largest employers in the country with just over two million people employed, approximately half of them in clerical positions.

The employment situation has been stable recently, but most analysts believe that demand for insurance products will continue to increase, thereby creating solid, long-term future job growth. Despite the 1991 failures of four huge life insurance companies—Executive Life, First Capital, Monarch, and Mutual Benefit—the insurance industry's worst crises appear to be over. An industry-wide shakeout is unquestionably in progress, yet its rigors may boost as many companies as it burdens. Strong insurers such as Northwestern Mutual, Prudential, New York Life, and Metropolitan Life will gain more policyholders from weaker firms.

In addition, demographic variables—conspicuously the aging of the Baby Boom generation—will raise demand sharply for products that provide retirement income and health care insurance. Health insurance seems likely to provide one of the strongest sectors of growth. Elected officials now voice concern over the plight of uninsured and underinsured citizens; even Americans with adequate coverage may upgrade their policies in response to escalating health care costs. Underwriters, adjusters, investigators, and claim workers seem likely to benefit from ongoing growth in this sector of the industry. Since insurance companies require large clerical staffs to function, growth in clerical job categories is also probable.

Actuaries The job outlook for actuaries seems strong, with three main factors contributing to the situation. First, actuaries are relatively rare; approximately 12,800 are accredited in the United States and Canada, of whom about 6000 work in the insurance industry. Second, the National Academy of Insurance Commissioners now requires that insurance companies appoint an actuary to provide opinions about loss reserves and other financial issues affecting firms' financial solvency. Third, actuaries' roles are broadening to include more managerial and marketing duties within the insurance industry. Jim Murphy, Executive Vice President of the American Academy of Actuaries, believes these combined factors bode well for actuaries' employment. "There's a significant need for the technical knowledge that actuaries possess, and the focus on competition and expenses these days also means that actuaries will be needed to plan and react to industry changes." Murphy also felt that the demand for actuaries would remain high both in property/casualty and life/health insurance sectors.

Underwriters Over the next decade the aging U.S. population should greatly increase the need for underwriters (there are about 110,000 now). The U.S. Bureau of Labor Statistics notes that two areas of particularly dramatic growth within the insurance industry are likely to be (1) insurance coverage for working women, and (2) expanding long-term health care and pension benefits for retirees. Since most people consider insurance a necessity regardless of economic conditions, underwriters are unlikely to be laid off during a recession.

Adjusters Roy Cervenka, President of the National Association of Independent Insurance Adjusters, regards the market for this job category as strong and getting stronger. "There's a shortage developing in the number of high-quality people in the field," according to Cervenka. The reason: "Companies used to provide good on-the-job training in this area, but this is no longer always true." Cervenka regards the shortage as essentially nationwide. Adjusters in line-of-claims, workers compensation, and casualty areas are in especially high demand.

Customer Service Representatives Katherine Hoffman, Associate Director of Public Relations for the National Association of Professional Insurance Agents (NAPSA), notes that CSR roles are changing and expanding, which bodes well for the employment outlook overall. CSRs are becoming involved in all aspects of the agency system, from marketing to management. Account development, telemarketing, and x-dating have all become part of the CSR's duties. Hoffman observes as well that "This is an appealing job category for women, especially those with children, and others who may not wish to work full-time."

Clerical Workers The overall situation for clerical workers seems good, given traditional high turnover and an ongoing need for support staff within the industry. An increased degree of computerization may reduce some firms' needs for personnel; on the other hand, precisely these same companies are likely to experience an increased need for computer-literate personnel. As noted earlier, the current crisis in health care suggests that this sector will undergo marked growth during the 1990s.

Brokers and Agents Approximately 50,000 insurance agencies operate in the United States, some of which employ hundreds of agents and brokers, some just a few. Since many of these brokers and agents operate on their own, it's difficult to project growth for this job category. The current mergers of insurance companies now in progress complicates the picture still more. However, the growing demand for health and insurance products, especially, suggests that the agent/broker category may be a likely growth area for people with strong entrepreneurial drive. As Catherine Hoffman of NAPSA points out, "The field for agents has great potential for minorities and women, since to date they have been under-represented.''

Publishing

Books Despite the ubiquitous presence of books in our lives (not in our homes of course, just on TV with Oprah, Phil, and Sonya), this is a relatively small industry. In 1991 book shipments totalled $16 billion and employment only about 72,000 nationwide, down from a peak of 74,000 in 1989. So anyone who feels he or she *must* have a job in this so-called glamour industry should take a hard look at the various areas of the business to see which offer the best opportunities.

The U.S. publishing industry has been in upheaval for nearly a decade. After dealing with the effects of corporate takeovers, publishers have had to navigate the recession. Burdened by overspending on advances to authors, over-production of titles, and overly optimistic printings, publishers are finally pruning their lists, and trimming their staffs as well. In 1990, new book output dropped 17 percent to an all-time low of 44,000 titles, although R.R. Bowker estimates that the number of new titles published in 1991 will have edged back up to 46,000–48,000 books and with it increased employment.

In this relatively small business, reports of layoffs of even 100 employees sends shockwaves through the industry, leaving people with the feeling that the job market in publishing is very grim. But, in *Publishers Weekly*'s 1991 salary survey, only 15 percent of the companies responding to the survey reported a decrease in staff. Nearly one-half of the respondents said that there was no change in staff size, and 36 percent increased their staff. For 1992, nearly 35 percent of the companies said they expected to hire additional staff during the year.

In recent years the strongest area of the business in terms of growth has been juvenile books, which in 1989-90 had an unprecedented growth spurt with sales increasing over 13 percent in both hardcover and paperback. While in general publishers have been cutting back on the number of titles they publish each year, children's books publishers have been *increasing* the number of new titles they issue. Sales of religious books and bibles increased nearly 11 percent—proving, once again, that bad economic times can be good for religious books. Increases in cover prices helped total sales go up despite the smaller number of general books published. Adult hardcovers and mass market paperbacks increased by 8.5 percent and 9.6 percent respectively. Educational publishing seems to have suffered the most in 1991, posting small increases for college textbooks (+ .3 percent) and elementary and secondary texts (1.7 percent).

Looking ahead, in a report entitled *Book Publishing at the Crossroads* compiled by Coopers and Lybrand, an international group of publishing executives predicted that the world book market would grow between 8.3–9.4 percent annually over the next three years. The American participants in the study felt that the lower number was a realistic expectation for growth in this country.

Susan Gordon, president of the Lynne Palmer Agency, an employment agency specializing in publishing placements, says that new jobs are coming up in children's books and in professional and scholarly publishing (which includes business, law, medical, scientific, and technical books). She also sees an increased demand for individuals who can bring specialized talent to nonfiction houses. Gordon says many publishers are looking for people who know everything there is to know about a subject, like gardening, or quarks.

Although New York City is still the publishing center of the country, the agency is increasingly recruiting for regional and specialty publishers around the country. For example, there is a large enclave of publishers in the Bay Area, and small publishers and university presses abound in the rest of California, Colorado, and other Rocky Mountain states. The center for computer book publishing is in Indianapolis, home of Macmillan Computer Publishing. This group publishes most of the bestsellers in the field and expects to increase its frontlist publishing by 35 percent in 1992.

Ms. Gordon also sees job opportunities with European publishers opening offices in New York, and with book packagers, an emerging force in the publishing world. Leaner in-house editorial and production staffs lead to a greater dependence on packagers to develop and produce books. Steve Ettlinger, president of the American Book Producer's Association, says that even publishers who have never dealt with packagers before are turning to them for ideas.

Magazines The bottom line: 1991 was the worst year financially in decades for the magazine industry. However, while newsweeklies and women's magazines may be losing advertisers and readers—and as a result, firing staff writers—other magazines are faring much better. More than 10,000 magazines are published annually in the U.S. with the number of new publications topping 500 every year. For every advertising-driven mega-magazine slashing staff, there are dozens of smaller, "niche" publications supported by readers, which are hiring writers and editors.

"Companies that have circulation-driven magazines have not been hit as hard," says Bob Farley, executive vice president of the Magazines Publishers Association. Circulation-based magazines are generally narrowly focused, with a specialized audience. Farley points to several healthy companies with "niche" magazines: Cowles in Harrisburg, Pa. with *Fly Fisherman, Bow Hunter,* and *American History Illustrated;* Elhert in Wayzata, Minn. with *Water Scooter* and *Snowmobile;* and Rodale Press in Emmaus Pa., with *Prevention, Runners World* and *Backpacker.*

Farley points to technology and computers as "hot" areas. Ziff-Davis, publisher of *MacUser* and *PC Computing* among other titles, posted gains last year.

Samir Husni, a University of Mississippi professor who tracks the industry, also finds there are openings. "Many are at small publications and start-ups where staff members are expected to know how to do everything from writing and editing to desktop publishing." Many of the start-ups publish with small staffs and use computers for pasteup, photos, and layout to cut costs. Popular categories for new publications include country, home, crafts and health.

Husni suggests trade and association journals as possibilities. The *Employment Roundup* published by the American Business Press recently had job listings for golf, food service, medical and technology publications. Associations such as the New York Academy of Sciences and the Institute of Electrical Engineers recently hired writers, pointing up another strong area: specialized writing. While the National Association of Science Writers admits that some major publications have let people go, there is still a fairly strong market for medical, health and technical experts. Two major universities, for example, were looking for specialized writers to head the communication offices for their medical and technical schools. The association has also found that newsletters, especially in the biotechnology, government relations and medicine, are looking for writers.

Another trend, which is good news for younger writers, bad news for veterans, has been observed by Edwin Diamond, media columnist for New York magazine. "The pattern I've begun to see is that magazines buy out older workers who have good benefits and salaries and in their places hire younger people on a contract basis, which usually means half the salary and no benefits like health or pensions."

The contract arrangement not only saves management money but also appeals to editors who need more staff during the frenzy prior to deadline. One contract writer was recently hired by a newsweekly to work two 15-hour days, Friday and Saturday, when the book closes.

The contract arrangement exists mostly at major publications in New York. But if writers are willing to relocate, full-time positions are in other areas of the country, especially at regional publications in California and Florida. Publishing pockets flourish in places like Des Moines, home of Meredith, publishers of 13 titles from *Better Homes and Gardens* to *Wood,* and Knoxville, headquarters for Whittle, publishers of a large number of special-interest, single-advertiser magazines. Husni suggests, ''Forget a job in New York City, but there are new and replacement jobs out there is other areas of the country.''

Disagreeing with Husni about New York is Ed Koller, president of the Howard Sloan-Koller Group, which places editors. ''Even in New York there are jobs for bright, aggressive people. Magazines are being more selective, they want more for their money. They are placing a premium on talent and people willing to work hard and long hours.'' Koller also says there is one perennial opening. ''Good copy editors are impossible to find. There are always openings for them.''

Newspapers   The headlines on the newspaper industry's economic health have spelled doom and gloom. While the drop in advertising revenues has forced cutbacks in all areas, the impact on editorial jobs has been lessened thanks to a perennial management headache: the high turnover rate of reporters and editors. Even though the economic climate has damped the wanderlust somewhat, newspaper industry observers say that editorial staffers are still moving around, creating openings, especially at smaller and mid-sized papers.

''There has been some whittling down and consolidations,'' says Lee Stinnett, executive director of the American Society of Newspaper Editors, ''but because of the high turnover rates there are opening all over.''

Experts points to several ''hot spots'' in newspapers. The Southwest and Midwest are two of the strong areas, according to John Blodger of the American Newspaper Publishers Association. "Most of the newspapers in the Southwest are holding their own. Some are even gaining in circulation," he said. Two newspapers in Indiana, one in Gary, the other Fort Wayne, recently posted several listings for positions ranging from sports copy editor to metro editor.

Papers with circulations under 100,000 are generally doing better than metro dailies. "Newspapers, especially in the 20,000 to 50,000 circulation range, seem to have more job openings than larger papers," says University of Missouri professor Daryl Moen. "These papers are all over the country, but especially concentrated on the eastern seaboard."

Moen also points to several other strong areas, especially copy editing and "info graphics." "Papers are becoming much more editor-intensive with news summaries and roundups. To save money papers can fire two reporters and pick up the slack with one good copy editor," he says. "Also anyone who has the combination of computer skills and artistic talents will find openings doing charts and other info graphics."

Newspapers also have openings for minority reporters and editors. "Even places with job freezes will make room for a minority reporter with the right credentials," says Moen.

John Garcia, a New York writer who tracks employment for the National Association of Hispanic Journalists, agrees that the market for minorities is good, judging from the turnout at two recent "job fairs" for minority reporters.

He agrees with Moen that jobs exist at smaller papers, citing openings recently at newspapers in Hartford, Conn. and Allentown, Pa. Garcia also has observed a steady market in news services, like the Dow Jones News Retrieval and Prodigy. "There are jobs out there, but you have to be good and willing to leave New York."

Real Estate

The plethora of "For Sale" signs in store windows and office buildings will continue to spell bad news for the commercial real estate market. With high double-digit office vacancy rates the norm these days, employment levels in commercial real estate have sunk, and the work has been confined to specialists. The best prospects in commercial real estate are for *development managers,* well-trained individuals with undergraduate and graduate degrees in real estate development who specialize in marketing and leasing.

In the residential market, however, realtors are seeing some signs of recovery. Home prices rose 7 percent in 1991, according to the National Association of Realtors, and are expected to rise another 5 percent in 1992. Mortgage rates are also at their lowest in more than 17 years, and analysts expect a substantial increase in the sales of homes.

A shift in the age of the population will also mean more people buying homes. As baby-boomers find themselves with children of their own, they have already begun moving out of one- and two-bedroom apartments and into three- and four-bedroom houses.

The real estate market is, of course, responsive to geographic shifts in populations. Consequently, despite patches of difficulty, real estate jobs are expected to thrive in the southeast as well as along the Pacific Coast, but will fare poorly in the northeast and parts of the midwest. Dallas-Fort Worth, Atlanta, and Houston are especially strong metropolitan areas for the early 1990s.

Prospective job seekers can improve their chances of employment by getting training in the increasingly specialized areas of the field, such as appraising and development management, where most growth is projected. Women, who account for more than half of the residential sales agents in the country, are expected to make gains in other segments of the real estate market as well.

Brokers Brokers must be licensed by the state after completing more than 90 hours of training. They must also have anywhere from 1–3 years of selling experience. Some states waive the experience requirements for applicants with college credit or a bachelors' degree in real estate.

Until the real estate market rebounds from the recession, jobs for brokers in the residential markets are expected to be more plentiful than those for the sales agents they employ. Real estate brokers numbered 69,000 in 1990 and are expected to grow more than 20 percent, to 83,000, in 2005.

Sales Agents In the residential markets, jobs for qualified agents should be easy to come by in the 1990s, primarily because of high turnover and the high level of training required to enter this field. Sales agents in all states must have a high school diploma and be licensed. The licensing requirements for agents, who almost always work for brokers, are not as stringent as those for their bosses. Candidates for sales agents must take an exam and complete 30 hours of classroom instruction.

There were 300,000 real estate sales agents in 1990. Jobs for agents should grow no faster than the national average for all jobs (11–19 percent). But many beginning agents leave the profession because they become discouraged by an inability to close deals. Thus openings are commonplace, especially with large nationwide franchises.

Appraisers The men and women whose job it is to determine property values are the fastest-growing segment of the real estate industry. There were more than 44,000 real estate appraisers in 1990, and their numbers are expected to swell by 24 percent, to 54,000, in 2005. As institutional clients with large mortgage portfolios seek to redevelop and revalue their properties, the appraiser's job will become even more important.

The federal government requires that appraisers be state licensed or certified. Certification requires appraisal experience and an examination, or college credit, and is required for involvement in any federally related transaction of $1 million or more. Licensed appraisers must meet less stringent requirements and may appraise residential properties of up to four units.

Retail Sales

America's true national pastime is not baseball, it's shopping. In second place is eating (and drinking) outside the home.

Before you argue consider that in 1991 the American people spent over $1.7 trillion (about $8,000 per capita) in 1.5 million retail establishments, including 12,000 department stores, 105,000 furniture and home furnishing stores, 150,000 apparel stores, 185,000 food stores, and nearly 400,000 eating and drinking places (see below). More than 19 million people are employed in this sector of the economy, perhaps the most vital in a society based on mass consumption.

Of course the slightest glitch in the machinery of such an economy will have rapid fire effects. During the latest recession, for example, about 400,000 jobs were temporarily lost between September 1990 and September 1991. Industry analysts are predicting a turnaround this year with annual sales increasing by as much as 2 percent, strong but still anemic by the mid–1980s level of 4 percent a year.

So despite all the recent headline-making events like the bankruptcy filings by such all-American names as Macy's and Bloomingdale's, the immediate future of retailing looks solid if not spectacular. It's just that there will be new leaders as well as new kinds of stores.

According to Jack Frasier, Vice President, Human Resources, National Retail Federation, ''Obituaries on the demise of department stores are greatly premature. Customers want one-stop shopping and, although several big name department stores have gotten themselves in trouble, many others have seen their profits rise. Without question, however, the biggest area of growth has been, and will continue to be, in the so-called 'category killers.' Specialty stores such as The Gap, Toys R Us, Dollar General, Home Depot, for example, are seeing a tremendous growth. And, the future in retailing isn't limited to the United States. The recent opening of Toys R Us in Japan is just the beginning of an international expansion. In America, the major areas of future growth are in regions such as the Sun Belt and the Southwest, places that have experienced an enormous population growth.''

In addition, retailers expect lower interest rates to stimulate sales and to increase job opportunities. These sales increases will be seen especially in stores such as Wal-Mart, whose sales are expected to increase by 9 percent, and Kmart, with sales increasing at a slightly lower rate. Both Wal-Mart and Kmart are expanding not only in sales but in the number and size of new stores being opened in 1992 and '93. Kmart, for example, is designing 110,000 sq. ft. stores rather than their former 76,000 sq. ft. facilities. Says a key Wal-Mart executive, ''Our big store growth was in the 1980s. We slowed it in the early 1990s to catch up but now we're revving it up again with the large super Wal-Mart combination stores and specialty stores.''

Some analysts predict that Wal-Mart will be jumping into the warehouse-type outlets in a major way with some 200 Sam's Wholesale Club outlets scheduled to be built over the next decade.

The U.S. Bureau of Labor Statistics predicts that most of the job categories for retail sales workers will increase much faster than the average for all occupations between 1990 and 2005. Here are figures for the most common jobs in retailing based on the Bureau's moderate growth projections:

Job title	Number of employees 1990	2005	% growth
Cashiers	2,633	3,318	26%
Counter and retail clerks	215	289	34
Salespersons, retail	3,619	4,506	24
Stock clerks, sales floor	1,242	1,451	17

Eating and Drinking Places More than 6.5 million Americans work in the restaurants, bars, pizza places, chili joints, et al., that seem to have sprung up in every nook and cranny of every little town, large urban area, and suburban mall. Despite the recession's negative effects on the $260 billion food-service industry, every analyst in every state as well as all the forecasters in Washington, D.C., project very strong job growth in this sector of the economy. In fact the Bureau of Labor Statistics asserts that by the year 2005, fully six percent of U.S. employees will work in eating and drinking establishments—some 8.7 million people. The current recession has slowed hiring somewhat, yet overall growth should occur at about 1.9 percent annually, well above average for the total labor force.

The most important question, however, is what kind of establishments will these millions be working in. Since 1989 the number of restaurant outlets has declined dramatically from 379,000 to 269,000 according to Restaurant Consulting Group Inc. in Evanston, Ill. The midlevel and upscale establishments appear to have been hit the hardest, although the most expensive restaurants in major cities (Bouley and Lutece in New York, Spago in L.A., for example) are always booked solid.

The strongest current industry trend is an enormous surge in the fast-food sector. McDonald's, Wendy's, and Burger

King all report dramatically improved sales for late 1991; Kentucky Fried Chicken and Arby's have also indicated better sales. Clearly people who cannot afford to eat in so-called "white-tablecloth" restaurants will at least treat themselves to an inexpensive meal. A recent Gallup survey indicates that 45 percent of adult Americans would eat out more often if they had the cash.

Both high- and low-end restaurants that are thriving in the present economic climate stress hearty fare at reasonable prices. Restaurants catering to cost-conscious Baby Boomers with children also seem most likely to prosper. Typical restaurants of this sort are Chili's, Buffets Inc., and Cracker Barrel Old Country Store.

Chefs and Cooks These occupations will have the highest growth rate for any food service occupation—a whopping 42 percent by the year 2005. The nation currently employs about 1.2 million non-short order cooks and 743,000 short order cooks; these numbers will increase to 1.6 million and 872,000, respectively. Job growth will occur partly because of older cooks' retiring or seeking other forms of employment. Growth seems probable both at the high and low ends of the market: the overall aging of the U.S. population will mean more people able to afford meals at restaurants offering table service; at the same time, the trend toward two-income families will create greater demand for fast-food places.

Other Food Preparation Workers Bread and pastry bakers, fast-food cooks, and food preparers of other sorts are each expected to gain more than 30 percent in the number of jobs between now and 2005. Given the strong growth evident in the fast-food sector, preparation workers of all kinds seem likely to encounter abundant opportunities for employment.

Bartenders, Waiters, and Bus Persons On the service side, dining room and cafeteria servers, helpers, bartenders, and fountain/food counter workers are each likely to post employment gains of 34 percent between now and 2005; server jobs of all kinds should reach about 2.2 million total. Most openings will arise from the need to replace the many workers who seek other employment in this high-turnover category.

Securities

While the economy seems to have been in free-fall since mid–1990, the securities industry has been in full-flight, defying economic indicators and gloomy prognosticators, and giving its people hope that the glory days of the mid–1980s might not be gone forever. But soaring profits and surging stocks don't necessarily mean great job opportunities.

Anyone who has had experience looking for a job in this business, especially on Wall Street itself, knows that there are two related obstacles to finding one: the relatively small size of the industry and the blatant nepotism that pervades every area. For although the size and scope of American business requires three major stock exchanges in New York alone (not to mention the mountains of government debt that gets funded through the industry) there are only 8,000 firms with about 215,000 employees in the whole country. And because the pay is so good (even retail brokers *average* $80,000 a year), and the work clean and mostly respectable, despite the continuous scandals, it's not surprising or unusual that the relatives of those who are on the inside should have the first crack at these jobs.

In 1992 the job market looks better than it has since October 1987 when the Dow plunged more than 500 points and the industry began a major contraction reducing the work force by 50,000 over the next three years. In 1991 the Dow-Jones Index surged to record levels, avoided radical swings, and helped bring greatly increased pre-tax profits to most securities firms. Increased business on the global level also brought hefty profits and helped the market see new future possibilities.

But the most important reason for the dramatic increase in market activity has been the lowering of interest rates at every level. Many investors are taking their money out of the banks where it is often earning less than 5 percent and seeking higher returns in stocks, mutual funds, collateralized mortgages, and a whole host of products that were once the province of only the most sophisticated players. As a result many of the largest firms, including Merrill Lynch, Dean Witter, and Prudential Securities, are actively seeking to increase their staffs of retail brokers. Others such as Shearson Lehman Brothers have resumed their training progams to meet future needs. Shearson plans to add some 800 brokers nationwide, and Charles Schwab, the well-known discount broker, has been recruiting salespeople on a nationwide basis.

If the business continues to expand, as is expected, many entry and support level jobs will open up again but keep in mind how small the business really is and why it gets to select the best. Finally, the computerization of the so-called "back-office," where clerical jobs once abounded, has reduced employment permanently except for highly-paid and heavily recruited computer specialists.

Travel

Despite fears over travelling during the Gulf War and the continued recession, spending on the various travel services grew 3.9 percent in 1991. This is a trend that is expected to continue through the 1990s. Further consolidation of the airline industry, new forms of travel lodging, and more effective security measures (to allay fears of terrorism) are expected to produce dramatic gains in travel service employment.

The travel services are comprised of the airlines, intercity bus companies, Amtrak (the national passenger rail system), passenger ship and boat operators, automobile services, commercial lodging places, campgrounds and trailer parks, eating and drinking places, amusement and recreation facilities, automobile rental and tax companies, travel agents, and general merchandise and miscellaneous stores. Employment in these areas stood at just over 5 million in 1991 and is expected to post growth of about 4 percent in 1992.

Although growth in this area is largely dependent on the economy—travel services represented six percent of the Gross National Product—many areas are already succeeding in the recession. Carnival and Royal Caribbean cruise lines are reporting record-breaking bookings. The merger of the 12 European Community countries into a single market has fueled increased business interest by Americans in European markets, and a consequent increase in Transatlantic flights. Travel to Hawaii and Florida are both very strong, and the winter of 1992 shows a 25 percent increase over 1991 at resorts like Taos Ski Valley in New Mexico.

The industry has also succeeded in targeting special niche markets, such as "budget," "luxury," "corporate meeting," or "all-suite" hotels. This last category is one of the fastest-growing segments of the hotel industry. The travel services industry has also responded well to Americans' changing vacation needs, offering special weekend rates and four- to seven-day packages to travelers who have neither the time nor money for a traditional two-week vacation. Such short-stay packages are expected to be offered in all segments of the travel services industry in the 1990s.

Travel Agents   High growth and high turnover means that jobs for travel agents should be plentiful in the 1990s. The number of travel agents stood at 132,000 in 1990 and is expected to grow by 82,000 jobs, a whopping 62 percent by the year 2005. Specialized training is important for travel agents, as few firms offer on-the-job training. But full-time training programs lasting anywhere from three to 12 weeks are widely available. Courses in accounting, business management, and foreign language are helpful to travel agents seeking jobs. Computer skills are essential.

According to P. Jason King, president of Yours in Travel Personnel Agency, most travel agent jobs will be found on the East Coast, particularly in New York City, Boston, Washington D.C. and Florida. California, Chicago, Dallas, Phoenix, and Denver will also offer good opportunities.

Growth in managerial, professional specialty, and sales representative occupations (the people who do the most business travel) will spark a corresponding increase in business related travel in the 1990s. Consequently, business travel specialists such as meeting planners and corporate travel agents are especially good job prospects for the 1990s.

Airlines The conflict in the Persian Gulf and the subsequent economic recession took a heavy toll on the airline industry in 1990–91. Reduced revenues from vacation and business travelers combined with sharply higher operating costs forced established airlines such as Eastern, Pan Am and Midway to cease operations, while carriers including America West, Continental and TWA are operating in Chapter 11 bankruptcy status.

Nonetheless, a number of successful companies are expanding to fill the void left by the airlines that are now defunct, and smaller national and regional airlines are enjoying some growth by providing service between cities throughout the United States and the hubs operated by the major airlines. American, United and Delta, the largest domestic carriers, are financially sound, and have recently positioned themselves to become major players in international travel. Industry analysts predict that by the year 2000, global travel will nearly double as Europe opens its borders and Asia becomes a more popular destination for tourists and business people. American and United in particular, have the fleet size and experience to move quickly into this lucrative and burgeoning market.

Airline industry analysts have predicted annual growth

of 5 percent over the next four years, but this may prove to be conservative. In January 1992 *The New York Times* reported an unexpected surge in travel to U.S. and overseas destinations. Six airlines—United, American, Delta, America West, TWA and Continental—had traffic increases over the previous year, which may point to a more dramatic recovery than was anticipated; and an increasing number of jobs.

Job opportunities grow as airlines add new routes to their schedules and new jet equipment to their fleets. What follows is a summary of the activities of the 10 major U.S. airlines that should lead to the creation of new jobs through the end of the decade.

America West will double service from Columbus, Ohio with flights to Chicago Midway, Orlando and Tampa. The airline has orders and options on 152 new jets for delivery between 1992 and 2005.

American purchased 12 of Midway's slots at Laguardia (NYC) and 10 slots at National (D.C.). The airline is scheduled to purchase 682 aircraft by 1995.

Continental began service from Newark-Mexico City, and Newark-Madrid, and plans service from Newark to Munich and Paris in the early summer. They intend to provide service to Spain by 1993 and have orders and options on 190 aircraft between 1992 and 1995.

Delta picked up Pan Am's New York-Mexico City route and has temporary authority for Pan Am's Detroit-London route. The airline began service from Atlanta-St. Thomas, Orlando-Mexico City, Atlanta-Barcelona/Madrid, and from New York Kennedy to destinations in India, Europe and the Middle East. Delta has orders and options for approximately 400 new aircraft for delivery between 1992 and 2001.

Federal Express has ordered 75 new aircraft for delivery between 1992 and 1996.

Northwest purchased 21 gates at Chicago Midway and is discussing a possible merger with KLM and British Airways. The airline will build two new maintenance facilities in Minnesota and will take delivery on approximately 250 new jets between 1992 and 1998.

Southwest plans new service to seven cities from Las Vegas, to two cities from Sacramento and has added five flights to Phoenix from Los Angeles and six from Las Vegas to Los Angeles. Work is underway on a new maintenance facility at Phoenix Sky Harbor Airport and the airline will take delivery on 41 new jets through 1996.

TWA filed for bankruptcy in February, 1992, but the company does not expect any layoffs or cutbacks in the existing flight schedule.

United purchased Pan Am's routes to Central and South America and the Caribbean, as well as their Miami-Paris route. The airline began flying from Orlando-Mexico City and Los Angeles-Paris Charles de Gaulle and will expand service to Singapore. They have agreed to lease 42 gates at the new Denver airport and will build a new maintenance facility in Indianapolis. United has orders and options on over 500 aircraft between 1992 and 2000.

USAIR expects to begin service from Baltimore-London, Philadelphia-London, and plans routes to Hartford-Tampa/West Palm Beach and Philadelphia-Paris. The airline reached an agreement with Aeroflot to forward freight between Russia and the United States and has orders and options on 258 new jets for delivery between 1992 and 1999.

Aviation Maintenance   Future Aviation Professionals of America (FAPA) estimates that 3,500–3,600 new positions for mechanics, aircraft inspectors or avionics technicians will be available in 1992. Approximately 2,000 openings will be with the major airlines and the balance with national and regional airlines and helicopter fleets. Based on information on known retirements and orders and options for new jet equipment, FAPA predicts that the airline industry will need 70,000 maintenance technicians in the next 10 years.

The average starting hourly pay at the major airlines for a mechanic is $12.47 with a maximum rate of $19.00 per hour. Premiums ranging from 45 cents to $2.60 per hour are paid to mechanics holding airframe and/or powerplant licenses. FCC licenses command premiums ranging from 60 cents to $2.00 per hour. Foremen can expect to earn between $41,199–$53,126 per year.

According to FAPA's January, 1992 Maintenance Job Report, the following airlines are accepting applications for possible hiring:

Major Airlines: American, Continental, Delta, Federal Express, Northwest, Southwest, TWA, United, UPS

National Airlines: Airborne, Alaska, Aloha, ASA, Comair, DHL, Evergreen, Horizon, Midwest Express, Tower

Turbojet and Regional Airlines: Air America, Air Niagara, American International Airways, Buffalo, Express One, Rich International, Sun Country, American Eagle, Florida Gulf, USAIR Express

Flight Attendants The airlines currently employ 95,000 flight attendants, over 90 percent of whom work for the major airlines. In 1990–91 a number of airlines were forced to furlough flight attendants in an effort to cut costs, but hiring has picked up again and in December 1991/January 1992, almost 1400 flight attendants were recalled. FAPA predicts a demand for an additional 80,000 flight attendants between 1992 and 2000.

The average starting monthly pay for flight attendants with the major airlines, based on 72 flight hours per month is $1,108, with a maximum of $2,295 per month after 13 or 14 years of service. In addition, airlines pay between $1.00 and $2.00 per hour in expenses.

According the FAPA's January, 1992 Flight Attendant Job Report, the following airlines are accepting applications for possible hiring:

Major Airlines: American, Continental, Delta, Northwest, Southwest, United

National Airlines: Air Wisconsin, Alaska, Aloha, ASA, Comair, Horizon, WestAir, World

Turbojet and Regional Airlines: North American Airlines,

Rich International, American Eagle, Business Express, Express Airlines, Mesaba, Skywest, TWExpress, USAIR Express

Airports in the following cities serve as the major airlines' bases of operations for dispatching flight attendants and are the locations in which job openings are most likely to be found:

America West: Las Vegas, Phoenix

American: Boston, Chicago, Dallas, Los Angeles, Miami, Nashville, Raleigh-Durham, San Diego, San Francisco, Washington, D.C.

Continental: Cleveland, Denver, Honolulu, Houston, Los Angeles, Newark, Seattle

Delta: Atlanta, Boston, Chicago, Cincinnati, Dallas, Fort Lauderdale, Houston, Los Angeles, Miami, New Orleans, New York City, Portland, Salt Lake City, Seattle

Northwest: Boston, Chicago, Detroit, Honolulu, Los Angeles, Memphis, Minneapolis, New York City, Seattle

Southwest: Dallas, Houston, Phoenix

TWA: Los Angeles, New York City, St. Louis

United: Chicago, Cleveland, Honolulu, Los Angeles, Newark, New York, San Francisco, Seattle, Washington, D.C.

USAIR: Baltimore, Boston, Charlotte, Greensboro, Los Angeles, Miami, Philadelphia, San Diego, San Francisco, Syracuse, Washington, D.C.

Pilots Approximately 70,000 pilots flew for commercial airlines in 1990, but nearly 7,000 were laid off or furloughed during 1990–91. However, FAPA estimates that U.S. airlines will hire between 52,000–62,000 new pilots through the rest of the 1990s. Not only will healthy carriers expand their service, but they will also have to replace roughly 20,000 pilots who are scheduled to retire over the next 10 years.

At the major airlines, the average starting monthly salary for pilots logging 80 flight hours is $2,146, rising to a maximum monthly salary for captains of $14,000.

According the FAPA's January, 1992 Pilot Job Report, the following airlines are accepting resumes for possible hiring:

Major Airlines: American, Delta, Northwest, Southwest, United, UPS

National Airlines: Airborne, Air Wisconsin, Aloha, ASA, Horizon

Turbojet and Regional Airlines: Air Transport International, Express One, Key,

Hotels and Motels Travelers' gross spending has continued to increase over the past several years, with favorable long-term implications for the lodging industry. Although many hotels and motels have experienced lower occupancy rates, companies are luring travelers with bargain rates, business-plus-pleasure package deals, and other marketing efforts. In addition, industry analysts predict that because the ratio of employees to rooms is creeping upward, job opportunities will improve at a rate faster than the pace at which new hotel and motel rooms are being constructed. The U.S. Bureau of Labor Statistics estimates that employment should increase throughout the lodging industry; jobs will total about 2.2 million by the year 2005.

One notably bright spot in the lodging industry is the low-priced sector. In an increasingly segmented market—facilities are categorized as "luxury," "mid-priced," "corporate/convention," "budget," etc.—the budgetpriced hotels operate in a healthier niche than the rest. Economy hotels are the fastest-growing segment of the industry, and their revenues are well above the national average. Some hotel companies have even created their own budget niches. The Marriott Corporation owns a chain of Residence Inns for travelers needing long-term lodging, for instance; Marriott also owns Courtyard Hotels, an economy chain.

Industry analysts indicate that the full-service chains will make a comeback within the next several years, with Hilton Hotels Corporation, ITT Sheraton Corporation, and Loews Hotels likely to do especially well.

Managers and Managers' Assistants   Approximately 100,000 Americans work as hotel/motel managers and managers' assistants. The need for managers is projected to grow by at least 20 percent by the year 2000. Job growth will occur both because of industry expansion and because many experienced managers will retire or seek other kinds of employment. According to the Bureau of Labor Statistics entry-level positions are especially favorable for persons with college degrees in hotel and restaurant management.

Hotel and Motel Clerks   Holding about 113,000 jobs nationwide, hotel/motel clerks will have opportunities similar to those available to managers. One additional advantage for clerks is that turnover in this job category is often very high; each year thousands of clerks within the lodging industry transfer to other positions or other occupations. In addition, the round-the-clock nature of many clerks' duties means that shift-work and part-time schedules potentially increase the number of job "slots" available.

Nonmanagerial Hotel and Motel Jobs   As noted earlier, the ratio of employees to rooms is increasing within the U.S. lodging industry. Most of the workers affected by this shift are non-managerial staff: room attendants, cleaners, bell persons, laundry workers, etc. According to Steven Hiemstra, Professor of Restaurant and Hotel Management at Purdue University, this shift may indicate either a drop in industry-wide productivity or an increase in service-orientation. Either way, however, the implication is that hotels and motels may be likely to hire more workers in each category to look after guests even if overall occupancy rates remain stable.

WHERE THE JOBS ARE

THE PUBLIC SECTOR

Federal Government

The government of the United States employs slightly more than 3 million civilians, so it should not be surprising that there are literally thousands of job openings all the time and in many parts of the country as well as overseas. In 1991 more than 500,000 people found jobs in the federal government, jobs spanning the entire employment spectrum from professional (the government employs over 25,000 lawyers, and more than 40,000 accountants), technical (there are over 100,000 engineers and 49,000 computer specialists) and clerical (there are over 100,000 secretaries) to almost every kind of blue-collar occupation (over 15,000 aircraft mechanics, 10,000 pipefitters, and 23,000 warehouse workers are among those employed as of 1991).

So, yes, federal jobs are plentiful but finding one can require arduous searching so it's important to overcome some common prejudices. The prospect of a "government job" has rather negative connotations for some people who conjure up images of an insurmountable bureaucracy and employees lost under stacks of paper. Opportunities in the federal government can, however, far exceed these expectations. Not only are salaries commensurate with similar positions in private corporations, but job security and excellent benefits are also strong incentives. The government continues to be an important employer of minorities, offering and enforcing equal opportunity programs which are often sidestepped in the private sector.

A trip to one of the 44 Offices of Personnel Management Federal Job Information Centers (FJIC) can be daunting for any prospective federal employee. Posted in these offices are the semi-monthly Federal Job Opportunities Listings. Published on the first and sixteenth of every month, these are long lists of current federal job vacancies although they are by no means complete.

The first list, *GPA 001*, contains the jobs in the region where the Federal Job Information Center is located; the second list, *Nationwide,* gives federal job opportunities anywhere in the nation or the world. These lists can also be requested through the mail by writing to the FJIC in a particular location (see list). The positions available can range from unskilled worker to nuclear physicist and run the gamut on the General Salary Schedule.

As a guide through the application procedure, the code and control numbers for each position are included on the Opportunities Listings. Each position also has a Qualifications Information Statement (QIS) which gives the required skills, education and experience necessary for each opening. Applications and QIS statements can be obtained at the FJIC window or by written request. These job centers may also have federal personnel manuals and other reference books on hand.

As incongruous as it may seem, the federal government does not keep a list of *all* federal jobs currently available. Many agencies of the federal government have direct-hire authority and will fill positions rapidly instead of going through the FJIC. To be aware of agency openings you must keep in contact with those agencies which are of interest to you. In recent months, for example, the Central Intelligence Agency has been actively recruiting economists, among other specialists, on many college campuses.

There are two privately run publications that can be very helpful. *Federal Jobs Digest,* a bi-weekly newspaper, tracks federal job vacancies, lists US Postal Exams and has articles about job fairs, a "College Corner" and veterans' information. Each issue contains an average of approximately 3,000 jobs (Phone: 1–800–824–5000). *Federal Career Opportunities* is a similar publication concentrating on the

G–5 level and above. It also catalogs federal job openings in a systematic manner (Phone: 703–281–0200). Both publications are also available at most major libraries.

Jobs for College Graduates   In November 1990, the federal government began a new program to attract college graduates into civil service jobs. The Administrative Careers With America (ACWA) program encompasses 100 types of entry level jobs which are on the GS5 to GS7 levels of the General Schedule (salaries range from $16,973–$27,332 per annum). The positions are divided into six occupational groups:

1) Benefits Review, Tax and Legal
2) Business, Finance and Management
3) Law Enforcement and Investigation
4) Personnel, Administration and Computers
5) Health, Safety and Environmental Occupations
6) Writing and Public Information

To be eligible for this program, the applicant must have a bachelor's degree (or expect to receive one within eight months) or a minimum of three years of work experience. A combination of education and experience is also acceptable. There is a written test for each of the six occupational groups. Each test is administered periodically across the nation.

After passing the test, the candidate's name is placed on a list from which agencies with vacancies select. A series of interviews is then conducted by the specific agency. According to the US Office of Personnel Management, as of December 1991, approximately 73,000 people had passed the test and were on the register although only 6,693 had been hired through ACWA.

To apply for Administrative Careers with America, first obtain a copy of the Qualifications Information Statement (QIS) for one of the six occupational groups. These can be obtained from any Federal Job Information Center located across the country and can be requested by mail. In addition, a College Hotline has been set up to provide information and list test centers: 1–900–990–9200 (40¢ per minute).

State and Local Government

The sheer numbers of jobs in federal, state, and local government can make it an enormous source of employment in every area of the country. In 1990 more than 15 million jobs were in state and local government—4.5 million in state government and 10.8 million in local government.

By far the largest group of government employees worked in education. More that 4 million (32 percent of all local government employees) worked in this field. Health and hospital personnel make up an additional 10 percent of public sector workers, while police account for about five percent. In all, 2.2 million people worked in county government in 1990, while 2.6 million worked for the various towns, boroughs, townships, and cities all collectively known as municipalities.

The growth of the public job market has roughly paralleled the population shift in America. Most growth has occurred in the western states, while eastern states, especially those in the northeast, have experienced contraction of public sector jobs.

Overall, the public sector grew by 165,000 jobs in 1991 or 9.88 percent. Nevada led the way with growth of 6.95 percent, while Florida added more than 39,000 jobs—an increase of 4.6 percent. On the flip side, public sector jobs in Massachusetts declined by 2.5 percent while New York lost more than 30,000 public sector jobs in 1991 alone, a drop of 2.1 percent.

Government Job Growth—
Top 5 States, 1991

Top 5 By Percent		*Top 5 By Number*	
1. Nevada	6.95%	1. Florida	+39,800
2. Florida	4.57	2. Texas	+28,700
3. Washington	3.89	3. Washington	+15,800
4. Arkansas	3.54	4. North Carolina	+10,600
5. Hawaii	3.29	5. Ohio	+10,400

Police

The public's increasing concern about drug-related crimes and public safety means that budget constraints will probably not translate into severe cuts in local police departments. But fierce competition for jobs means that opening for police officers around the country are likely to be plentiful in the 1990s. Police jobs, which numbered 655,000 in 1990 according to the Department of Labor, are expected to grow by about 24 percent by the year 2000—slightly faster than the national average of 11–19 percent for all occupations. In an expanding economy, though, jobs for police could increase by as much as 30–35 percent.

Most police jobs are filled through attrition. Attractive salaries, retirement with a pension before the age of 50, and the opportunity to do exciting, valuable work contribute to a profession that has one of the lowest turnover rates in the country. Moreover, many of the more than 17,000 state and local police departments nationwide recruit new officers only once a year. Applicants who miss the police examination therefore must wait an entire year even to be considered for a position.

Concern for public safety means that police budgets are one of the last items to be redlined. Layoffs, therefore, are rare. Instead, police departments are looking for other ways of cutting costs. One cost-cutting method being adopted by some departments is shifting of routine duties like crowd control and airport surveillance to private security firms.

The number of police jobs usually correspond to the size of the city, with fast-growing cities adding more jobs than slow-growing or contracting cities.

Correction Officers

Jobs for correction officers should be plentiful in the 1990s. Legislation requiring mandatory minimum sentencing for convicted felons will mean more and longer prison sentences, and a correspondingly greater need for prison guards. Jobs for corrections officers should increase significantly by the year 2000. The Department of Labor projects a growth rate of 61 percent, with a maximum of 74 percent in an expanding economy. The average for all jobs is only 11–19 percent.

The prison population increased steadily—some might say alarmingly—during the 1980s and many prisons were built every day. The high risk and comparatively low pay for correction officers also means that jobs open frequently. Correction officers face many of the same life and death situations as police officers, but their salaries are almost always lower.

About 60 percent of America's 230,000 correction officers worked for state correctional facilities in 1990, according to the Department of Labor. The rest are split between city and county jails and federal prisons. Concern for public safety means that correction officers are not usually subject to budget cuts, and are rarely laid off.

Fire Fighters

Like jobs for police officers, firefighter positions are high-demand occupations with low turnover. The most important job requirements—bravery and a high school education—mean that the number of qualified applicants almost always exceeds the number of openings. The uncountable number of volunteer firefighters should also give an indication of how sought after these jobs are.

Firefighters numbered more than 280,000 in 1990. More than 90 percent of those jobs were with municipal fire departments. The rest consisted of a few private fire departments, and state and federal fire departments, which put out fires at airports and other state and federal installations.

The Department of Labor projects 24 percent growth in firefighting jobs—slightly larger than the national average—and suggests the field could grow by as much as 34 percent in an expanding economy. Some of that growth will take place in large urban fire departments, but a vast majority will come in small communities that are rapidly expanding their population base.

Layoffs are rare in fire departments as well. If budget considerations force local governments to trim their fire fighting budgets, they usually do it through attrition, choosing not to replace retired workers. Some municipalities are expected to cut costs by contracting with private firefighting companies, though this clearly will be the exception, rather than the rule for the future.

Bus Drivers

Bus driving will continue to present good job opportunities for anybody with a good driving record who can qualify for a commercial driver's license. Overall, jobs for bus drivers, which stood at 561,000 in 1990, will increase by about 32 percent by the year 2000. In an expanding economy, jobs for bus drivers could grow as much as 41 percent.

Bus drivers are divided into three main categories. The largest of these groups is school bus drivers, which constitute 70 percent of all bus drivers. Another 18 percent drive local transit buses, and an additional 6 percent drive intercity buses. Of these groups, school bus drivers are expected to grow the most. The increasing elementary and secondary school populations will create a growing need for school bus drivers throughout the 1990s. And the move by Americans to the suburbs will mean that a greater percentage of school children travel to school by bus.

Local transit drivers will also increase, but not as fast. In general, jobs for bus drivers will correspond to population growth in each city. Jobs for intercity bus drivers should also increase slightly, but air and auto travel are both expected to grow much faster than bus travel over the decade.

Because most school bus drivers are part-time, turnover is high and layoffs, especially in summer, are common; nonetheless, competition for local transit jobs is relatively high because wages and benefits are both good. Full-time drivers are rarely laid-off, though part-time drivers are often laid off even in winter months when service is cut back.

Highway Maintenance Workers

Jobs for highway maintenance workers will increase in the 1990s, but not as fast as the average for all other government jobs. More than 151,000 people worked for various state and local governments as highway maintenance workers in 1990. By the year 2000, their numbers are expected to increase by 24 percent. In an expanding economy, jobs for highway maintenance workers could increase by as much as 30–35 percent.

Subway and Streetcar Drivers

Subway and streetcar drivers are the only group of Rail Transport Workers that are expected to experience growth in the 1990s. The entire industry is expected to decline by as much as 11–19 percent by the year 2000, but jobs for subway and streetcar drivers should grow by a whopping 66 percent. In an expanding economy, this segment of the industry could grow by as much as 79 percent, more than 4 times the 11–19 percent average for all jobs.

There were more than 14,000 subway and streetcar operators in 1990 according to the Department of Labor. The growth of intercity rail systems and additional new lines to old systems will fuel the extraordinary growth rates. Competition for these jobs is considerable, as they provide high and good benefits with relatively few educational requirements.

Human Service Workers

"Human service worker" is a generic title for those who provide help of all kinds to people in need, whether it be from alcoholism, child abuse, mental retardation, or the effects of aging. They are often employed in support positions that assist social workers and mental health professionals. Under this classification fall people who work in homes for the retarded, in halfway houses, and in social services offices performing functions such as screening applicants, recordkeeping, etc.

Opportunities for human service workers should abound in the 1990s due to rapid growth and high turnover in the business. The growth of the elderly population will be primarily responsible for a 71 percent increase in the number of human service workers by the year 2000. That number could be as high as 82 percent in an expanding economy.

The Department of Labor reported 145,000 human service workers in 1990. One fourth of those were employed by state and local governments for work in hospitals, outpatient clinics, and health clinics. Because salaries are low and qualifications are high, competition for jobs is almost nonexistent, and applicants with high school and college educations find work very easily.

Social Workers

A growing, aging population means that jobs for social workers in the 1990s should increase by as much as 35 percent, faster than the national average of 11–19 percent, according to the Department of Labor. An expanding economy could bring a maximum increase of 43 percent. But an extended recession cold take its toll on the profession, as social worker positions are usually the first to be cut in a budget crisis.

Almost all of the 438,000 social workers employed in 1990 worked in the public sector. About 40 percent of them worked for state, county or municipal government agencies. A few others worked for the federal government. Social workers tend to be concentrated in urban areas, but recently they have begun working with families in more rural areas.

The biggest growth will be due to the aging population. More and more social workers are spending time with lonely and poor people without care and access to social services. Other areas of social work that are likely to increase are child care protection and community-based service for the retarded and the chronically ill. On the other hand, social workers at state mental hospitals and specialized training schools for the retarded are most likely to fall victim to the budget knife when jobs are cut.

The public's growing willingness to finance psychological help programs should help stave off some cuts in social work programs. The willingness of health insurance programs to pay social services should also keep these programs funded.

Librarians

Job prospects for librarians are actually much stronger than one might expect given all the talk about financial cutbacks. Of course cutbacks for libraries have been a regular part of state and local budgeting politics ever since Richard Nixon was president. With the prospect of fewer jobs back then the number of people entering the field declined quickly so the total number of librarians has remained relatively constant at about 150,000 after having more than doubled during the 1960s. Now, with many of the older group preparing to retire there are openings in many areas of the country and especially in certain fields.

Children's librarians are in great demand everywhere and the American Library Association recently reported actual shortages in Arkansas, California, Connecticut, Massachusetts, Michigan, New Jersey, Ohio, and Washington. Academic librarians, those who work in special areas of university institutions (and who usually hold two advanced degrees), are also in demand, especially in the northeast and midwest. The recent explosion of information sources and of new media to convey it to users had created a much greater need for libraries with specialized knowledge of medicine, law, and the sciences, including computer science. Many large corporations are also hiring experienced, highly-trained librarians to help them organize their own information and to tell them what outside sources they should utilize.

There are also openings for school librarians (who almost always must be certified teachers as well) and for public librarians, especially if they have a special skill such as cataloging, which the ALA reports have many positions available.

None of the above is meant to suggest that finding the right job as a librarian will be easy. On the other hand if the jam-packed employment opportunity pages of *Library Journal American Libraries,* and the other leading professional journals are valid indicators, it is safe to say that there are many jobs for librarians today. Here's a list of associations and agencies that can help.

Associations

American Library Association,
Office of Personnel Resources (Chicago).
Various state library associations
Medical Library Association (Chicago)
American Association of Law Libraries (Chicago)
Association of College and Research Libraries (Chicago)
Special Library Association (Washington D.C.)

Agencies

Theresa Burke Employment Agency (New York)
Gossage & Regan Associates (New York)
HBW Library Recruiters (Denton, Texas)
Library Associates (Beverly Hills, California)

Teachers

About 2.7 million school teachers were engaged in classroom instruction in the fall of 1990, the latest year for which final figures were available at the time of this writing. About 1.6 million teachers were teaching elementary school, while about 1.1 million were employed at the secondary level. About 2.4 million were in public schools and about 0.4 million were in private schools.

The 1991–92 recession hit public education hard, forcing teacher layoffs and increasing student-teacher classroom ratios. For example, New York City laid off 5,000 teachers in 1991. In the spring of 1991 Los Angeles was forced to lay off 2,000 teachers but by October hired all 2,000 back but with a small pay cut across the board.

But the outlook for teaching jobs in the near future is very good. The National Center for Education Statistics (NCES) projects that between 1990 and 2002, the number of classroom teachers in elementary and secondary schools will rise significantly primarily due to the upswing in school enrollment resulting from a sudden increase in the number of births in recent years.

The center estimates that the number of public and private school teachers will grow by at least 1.2 percent and perhaps by as much as 1.7 percent. Elementary teachers are thereby projected to increase by at least 240,000 and by as much as 370,000 by the year 2002. Secondary teachers are expected to increase by 220,000 to as much as 280,000 by the year 2002. The number of private school teachers is projected to increase by approximately 64,000.

Half of all the elementary and secondary education students in the United States reside in eight states: Texas, California, Florida, Illinois, Michigan, Ohio, Pennsylvania, and New York. Add another six states—Indiana, Maryland, New Jersey, Virginia, North Carolina and Georgia—and you have two-thirds of all the students in this country.

The National Center for Education Statistics estimates that between 1990 to 1996, 23 states will have double digit growth in student enrollment with Arizona having the largest projected growth rate of 28.3 percent. Also having high projected enrollment rates are New Hampshire 28.0 percent, Hawaii 24.9 percent, Virginia 23.1 percent, Maryland 22.4 percent and Florida 20.4 percent. As student enrollment increases, teaching positions also increase.

Because education policy is determined by state legislatures and community districts, each jurisdiction is different. In early 1992 state legislatures and governors were groping with smaller budgets and struggling to determine spending priorities. Some states seem to be deciding that education is a high priority while others are putting schooling further down on the list. Tennessee, Kentucky and New Jersey governors have expressed a strong desire to preserve education budgets. Florida seems to have no money but more students.

Big city school systems almost always need teachers. Los Angeles traditionally hires 3,000 teachers each fall—that's the total number of teachers in Pittsburgh. Chicago usually hires approximately 2,000 new teachers annually and Houston has 500 vacancies virtually every day of the school year.

Florida and Georgia traditionally hire half of their teachers from outside their state borders because their universities do not produce enough education graduates.

States Increasing Elementary and Secondary Teaching Positions, 1989–1990

State	Classroom Teachers 1985 (fall)	Classroom Teachers 1990 (fall)	Teaching jobs increased from 1989–90
TOTAL	2,355,963	2,390,771	1,034,808
Texas	199,397	206,399	7,002
Florida	104,127	108,422	4,295
Georgia	61,487	65,067	3,580
California	212,687	215,799	3,112
Wisconsin	49,329	52,378	3,049
Maryland	41,646	44,373	2,727
Tennessee	42,824	44,491	1,667
New Jersey	79,597	81,934	1,437
N. Carolina	63,160	64,331	1,171
Kentucky	35,731	36,847	1,116
Colorado	31,954	32,600	354

Note: Excludes teachers in private schools.

States Losing Elementary and Secondary Education Teaching Positions, 1989–1900

State	Classroom Teachers 1985 (fall)	Classroom Teachers 1990 (fall)	Teaching jobs lost from 1989–90
Massachusetts	59,040	56,678	− 2,362
N. Dakota	7,809	6,593	− 1,216
Pennsylvania	105,415	104,800	− 615
Ohio	101,627	101,032	− 595
West Virginia	21,653	21,251	− 402
Arizona	32,134	31,799	− 335
Wyoming	6,697	6,553	− 144
New York	174,610	174,500	− 110
Connecticut	35,308	35,260	− 48
Oklahoma	35,631	36,600	− 31

Note: Excludes teachers in private schools.

The 10 Largest School Districts, 1989 Fall

District	Classroom Teachers	Student Enrollment	No. of Schools
New York City	54,969	930,440	998
Los Angeles Unified	25,778	609.746	630
City of Chicago Schools	22,177	408,442	608
Dade County, Fla.	15,388	279,420	301
Philadelphia City	10,951	189,451	256
Houston ISD	10,429	185,566	244
Detroit City	9,631	175,436	259
Hawaii Dept. of Ed.	8,830	169,493	234
Broward County, Fla.	8,022	148,803	176
Fairfax County, Va.	7,643	126,790	188

Percent change in grades K-12 enrollment in public schools, by state, projected 1990 to 1996

State	*Percentage of enrollment increase projected, 1990–1996*
United States	9.9%
Arizona	28.3
New Hampshire	28.0
Hawaii	24.9
Virginia	23.1
Maryland	22.4
Florida	20.4
Delaware	17.2
New Jersey	17.1
Nevada	16.9
North Carolina	16.2
California	16.1
Georgia	16.0
New Mexico	15.5
Massachusetts	13.5
Alaska	13.0
Maine	12.8
Connecticut	11.7
Missouri	11.4
Vermont	11.3
District of Columbia	10.2
Colorado	9.9
Washington	9.8
South Dakota	9.3
South Carolina	9.2
Illinois	8.3
Minnesota	8.3
Tennessee	7.7

Percent change in grades K-12 enrollment in public schools, by state, projected 1990 to 1996 (cont.)

State	Percentage of enrollment increase projected, 1990–1996
Utah	6.7
Kansas	6.1
Arkansas	5.4
Alabama	5.0
Michigan	4.8
Texas	4.8
Oregon	4.4
Ohio	4.2
Indiana	3.5
Mississippi	3.5
Wisconsin	3.3
Louisiana	2.9
North Dakota	1.7
Nebraska	1.4
West Virginia	−9.1
Wyoming	−6.0
Iowa	−4.4
Oklahoma	−3.3
Idaho	−2.4
Kentucky	−1.4
Montana	−1.1

Source: U.S. Dept. of Education, *National Center for Education Statistics,* Digest of Education Statistics 1991.

Alternative Certification Programs States report that more than 20,000 people have been licensed through alternative certification programs since 1985. In just the last two years, more than 12,000 people have entered an alternative teacher certification program. This represents a 120 percent increase from two years ago and a 31 percent increase from 1989 to 1990. This trend is expected to expand as more states establish alternative certification programs. And, as part of The America 2000 Excellence in Education Act of 1991, Congress is to provide grants to states and districts to develop alternative certification systems for teachers and principals.

The National Center for Education Information (NCEI) reports that as of September 1991, 11 states have an alternative certification program designed for the explicit purpose of attracting talented individuals who already have at least a bachelor's degree in a field other than education into elementary or secondary education. These programs are not restricted to shortages and involve teaching with a trained mentor and formal instruction dealing with content and practice teaching during the school year and sometimes summers. The 11 states offering the most open programs for adults in other careers to move into teaching are: Colorado, Connecticut, Kentucky, Maryland, Minnesota, New Hampshire, New Jersey, Tennessee, Texas, Washington, West Virginia. In addition, Arizona, Idaho, Mississippi and Ohio have alternative certification programs only for high school job openings. Another four states offer alternative teaching certificates only when there are shortages: Arkansas, California, Georgia, Missouri. North Dakota and New York are the only states that say in 1991 that they are not even considering alternative routes to classroom teaching positions.

A total of 39 states *say* that they are implementing alternatives to the approved college teacher education program route for certifying teachers. Twenty-eight of these states have various types of criteria and restrictions to their programs.

The alternative teaching certification programs are the major vehicle for minority persons to enter the teaching profession. Approximately 95 percent of college graduates in education are white, while 20–30 percent of those in the alternative teaching certificate programs are members of minority groups.

College and University Faculty

There are approximately 846,000 college and university faculty positions in America. During the 1989–90 academic year, 10,606 institutions offered post secondary education (2,127 4-year colleges, 1,408 2-year colleges and 7,071 vocational and technical institutions). Over 70 percent were in public institutions. About one-third of these positions were part-time because some faculty had primary jobs outside academia—in government, private industry or in nonprofit research—and others could not find full-time jobs.

The National Center for Education Statistics (NCES) estimates that in 1990 there were 13.9 million students enrolled in higher education and it projects that enrollment in 2002 will be between 15.2 million to 17.4 million. On this basis and on the fact that many professors will retire, many people are projecting a significant increase in college and university faculty positions.

A 1989 study, *Prospects for Faculty in the Arts and Sciences,* cowritten by former Princeton president William G. Bowen, projected that by the year 2000 there might be only 30,934 new faculty members to fill 37,091 positions. Colleges and universities need to issue two-thirds more doctorates than they currently are to meet anticipated demands for faculty to avert a shortage towards the end of this decade.

Current job prospects are better in business, engineering, computer science, physical sciences and mathematics largely because attractive jobs in the private sector are also available.

A recent study by Mr. Bowen, *In Pursuit of the Ph.D.* (Princeton University Press), discovered that we will probably run short of college professors and researchers in the arts and sciences. During the last decade there was a serious drop in the number of doctorates awarded in economics, English, history, mathematics, physics and political science. Having a doctoral degree is almost always a requirement for appointment as a professor or researcher. The study called for colleges and universities to improve the effectiveness of these programs.

WHERE THE JOBS ARE

SPECIAL AREAS

New College Graduates

After four years of college, many of the one million members of the class of '92 hope to find a good job with a decent salary. Instead, they are facing the toughest job market in 20 years as corporations and government slash hiring. No longer is a bachelor's degree a surefire ticket to an entry-level job.

Who will get hired? The cream of the crop, with high grade point averages and some job experience. Employers are being more selective and establishing higher standards for new employees, according to L. Patrick Scheetz of the Michigan State University's annual report on national hiring trends for college graduates. A student with a 2.5 average will face a very difficult job search. Employers also expect students to have gained some career-related experience through summer jobs, internships, and cooperative education programs.

"There are some jobs out there but not enough for all the new graduates," Scheetz says. "Graduates who have been hardworking students and planned for life after graduation will find jobs." Young people who will have the easiest time finding jobs majored in math, engineering, computer science or health-care related fields like nursing. Opportunities are also good where firms are expanding—and hiring—including public utilities, metal products, petroleum, construction and building material manufacturing, and printing, publishing and information services. Decreases in hiring are expected in automotive and mechanical equipment, electronics, government administration, the military, and diversified conglomerates.

Among the fields with the highest demand are new and emerging careers such as laser technology and research, computer applications and graphics, database designing and desktop publishing. Perennially in high demand are chemical, electrical, mechanical, and industrial engineers. Women and minorities are especially in high demand in the engineering fields. Scheetz also found that demand was high for accountants, chemists, computer scientists, quality control engineers, toxic waste specialists, emergency care nurses, occupational and physical therapists, and speech and language pathologists.

According to the Michigan State survey job opportunities for new graduates will be strongest in the southeast, the southwest, and the upper midwest. The places hardest hit by the recession, especially New England, will of course offer the fewest job possibilities.

The negative impact of the recession cannot be overstated. "An overwhelming 60 percent of corporations expect their business to decline—or at best stay even this year," reports Victor R. Lindquist, director of placement at Northwestern University and author of its 46th annual survey of business and industry. The survey found that 47 percent of businesses will decrease their hiring at the bachelor's level and, overall, job opportunities will fall 4 percent.

The Michigan State University survey concurs and predicts that hiring will be off by 10 percent in 1992, the third year in a row of decreases. Business and industry hiring is expected to decrease the least, 1.9 percent, while government and military hiring will decrease the most, 20.7 percent. The reasons are "layoffs in many industries, preference for graduates who already have two or three years of experience, fewer job openings and the current recession."

The Northwestern Lindquist-Endicott report surveyed 259 mid-to-large-size businesses and the MSU report, 464 employers in business, industry and government agencies.

What distinguishes this recession is that white collar jobs

have been lost. According to the federal Bureau of Labor Statistics, in the 1981 recession 838,000 new white collar jobs were created while in the 1990s 209,000 have been lost.

Hardest hit will be graduates with degrees in economics and finance, with a 16 percent drop in demand, according to the Northwestern report. Demand for graduates with degrees in business administration and liberal arts will each be down between 4 and 5 percent.

One bit of good news is that starting salaries will increase slightly. MSU found salaries for new college graduates with bachelor's degrees will average $27,037, an increase of 2.3 percent. The highest salaries, above $32,000, will go to students with degrees in engineering and computer science. The lowest salaries, about $21,000, will go to graduates with degrees in liberal arts, home economics, journalism, and retailing.

Both surveys also examined what potential employers view as the weaknesses of new college graduates. "Unrealistic expectations of all kinds are cited as the greatest shortcoming," says Lindquist, adding that many students believe they have "already paid their dues" and expect job offers a step up from the bottom rung of the corporate ladder. Other shortcomings include marginal writing and speaking skills, lack of career-related experience, overconfidence in abilities, and insufficient commitment to the job.

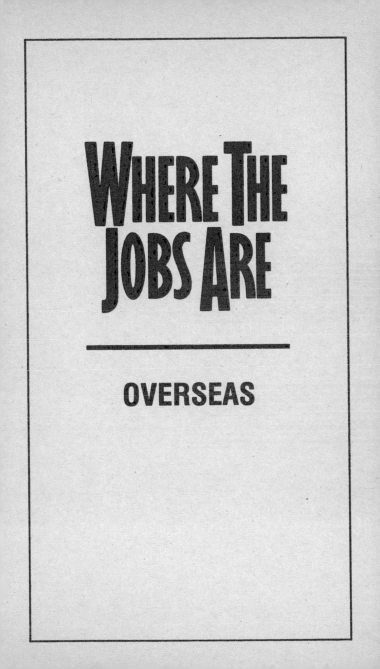

WHERE THE JOBS ARE

OVERSEAS

In addition to the tens of thousands of military personnel still stationed outside the U.S. and the 50,000 students studying abroad, more than two *million* Americans live and work overseas. More and more Americans are discovering that by combining the good salaries paid in many foreign countries with the tax advantages of living outside the U.S., it is possible to save and return home with a substantial nest egg.

The kind of jobs available to Americans overseas usually require particular skills or training not available locally. This rules out such jobs as truck drivers and laborers but often includes specialized equipment operators and journeymen. There are jobs overseas for just about any profession, discipline or craft, and in almost any field including construction, engineering, health care, education and training.

Education, training and experience are the keys to getting a job overseas, just as in the U.S. Most jobs tend to be for management and supervisory personnel or the highly technically trained and experienced professional. In the construction field, for example, there are jobs for managers and engineers, of course; but there are also jobs for superintendents and foremen, estimators and office managers, equipment operators and surveyors. Most of the craft jobs will be filled by locals or third country nationals, e.g., Filipinos or Indians. But often these workers are supervised by experienced American craftsmen.

The same is true in most other fields. There is a strong demand for doctors, nurses, and technicians, but jobs for practical nurses, aides, orderlies, etc., are usually filled by locals or third country nationals. American teachers can find jobs overseas teaching American children or teaching English as a second language. There are also opportunities for experienced American servicemen and women in training foreign military forces. And the list goes on and on.

Middle East

Saudi Arabia, Kuwait, United Arab Emirates, Bahrain, Quatar, Yemen all have large populations of Americans living and working there. These jobs tend to be the highest paying and most plentiful of job opportunities currently for Americans. David Lay, author and veteran expatriate, reports, "If you're willing to go where the work is, the Middle East has by far the most lucrative employment opportunities in the world for Americans overseas!" Lay further states that not only do salaries often range up to 50 percent higher than the U.S., but Americans who are out of the U.S. for 330 days of 12 consecutive months are eligible for a tax exemption of $70,000 per year. He cautions, however, that Americans are often subject to the income tax of the host country. Fortunately, most Middle East countries do not tax foreigners, or their own citizens in most cases. Lay's current book, *Getting Your Job In The Middle East,* is available through DCL Publishing Company (P.O. Box 16347, Tampa, Fl. 33687–6347 or by calling toll free 1–800–835–2246 ext. 73).

Far East

Indonesia, China, and even Hong Kong and Singapore offer many opportunities for Americans. *The Wall Street Journal* prints an edition just covering this part of the world and many jobs are advertised there each week.

Africa

Most of the African nations are still in a developing state and offer many jobs to Americans. There are also many non-profit organizations that send Americans to Africa, such as the World Health Organization. Many of these jobs are available through the United Nations and information may be obtained through its various organizations, most of which are in New York City.

Central and South America

Although fewer jobs exist here than in other regions, in the mining and petroleum producing countries such as Venezuela, Chile and Peru, many American companies hire U.S. citizens. Most large U.S. companies that export products or services overseas have representatives and sometimes manufacturing plants in Central and South America.

Europe

Countries in western Europe have people well qualified for most jobs, but there are opportunities for Americans to work with American companies. (Language capability obviously becomes more important in European countries other than the United Kingdom.) Jobs for computer specialists and systems analysts are usually available, so too are marketing and sales positions either for U.S. companies or foreign companies representing or utilizing American products and services. Jobs for teachers of English as a second language as well as many higher education openings for engineers and scientists are usually plentiful, but competition can be keen.

Most European countries have the same difficulties as the U.S. in filling highly technical or professional positions and often make exceptions to immigration policies to facilitate recruiting of foreign nationals.

Many jobs in eastern Europe should become available to Americans once the national economies rebound and especially after U.S. companies begin operations there.

Further Information for the Serious Job Seeker

Where to Start

Whether you are young and just beginning to look for your first job or a bit older and returning to the work force after an illness or staying home with the young children, the best way to start your search is with a visit to your local library. The same is true for the 10 million Americans who change occupations each year.

If you are like most people you are puzzled or confused by the incredible assortment of jobs that exist in the U.S. and the best way to overcome those feelings is by educating yourself about the job market. What jobs interest you? Are you qualified? What jobs are actually available?

The two most comprehensive books are the 1,000-page *Professional Careers Sourcebook* (Gale Research Publishing), and *The Occupational Outlook Handbook, 1992–93*, produced by the U.S. Department of Labor (this book can also be purchased at any U.S. Government Bookstore, or by calling the office of the Superintendent of Documents in Washington, 202-783-3238. It costs about $25). Both books contain job descriptions, and the names and addresses of associations that can provide further information on career possibilities.

The best and least expensive book available for comprehensive and up-to-the-minute information about jobs as well as their current pay rates is my own *American Almanac of Jobs and Salaries* (Avon Books) currently in its fourth edition. This book, like the one you are reading, is also concerned with local and regional variations of pay and job growth.

If You Are Moving

The best place to obtain general information about local job markets is through the labor departments of each state. Every state produces something and some (California, Florida, Arizona, New York, for example) devote a great deal of time and energy to creating large amount of data. A full listing of state offices with addresses, phone and fax numbers is given below. If you write or call be sure to ask for local area information as well; the larger states have branch offices in major cities too, so ask for those numbers. Of course, you should also contact the local chamber of commerce in the area, and it's always worth calling the mayor's office as well, since the people there will often direct you to the appropriate department.

State Labor Departments

ALABAMA

Labor Market Information
Department of Industrial Relations
849 Monroe Street, Rm. 422
Montgomery, AL 36130
205/242-8855 (FAX # 205/240-3070)

ALASKA

Research & Analysis
Department of Labor
P.O. Box 25501
Juneau, AK 99802-5501
907/465-4500 (FAX # 907/465-2101)

ARIZONA

Department of Economic Security
1789 West Jefferson
P.O. Box 6123, Site Code 733A
Phoenix, AZ 85005
602/542-3871 (FAX # 602/542-6474)

ARKANSAS

State & Labor Market Information
Employment Security Division
P.O. Box 2981
Little Rock, AR 72203
501/682-1543 (FAX # 501/682-3713)

CALIFORNIA

Employment Data & Research Div.
Employment Development Dept.
P.O. Box 942880, MIC 57
Sacramento, CA 94280-0001
916/427-4675 (FAX # 916/323-6674)

COLORADO

Labor Market Information
393 So. Harlan, 2nd Floor
Lakewood, CO 80226
303/937-4935 (FAX # 303/937-4945)

CONNECTICUT

Research & Information
Employment Security Division
Connecticut Labor Department
200 Folly Brook Boulevard
Wethersfield, CT 06109
203/566-2120 (FAX # 203/566-1519)

DISTRICT OF COLUMBIA

Chief of Labor Market Information
Dept. of Employment Services
500 C Street, N.W., Rm. 201
Washington, D.C. 20001
202/639-1642 (FAX # 202/639-1766)

DELAWARE

Office of Occupational & LMI
Delaware Department of Labor
University Plaza, Building D
P.O. Box 9029
Newark, DE 19702-9029
302/368-6962 (FAX # 302/368-6748)

FLORIDA

Bureau of Labor Market Information
Department of Labor & Employment Security
2012 Capitol Circle, S.E., Rm. 200
Hartman Building
Tallahassee, FL 32399-0674
904/488-1048 (FAX # 904/488-2558)

GEORGIA

Labor Information System
Department of Labor
223 Courtland Street, N.E.
Atlanta, GA 30303
404/656-3177 (FAX # 404/651-9568)

HAWAII

Research & Statistics Office
Dept. of Labor & Industrial Rel.
830 Punchbowl St., Rm. 304
Honolulu, HI 96813
808/586-8999 (FAX # 808/586-9022)

IDAHO

Research & Analysis
Department of Employment
317 Main Street
Boise, ID 83735
208/334-6169 (FAX # 208/334-6427)

ILLINOIS

Economic Information & Analysis
Department of Employment Security
401 South State Street, 2 South
Chicago, IL 60605
312/793-2316 (FAX # 312/793-6245)

INDIANA

Labor Maket Information
Dept. of Employment & Training Services
10 North Senate Avenue
Indianapolis, IN 46204
317/232-8456 (FAX # 317/232-6950)

IOWA

Audit & Analysis Department
Department of Employment Services
1000 East Grand Avenue
Des Moines, IA 50319
515/281-8181 (FAX # 515/281-8195)

KANSAS

Labor Market Information Services
Department of Human Resources
401 Topeka Avenue
Topeka, KS 66603
913/296-5058 (FAX # 913/296-0179)

KENTUCKY

Labor Market Research & Analysis
Department for Employment Services
275 East Main Street
Frankfort, KY 40621
602/564-7976 (FAX # 502/564-7452)

LOUISIANA

Research & Statistics Division
Dept. of Employment & Training
P.O. Box 94094
Baton Rouge, LA 70804-9094
504/342-3141 (FAX # 504/342-9193)

MAINE

Division of Economic Analysis & Research
ME Department of Labor/BES
20 Union Street
Augusta, ME 04330
207/289-2271 (FAX # 207/289-5292)

MARYLAND

Office of Labor Market Analysis & Information
Dept. of Economic & Employment Development
1100 North Eutaw Street, Rm. 601
Baltimore, MD 21201
301/333-5000 (FAX # 333-7121)

MASSACHUSETTS

Division of Employment Security
19 Staniford Street, 2nd Floor
Boston, MA 02114
617/727-6868 (FAX # 617/727-0315)

MICHIGAN

Bureau of Research & Statistics
Employment Security Commission
7310 Woodward Avenue
Detroit, MI 48202
313/876-5445 (FAX # 313/876-5244)

MINNESOTA

Research & Statistical Services
Department of Jobs and Training
390 N. Robert St., 5th Floor
St. Paul, MN 55101
612/206-6546 (FAX # 612/296-0994)

MISSISSIPPI

Labor Market Information Dept.
Employment Security Commission
P.O. Box 1699
Jackson, MS 39215-1699
601/961-7424 (FAX # 601/961-7405)

MISSOURI

Research & Analysis
Division of Employment Security
P.O. Box 59
Jefferson, City, MO 65104
314/751-3591 (FAX # 314/751-7973)

MONTANA

Research & Analysis
Dept. of Labor and Industry
P.O. Box 1728
Helena, MT 59624
406/444-2430 (FAX # 406/444-2638)

NEBRASKA

Labor Market Information
Department of Labor
550 South 16th Street
P.O. Box 94600
Lincoln, NE 68509
402/471-9964 (FAX # 402/471-2318)

NEVADA

Employment Security Research
Employment Security Department
500 East Third Street
Carson City, NV 89713
702/687-4550 (FAX # 702/687-3424)

NEW JERSEY

Policy & Planning
Department of Labor
John Fitch Plaza, Room 1010
Trenton, NJ 08625-0056
609/292-2643 (FAX # 609/292-6692)

NEW HAMPSHIRE

Labor Market Information
Department of Employment Security
32 South Main Street
Concord, NH 03301-4587
603/228-4123 (FAX # 603/228-4172)

NEW MEXICO

NM Department of Labor
401 Broadway Boulevard, NE
P.O. Box 1928
Albuqueque, NM 87103
505/841-8645 (FAX # 505/841-8421)

NEW YORK

Div. of Research & Statistics
NY State Department of Labor
State Campus, Bldg. 12, Rm. 400
Albany, NY 12240-0020
518/457-6181 (FAX # 518/457-0620)

NORTH CAROLINA

Labor Market Information Division
Employment Security Commission
P.O. Box 25903
Raleigh, NC 27611
919/733-2936 (FAX # 919/733-8662)

NORTH DAKOTA

Research & Statistics
Job Service North Dakota
P.O. Box 1537
Bismarck, ND 58502
701/224-2868 (FAX # 701/224-4000)

OHIO

Labor Market Information Division
Bureau of Employment Services
145 S. Front Street
Columbus, OH 43215
614/644-2689 (FAX # 614/644-3579)

OKLAHOMA

Research Division
Employment Security Commission
308 Will Rogers Memorial Ofc. Bldg.
Oklahoma City, OK 73105
405/567-7116 (FAX # 405/557-7256)

OREGON

Research & Statistics
Oregon Employment Division
875 Union Street, N.E.
Salem, OR 97311
503/378-3220 (FAX # 503/373-7515)

PENNSYLVANIA

Research & Statistics Division
Department of Labor & Industry
1216 Labor & Industry Building
Harrisburg, PA 17121
717/787-3265 (FAX # 717/772-2168)

PUERTO RICO

Research & Statistics Division
Dept. of Labor & Human Resources
505 Munoz Rivera Ave., 20th Floor
Hato Rey, PR 00918
809/754-5385 (FAX # 809/751-7934)

RHODE ISLAND

Labor Market Information
  & Management Services
Department of Employment
  & Training
101 Friendship Street
Providence, RI 02903-3740

SOUTH CAROLINA

Labor Market Information
Employment Security Commission
P.O. Box 995
Columbia, SC 29202
803/737-2660 (FAX # 803/737-2838)

SOUTH DAKOTA

Labor Information Center
Department of Labor
P.O. Box 4730
Aberdeen, SD 57402-4730
605/622-2314 (FAX # 605/622-2322)

TENNESSEE

Research & Statistics Division
Department of Employment Security
500 James Robertson Parkway
11th Floor
Nashville, TN 37245-1000
615/741-2284 (FAX # 615/741-3203)

TEXAS

Economic Research & Analysis
Texas Employment Commission
15th & Congress Ave., Room 208T
Austin, TX 78778
512/463-2616 (FAX # 512/475-1241)

UTAH

Labor Market Information & Research
Department of Employment Security
140 East 300 South
P.O. Box 11249
Salt Lake City, UT 84147
801/536-7400 (FAX # 801/536-7420)

VERMONT

Policy & Information
Department of Employment
  & Training
5 Green Mountain Drive
P.O. Box 488
Montpelier, VT 05602
802/229-0311 (FAX # 802/223-0750)

VIRGIN ISLANDS

Research & Analysis
Department of Labor
P.O. Box 3159
St. Thomas, VI 00801
809/776-3700 (FAX # 809/774-5908)

VIRGINIA

Director
Economic Information Service Division
VA Employment Commission
P.O. Box 1358
Richmond, VA 23211
804/786-7496 (FAX # 804/225-3923)

WASHINGTON

Employment Security Department
212 Maple Park, Mail Stop, KG-11
Olympia, WA 98504-5311
206/753-5114 (FAX # 206/753-4851)

WEST VIRGINIA

Assistant Director
Labor & Economic Research
Bureau of Employment Programs
112 California Avenue
Charleston, WV 25305-0112
304/348-2660 (FAX # 304/348-0301)

WISCONSIN

Labor Market Information Bureau
Department of Industry, Labor
  & Human Relations
201 East Washington Ave., Rm. 221
P.O. Box 7944
Madison, WI 53707
608/266-5843 (FAX # 608/267-0330)

WYOMING

Research & Planning
Division of Administration
Department of Employment
P.O. Box 2760
Casper, WY 82602
307/235-3646 (FAX # 307/235-3293)